My Amish Childhood

JERRY S. EICHER

HARVEST HOUSE PUBLISHERS
EUGENE, OREGON

All Scripture quotations, unless otherwise indicated, are taken from The Holy Bible, *New International Version®, NIV®.* Copyright © 1973, 1978, 1984, 2011 by Biblica, Inc.™ Used by permission. All rights reserved worldwide.

Cover photos © Neil Wright
Cover by Garborg Design Works, Savage, Minnesota

Acknowledgments

Two books were used to help me keep the dates straight. I owe a thank you to Monroe Hochstetler for his book *Life and Times in Honduras* and to Joseph Stoll for his book *Sunshine and Shadow.* Any errors in dates or events in *My Amish Childhood* are my own.

MY AMISH CHILDHOOD
Copyright © 2013 by Jerry S. Eicher
Published by Harvest House Publishers
Eugene, Oregon 97402
www.harvesthousepublishers.com

Library of Congress Cataloging-in-Publication Data
Eicher, Jerry S.
    My Amish childhood / Jerry S. Eicher.
        p. cm.
    ISBN 978-0-7369-5006-0 (pbk.)
    ISBN 978-0-7369-5007-7 (eBook)
    1. Eicher, Jerry S.—Childhood and youth. 2. Eicher, Jerry S.—Religion. 3. Eicher, Jerry S.
—Travel—Honduras. 4. Amish—Ontario—Biography. 5. Amish—Honduras—Biography.
6. Authors, American—20th century—Biography. I. Title.
PS3605.I34A3 2013
818'.603—dc23

                                                                                    2012028996

Printed in the United States of America

    13 14 15 16 17 18 19 20 21 / LB-JH / 10 9 8 7 6 5 4 3 2 1

The Two Amish Farms in Honduras

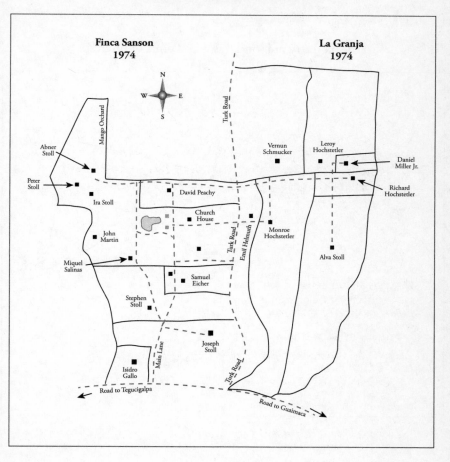

Finca Sanson
1974

La Granja
1974

Mango Orchard

Turk Road

N
W E
S

Abner
Stoll

Peter
Stoll

Ira Stoll

David Peachy

Church
House

John
Martin

Miquel
Salinas

Vernun
Schmucker

Leroy
Hochstetler

Daniel
Miller Jr.

Richard
Hochstetler

Monroe
Hochstetler

Turk Road

Emil Helmuth

Alva Stoll

Samuel
Eicher

Stephen
Stoll

Main Lane

Joseph
Stoll

Turk Road

Isidro
Gallo

Road to Tegucigalpa

Road to Guaimaca

The Country of Honduras with Points of Interest

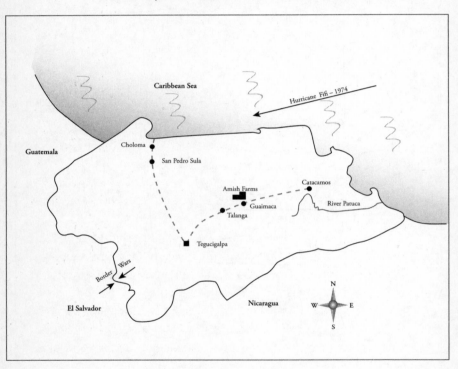

Chapter 1

I can still see his face. Lean. Determined. Framed by his lengthy beard. I can see him running up the hill toward our house. He was carrying his bag of doctor implements.

Mom was having chest spasms, and any real doctor was miles away—across four hours of the broken, rutted, dusty Honduran road we took only as a last resort.

The running man was my Uncle Joe. The smart one of the family. The older brother. The intellectual genius. When Uncle Joe walked by, we stopped talking and listened intently when he spoke. On this day, he rushed by, not paying any attention to us children.

I knew he was coming about Mom, but I recall experiencing no fear for her life. Perhaps I wasn't old enough to have such a fear. To me, Uncle Joe's haste seemed more entertainment than emergency. After all, Mom had looked fine to me a few minutes earlier.

When Uncle Joe left the house some time later, he issued a favorable report that I never questioned. Nor did anyone else. The mysteries of the *Englisha* world of medicine were even further removed from us than the four hours to town. Uncle Joe studied the books, and we trusted him.

Years later, when our little Amish community in Central America was on its last legs and held in the grip of terrible church fights over cape dresses, bicycles, singing in English or Spanish on Sunday mornings, and other horrors that the adults spoke of with bated breath, it was the look on Uncle Joe's face as he talked with Mom and Dad by the fence on Sunday afternoon that made things clear to me. If Uncle Joe thought something was over, then it was over.

Uncle Joe lived below us, across the fields, in a house smaller than ours even though his family was much larger. How they managed, I never thought to wonder. Their house never looked crowded. It was kept spotless by his wife, Laura, and their oldest daughters Rosanna and Naomi. We didn't visit often on Sunday afternoons. Mostly we children dropped by on weekdays, sent on some errand by Mom or we wandered past on our meanderings around the countryside.

They kept goats in the yard, all of them tied with long ropes to stakes. One of them was named Christopher. We didn't have goats. Dad ran a machine shop, and Mom took care of the garden. Goats were foreign to us. Smelly creatures. Mom scorned goat's milk, even when Uncle Joe said emphatically it was far superior to cow's milk.

We all lived near each other in those days—part of a grand experiment to see if the Amish faith could survive on foreign soil.

My grandfather, Peter Stoll, an Amish man of impeccable standing, had taken it upon himself to lead an Amish community to the Central American country of Honduras. He wasn't an ordained minister, and I don't remember seeing him speak in public. Still, the integrity of his life and his ideas so affected those around him that they were willing to follow him where few had gone before.

At the height of the experimental community, we ended up being twenty families or so. We all lived on two neighboring ranches purchased in a valley below a mountain. Most of us had come to Honduras from the hot religious fervor of the small Aylmer community along the shores of Lake Erie in Southern Ontario or from the detached coolness of Amish country spread over Northern Indiana. Plans were for the two to become one in mind and heart. And for awhile we did.

Those were wonderful years. The memories of that time still bring an automatic gathering of hearts among the Amish who were there—and even some of us who are no longer Amish. All these years later, most of us are scattered across the United States and Canada—except for the few of the original group who stayed behind.

Some of the people credit the joy of those days to the weather in our Honduras valley. And lovely weather it was. Balmy. Hardly ever above ninety or below forty. Others credit the culture. Some attribute our happiness to being so far from the States that we only had each other. I don't know the full reason for our happiness. Perhaps it isn't possible to know. But I do remember the energy of the place—its vibrancy. I do know the years left their imprints on us all.

This was my childhood. Those hazy years when time drags. When nothing seems to come soon enough. And where everything is greeted as if it had never been before. To me that land—that valley—was home. I absorbed it completely. Its sounds. Its language. The color of the dusty towns. The unpaved streets. The pigs in the doorway of the huts. The open fires over a metal barrel top. The taste of greasy fried beans. The flour tortillas and meat smoked to perfection. In my heart there will always be a deep and abiding love for that country.

Around us were mountains. To the north they rose in a gradual ridge, coming in from the left and the right to meet in the middle, where a distinctive hump rose into the air—officially named Mt. Misoco. But to us it was simply what the locals called it: La Montaña. The Mountain. *Our* mountain. Which it was in ways we could not explain.

To the south lay the San Marcos Mountains. At least that's what we called them. Those rugged, jagged peaks lying off in the distance. I never climbed those mountains, but I often roamed our mountain— or rather our side of it—from top to bottom. On its peak, looking over to the other side, you could see lines and lines of ridges running as far as the eye could see.

A party of courageous Amish boys, along with a few visiting Amish youngsters from stateside, once decided to tackle the San Marcos Mountains. They threw their forces together and allowed two days for the trip. I was much too young to go along—and probably wouldn't have anyway. But I waited for news of their adventure with interest. They came back soon enough— defeated and full of tales of dark jungles and multiple peaks that disoriented the heart. No one even caught sight of the highest point, let alone the other side.

In the summer, around five in the morning, the Southern Cross— that symbol of Christianity—hung over the San Marcos Mountains. Its haunting figure made of stars swung low in the sky. I would stand for long minutes gazing at the sight, caught up in the glory of it.

I was eight when we arrived in Honduras. We were one of the first families there after Grandfather Stoll had purchased and settled on the Sanson ranch. Dad seemed driven to the move by motives other than adventure. He was unhappy with the *ordnung* rules in the Amish community at Aylmer, and he wanted change. Change that didn't include the great sin of joining a more liberal Amish church, of course.

In time Dad came to love the land along with the rest of us. And strangely, he came to love what he didn't expect—the old ways, imperfect though they had been. My most enduring memory of Dad in those days is hearing him sing the old German songs at the top of his voice over the roar of his machine shop motors. And in the end, it came down to that question for all of them. A choice between what they loved and what they loved the most.

I grew up surrounded by men dedicated to an old faith. I saw those men, most of them my uncles, tested to the core. I saw them wrestle with the old and with the new, trying to figure out where everything fit together. I lived among giants of faith. I saw their agony and their sacrifice. I saw their choices, and it affected me deeply. Their faith had been hammered out back in the sixteenth century, in the old town of Zurich, Switzerland. Back during the time Ulrich Zwingli thundered his sermons in the old Grossmunster Church.

But in the days of my childhood, those stories of long ago were not mine yet. Those gallant tales of deeds done under fire and sword. Of imprisonment in noblemen's castles. Of narrow escapes into the Swiss countryside from the murderous Berne Anabaptist hunters. Instead, my memories are of men in my own time. Men who believed that life was not worth living if you didn't believe in something worth dying for. I was surrounded by men of passion. And if someone should make the claim that these men were misguided, I would insist the fault lay not in caring too much about religious matters. For I learned while growing up among them that this is how a person should live. That true believers follow God with all of their hearts and souls.

Chapter 2

I was born in 1961 to a nineteen-year-old Amish woman. Her wedding in August of the prior year had been agreed to by her father only after a special arrangement was made. She would work at home the following summer to help with the family's vast strawberry pickings. Because I arrived in May—nine months and a few days after the wedding—this didn't happen. Grandfather Stoll was left to pick his strawberries without his married daughter's help. And I'm now haunted by a characteristic that seems to follow me always. I disrupt the lives of those around me.

Dad said he wanted a healthy wife. One who wasn't always down with some ache or pain. I'm not sure how he ascertained that Mom did or didn't fit these qualifications, but he got his wish for the most part. Even with her heart trouble later in life, I always remember Mom on her feet and fully in charge.

Mom was a Stoll. Grandfather Stoll was a regal, jolly man with a fiery temper. He took on Amish bishops in his frequent complaints over the lack of missions and outreach. Somehow he survived those clashes. Often during his lengthy exchanges with church authorities, he would say too much. But once his temper had cooled, he'd get into his buggy and make return trips to apologize. And for awhile things would be smoothed over.

In the end it was his actions and not his words that would change so many of our lives. Grandfather Stoll had married a Wagler—Anna

Wagler. Her brother, the towering Amish intellectual David Wagler, along with several of Grandfather Stoll's sons, founded Pathway Publishers, an Old Order Amish publishing house. They were all men who bore themselves with a confidence born deep in their souls. Intellectuals, most of them. If they doubted their faith, the world never found out. The Waglers came with a stable, steady constitution, while the Stolls often flirted with brashness.

On the other side of my family, Grandfather Eicher was the opposite of the Stolls and Waglers. He was jolly and industrious. Few of his thirteen children showed any literary inclinations. Such things take a certain boldness of spirit, a willingness to work in the sunlight, and enough bravado to stare down critics. Grandfather Eicher ran underground like a mole. He had work to do. So while the Stolls and the Waglers wrote for Pathway and set forth on great ventures to change the world as they knew it, Grandfather Eicher ran the machinery at the print shop.

From left to right: Susanna, Sarah, John, Miriam, and Junior.

I'm the recipient of these dueling natures. Like Grandfather Eicher, I would rather stay out of sight and work with my hands. But then things stir in my spirit. Voices that must be obeyed. And up to the sunlight I go. It's Mom's fault really. She was the princess who married the stable help.

After their wedding, Mom and Dad set up house in one wing of Grandfather Stoll's home. The place was massive—a long, rambling house with high ceilings and huge rooms. My earliest memories begin there. I can see the house in the background while I'm wielding a stick and trying to chase a stray dog out of our yard. I don't think he was very frightened by my feeble efforts.

We moved after the birth of my brother John, the third child. All of us arrived in more or less yearly increments in those first years. My sister Susanna came second and was named after Stephen Foster's song *Oh Susanna*, written in 1847. Somewhere Dad heard the song and fell in love with the line of the chorus: "Oh, Susanna, don't you cry for me." I doubt if Mom and Dad ever told anyone about this un-Amish source of Susanna's well-known Amish name—at least not at the time.

During those years, Dad had a prosperous construction business, primarily working in the town of Aylmer where he contracted residential housing. Things went so well, Dad built his growing family a white two-story home across from the South Amish schoolhouse. Our house had a nice porch on the front and a basement. Across the lawn, a new barn went up. I think Dad planned to raise pigs on the side because there wasn't enough acreage for cows.

My Aunt Magdalena, from the Eicher side of the family, taught school in the two years I attended there. I arrived eager to learn and experience this new phase of life. I loved the schoolhouse's tall ceilings and the desks that were set in long rows. I loved the noise I could make with my shoes on the hardwood floors, the vast ceiling amplifying the sound. I remember a woodstove in the back and a shaggy woodshed outside. With our house just across the road, I didn't pack a lunch like the other children did. I ran home at lunchtime for whatever Mom had ready for me.

How I fared at my studies, I don't remember. There are no report cards saved from those days. What I do remember is standing beside my desk during recess. My schoolbooks are open in front of me. I glance across the aisle where one of Uncle Stephen's boys had his workbook open to the same place. His answer to one question was clearly different from mine. And since I knew him as someone whose answers were correct most of the time, I eagerly grabbed my eraser and corrected my mistake.

My cousin's eyes widened in horror. He didn't say anything as his mouth worked. When he had sufficiently collected himself, he rushed up front to report this clearly horrible offense to teacher Magdalena. I stood frozen at my seat, trembling inside as I awaited the approach of doom, which I knew would be followed by the gloating of my Stoll cousin. Indeed, he looked as if he had just cleansed the temple and was glad to have had a hand in the matter.

Magdalena looked things over, asked a few questions, and led me outside by the hand. I fully expected to be strapped on the spot. Instead, she asked me if I could explain why I'd changed my answer. I told her some version of what I just recounted.

"Don't do that again," she told me. And that was the end of it.

I was thunderstruck. I silently followed her back inside the schoolhouse, unable to believe this turn of events. I can't recall how my Stoll cousin took the verdict—I was too happy to care. But I never pulled that particular stunt again.

After school I was free to roam around the house or in the barn. I can't remember having any chores assigned to me, mostly because we didn't have any livestock beyond our horses. There was no hay in the mow, the empty expanse vast where sparrows chirped and nested.

As dusk fell, we would wait for Dad to come home from work. In the summertime he drove a cart with a toolbox attached underneath. Once the weather grew cold, he switched to his enclosed buggy.

The road we lived on was spotted with Amish homes all along the stretch. The first place west was the huge, two-story house dubbed the "Red Mansion." Why, I don't know, except it was made of red brick. It certainly wasn't for luxury reasons and it wasn't a third the size of Grandfather Stoll's place. It was inhabited at that time by Uncle Joe's family, with Uncle Stephen's family living in the next place on the right.

In those early years I saw my first set of Tinker Toys in front of the Red Mansion. They were in a round box leaning against the mailbox post. Some Stoll child had been given it as a gift, I was told. That day I wanted a box of Tinker Toys more than I'd ever wanted anything. Why I didn't say so, I have no idea. It simply seemed an unobtainable dream. Mom and Dad weren't poor by any sense of the word, and looking back now, I suspect they would have willingly purchased a set for us children.

In the other direction was Johnny Gascho's place. Uncle Johnny had married Mom's older sister Martha. He was a thin wisp of a man and mild-tempered to a fault—a trait that followed in his sons. It was the women who made the noise around the place.

Uncle Johnny's two oldest boys, Luke and Noah, were good friends of ours. They would sometimes invite my brother John and me to stay overnight. These visits we greatly enjoyed. One morning at breakfast I became aware of Uncle Johnny regarding me intensely. They had served pancakes along with real maple syrup made from their own trees. That was something we didn't get at home. I loved maple syrup and had poured liberal amounts on my pancakes. Clearly Uncle Johnny didn't approve of visiting little boys making off with his maple syrup. But he never said a word. I quickly finished eating, but I didn't pour any more maple syrup on my pancakes.

From there—to the east and north again—the hallowed grounds of Pathway Publishers were just around the corner. The building was low, hugging the ground. It was unpretentious compared to what went on inside. Pathway put out three monthly magazines designed especially for Amish readers. The aim was to contend for the faith primarily through the medium of story. Pathway printed our generation's first Amish fiction, and people came from far and wide to visit the place.

Inside, the assembly line hung from the ceiling—long spindly arms of wires and metal tracks. Grandfather Eicher, his hands stained with ink and his smile spread from ear to ear, would show us around the printing presses. Each page of the magazine had been transcribed to a master sheet and was spun around on rollers to create others like it, all in ways I didn't understand at the time. It was a land of wonder for me. A place where words spoke from paper. I already knew I loved books and stories. I hung out for long moments in the small bookstore off to

the right of the main door. I had no money to spend, but being close
to the stories was joy itself.

The place where my desire for books reached fever pitch was further down the road. I went there with my friend Ira Wagler on occasion. His father, David Wagler, had a red railroad caboose parked in
his front yard. It was loaded with books to sell—lots of them. Huge
shelves full of worlds that beckoned me away from the world in which
I lived. There the entire Mother West Wind series by Thornton Bur-
gess was on display. There I discovered the adventures of "Reddy Fox,"
and "Jimmy the Skunk," and "Peter Rabbit." I made do with the occasional copies people gave me—Ira, mostly. He allowed me to choose
a book for free when I went home with him as an overnight guest. I
dreamed of the day when I would own the entire set, which, for some
reason, never happened. Likely because I spent most of my childhood
far removed from such luxuries.

Friends like Luke and Ira were precious to me. More so on my part
than theirs, I'm sure. I was already tall and skinny for my age. I was
clumsy and spoke with a terrible stutter I didn't even realize I had at
that point. That, coupled with a naturally aggressive personality, meant
I wasn't always the most pleasant child to have around.

Chapter 3

My memories of Grandfather Stoll's house return in flashes. I see strawberry patches—long, long rows of them. And I'm tagging along with the adults as they harvest the berries. I must have been quite young to not be helping. All Amish children begin working early.

Aunt Mary claims I was always a sad child. Coming from her I don't doubt it, but I have no idea why I was that way. She always had a soft heart for people, and I was drawn to her. Outside of my immediate family, she was the person I felt the greatest affection for in my childhood—a feeling that seems to have gone both ways. Aunt Mary was a special woman. If there was someone hurting, she would be the first one there. She would go where others dared not. Even with excommunicated people, she was allowed special privileges.

Once when Uncle James—who had been placed in the *bann*—visited, Aunt Mary was the first one to cross the fields to greet him and give him some degree of welcome. Only then did a few of his brothers approach. A year or so earlier, Uncle James's wife had left him, and he'd been unable to resist the charms of a neighboring *Englisha* woman. Adding tragedy to tragedy in Amish eyes, a second marriage had ensued, and the result was Uncle James being put in the *bann*.

Aunt Mary also has the rare distinction of being married to a converted *Englisha*, David Luthy. Uncle David, as a young man, had studied for the Catholic priesthood, but through contact with my Uncle Elmo, David was drawn to the Amish lifestyle. He visited and liked the Aylmer community, eventually settling there. And not unlike many converts, he turned out more Amish than many a born-Amish man.

Today, Uncle David still works at Pathway, and he's collected the largest Amish historical library in existence—the Heritage Historical Library. I've seen him quoted for background material in Amish novels and in prestigious university works on the Amish. Stoll and Wagler bravado aside, it was David Luthy, with his *Englisha* education, who supplied the refining touches to the Pathway endeavor.

The last of Grandfather Stoll's natural-born children, Aunt Sarah, was a fragile girl. She suffered an injury in a buggy wreck prior to the Honduras move and spent months in bed recuperating, never seeming to fully recover. I remember visits to her sickbed with Mom. One of them was made memorable by the thrashing I received afterward. I had been told to be quiet during the visit. Instead, I ran up and down the stairs the whole time. Mom didn't make much of a fuss, which I calculated would have ensued if the matter were truly serious. My miscalculation became apparent once we were home. I ended up with my behind warmed that night. And I was never one to take spankings graciously.

Just beyond Pathway lay Grandfather Eicher's place. The family lived in a long, white house with large windows in the front. Toward the back, the house had a wing attached that included the mudroom and woodshed. A portion of the house had an upstairs, the roofline leaving the welcoming sweep of the front windows unaffected. Here the sustained memories of that period of childhood reside. I find that strange now. I would have thought they'd be at Grandfather Stoll's place or even at home. But they are not.

I remember the prayers at mealtimes around the long table. Grandfather Eicher would lead out in his singsong chant that charmed and fascinated me. It was as if he knew a secret he wasn't telling us. Some hidden pleasure he'd found that we could not yet see. I remember him always laughing. That was how he approached us grandchildren, his white beard flowing down his chest, his face glowing. And it didn't take a special occasion to put him in such a mood. It was as if *we* were the occasion.

Grandfather Eicher was a minister back then. Once, after we'd returned from Honduras, our hearts aching in sorrow, he approached me in the washroom and said there had been complaints that I was singing parts at the Sunday-night hymn singings. He told me, "We don't do things like that around here." He laughed as he said it, and I knew someone else had put him up to it. Grandfather Eicher wouldn't have cared one way or the other whether a few bass notes were growled at the hymn singings. But I nodded my agreement. There would be no more parts singing on Sunday nights.

I never knew another man who could make a person feel so at home, yet he never drew close, as if his heart was always far away.

His preaching is still a distinct memory. When I remember him speaking, I see his face lifted toward the ceiling, his hands clasped in front of him, his white beard flowing over his arms. He could chant a thousand miles an hour, or so it seemed to me. A person could lose himself in that voice. It was as if I were enveloped in love and acceptance. In his preaching, he was never going anywhere particular. He had no agenda. He simply exalted in the holy words, as if he were glad to be part of such a great thing.

Grandmother Eicher could chatter during the week about as fast as Grandfather Eicher did on Sundays. She'd say hi, give out a long stream of words, and then bustle on. There was always something going on at her house. She came from Arthur, Illinois. Grandfather made contact with her from his world in Davies County, Indiana. My guess is they met when he visited Arthur on weekends for weddings or funerals, typical Amish reasons to travel to another town. Grandmother Eicher had a great sorrow in life. She'd lost her first love under tragic circumstances before she could marry him. She never forgot that.

The Eicher men worked during the day, either in the fields or on construction jobs, so my visits to Grandfather Eicher's place were always populated with women.

Aunt Rosemary, the youngest aunt on the Eicher side was petite, the prettiest of the sisters. She would end up marrying a rather cultured Amish man from one of the trackless Northern Ontario Amish communities.

Aunt Nancy could move about as fast as Grandfather and Grandmother could talk. She was the shy one, even with us children. She would tilt her head in that peculiar way of hers, as if to deflect some incoming missile. She would marry one of the Stoll cousins, a man who stuttered as I did, although not as severely. Perhaps she had her own sorrows from which her heart reached out to a fellow sufferer.

Aunt Martha was the jolly one, always smiling and happy. I never saw her that she wasn't bubbling with joy. She was also a diabetic from early childhood. I remember she gave herself insulin shots in the leg and allowed us children to watch. I knew nothing then of the sufferings of a diabetic, and still don't, except from secondhand sources. But it could not have been easy for her. She never married. I don't think I ever heard of a suitor, either. It was just one of those things. Her kidneys gave out in her early fifties, and she soon chose to forgo dialysis rather than hire a driver to make the long trips into town. Her decision was influenced perhaps by the expense or simply from the weariness of suffering.

It must have taken great courage to walk so willingly over to the other side. But then I can imagine Aunt Martha facing it in her life lived in cheerful acceptance. I suppose she was welcomed home with more joy than many of the earth's great people. I know she lived close to the Father's heart.

Though most of my childhood was spent in Honduras surrounded by the vigorous intellectual life of the Stoll relatives, it was from here, at Grandfather Eicher's home, that I draw the characters for my Amish fiction writing. The white walls, the long dinner table, the open living room, the small spotless bathrooms, the yard outside with its swing tied high in the tree. And above all, from the feeling of simple living. It's here that life slows down. It's unpretentious. These people profess to be nobody special. There's a minister in the house, and later a bishop, but you wouldn't know it. They laughed a lot.

I've not always lived like that. Being honest, I've hardly ever lived like that. Life has been a hard climb, and each peak only reveals another. In those moments when I come home, this is where I come to. To Grandfather Eicher's house.

I shouldn't be surprised, but I am.

Chapter 4

On a typical day, Dad would drive his cart or buggy into the town of Aylmer, where most of his construction projects were. The distance was considerable for horse and buggy travel but doable. I suppose that's why the rules of the *ordnung* were later strengthened to state that no *Englisha* driver could be hired by the men who worked in construction. Rules made by farmers who viewed all work outside the family acreage with suspicion. Rules made to limit Amish involvement in *Englisha* endeavors.

Dad often brought home store-purchased ice cream wrapped in layers of paper bags to keep it cold. I know that homemade ice cream is now considered a delicacy, and I can't say I disagree. Perhaps the recipes have changed since those days, but back then we children gathered around *Englisha* ice cream with our mouths watering. There were few things we appreciated as much as Dad bringing home this treat in his toolbox.

Mom increased our delight in the goodness of our father by telling us that Uncle Leroy, Dad's brother, ate the ice cream he bought before he arrived home, leaving none for his family. Whether this was true or not, I never inquired. But the tale served its purpose, and Dad's gift grew large in our eyes. I could easily imagine Uncle Leroy licking the last of the melting ice cream from the paper wrapping minutes before he arrived home.

Our other taste of *Englisha* life was when a salesman stopped by to sell Mom some sort of nutritious orange drink. At least that's what he claimed it was. Good for what ails you, and absolutely necessary in the development of growing children, he said. We gathered around, wide-eyed, at the kitchen table as precious samples were measured out for our tasting. But that was as far as things went. The salesman left without his purse fattened, and we without our hearts gladdened for the coming day. Mom always sent him away with no orange drink left behind.

Our barn stood to the west of the house, a nice affair as barns go. New construction, of course, as all our buildings were. Dad had applied considerable thought to our place, pushing the limits of design a little for an Amish man. He was like that, always nudging the *ordnung's* fence when it came to his business.

There was even talk in those days of joining a more liberal church within the Amish world. Talk on Dad's part, that is. Mom would never have consented.

Dusk was falling by the time Dad arrived home on winter evenings, the glow of the gas lantern shining and welcoming in our kitchen window. He unhitched near the barn while we children raced outside to meet him, glad for a diversion after our day at home with Mom. After Dad took care of the horse, we trooped back inside with him.

Our house had a back door that opened to split-level stairs, one half going to the main level, the other to the basement. It was the only Amish home in the area with that feature that I know of. Probably a design taken from one of Dad's construction projects in town. Another reason, I suppose, he unwittingly contributed to later efforts by the Amish farmers to stop the further influence of the *Englisha* world by adding more limits to interactions between the two cultures.

Mom had supper on the table by then, set up just inside the stair door. I remember only silence at supper, our vague forms sitting around the table. We were a quiet bunch. There were six of us children by the time we left for Honduras. Sarah Mae, the seventh and youngest and cutest, would be born on foreign soil.

After supper Dad would work in his small machine shop he'd built between the barn and the road. Already he'd begun to tinker with what would become his main businesses when we moved to

Honduras—welding, metal lathe work, and basically anything else that involved metal.

People were always bringing over things to be worked on, and one day someone dropped off a lawnmower—the old self-propelled kind with a rolling drum blade. It was after dark that evening, and I was playing outside while Dad worked in his shop. I pushed the lawnmower around in the yard, playing at cutting grass. The machine must have needed its handle fixed, because there wasn't one attached. And somewhere in the midst of my fun, with my back bent over and hands holding the frame to propel the mower, my foot ended up in the drum blade. I remember no blinding flash of pain—just running into the shop to report that something was wrong. What, I was uncertain of.

I don't know where all the people came from so quickly, but suddenly they were there, gathered around me. A sizable number of them followed as I was carried over Dad's shoulder into the house. He set me down and examined my foot. Half a toe was gone. Someone ran over to the schoolhouse to make a phone call, and a car soon appeared. A neighbor, probably summoned from his dinner table, arrived. From there things get dim. I wasn't in pain that I can remember, but soon hospital walls appeared, and someone placed a mask over my face. And then I was out cold. I spent several days in the hospital with nothing memorable happening. Half of my toe was gone, but I don't remember being all that concerned. But obviously I haven't forgotten it either.

In the lore that passes through Amish mouths, I heard years later that a child under seven will grow back such shorn extremities if the body part is left alone. Apparently such wisdom was unknown to Mom and Dad—or disbelieved if it was. With a choice in the matter, I would have taken the chance. The injury can always be sewn up later if necessary.

It was from this house that Susanna and I set out one wintry afternoon. Mom had broken her last glass shade used on kerosene lamps—the only light we had for the bedrooms. For some reason it seemed important to Mom that those lamps be lit. So Mom wanted us to walk down to Bishop Pete's little store, a sort of all-around Amish specialty place the bishop kept in the middle of the community.

We weren't very old, obviously, and hard to convince of the wisdom in this journey. Finally Mom prevailed, and we were wrapped up and on our way. We were shivering, not from the cold but because there had been tales in the community of wolves spotted running in the woods up north. It didn't take much for me to see them hungrily devouring two small Amish children. Susanna's imagination wasn't that difficult to arouse either. (When I began writing fiction, she told me she was glad to see at least one of us doing something profitable with the wild Eicher imagination.)

Susanna and I pressed on in our journey, convinced to proceed not by the goodness of our hearts or from forced obedience. Mom had bribed us with a silver dollar apiece, so we didn't think of turning back. I remember snow blowing across the road, but we were well bundled up. We'd suffered no harm from the weather by the time we arrived at Bishop Pete's little store.

The bishop wrapped the purchased lampshades in paper bags and took the money Mom had sent along. We told him nothing about the silver dollars. The trip back was as uneventful as the coming had been. I've never forgotten the terror of watching the north woods with a pounding heart or peering across the fields for the first sight of long-legged wolves taking form in the driving snow.

Childhood must be a place where all children face their first nightmares. Is it not the world where the tales of *Little Red Riding Hood* and *The Three Little Pigs* are read? My own nightmares came at night after I'd see shadows on the walls that sent me racing into Mom's bedroom and calling for help. "There is someone in the house!" I reported. "He is very evil." She'd take me back to bed, comfort me, and tell me everything was okay.

Only years later, once I was grown, did Mom confess to seeing apparitions standing at the foot of her own bed. She even spoke to one once, but it vanished. That probably was the real reason we had the nightlight burning in the hallway every night. And why two Amish children faced the wolves during the day to escape the terrors during the night.

Chapter 5

We saw the red glow that evening after we'd finished supper. The distinct splash of crimson reached high into the southwestern sky. Red color where there should have been blue sky. We all gathered out in the yard and stared off into the distance. Clearly someone's place was on fire. We watched as the air around us seemed to tingle with excitement.

Out on the road, traffic had increased, lines of cars driving by. *Englisha* people who had seen the same thing we had. Dad ran out to the road and flagged down the car of someone he knew and left with him. We continued standing there watching the glow until Mom herded us inside for bed.

Dad must have come home in the late hours of the morning, but none of us children heard him. We were told the news the next morning when we awoke. Grandfather Stoll's big house had burned up. Aunt Mary had been cooking on their old wood kitchen stove, alone in the house while the others did the chores. An explosion had occurred— thankfully while Aunt Mary was out of the kitchen. By the time the phone call was made at an *Englisha* neighbor's place and the fire department arrived from Aylmer, not much could be done. The wood and other burnable materials in the long, rambling brick building had been a tinderbox.

Mom took us over in the buggy after breakfast. I climbed out to stare at the smoldering ruins. Bricks lay scattered everywhere, tall stacks of them where the walls had not completely collapsed. The yard was full of household items scattered all over the place. Several of the Stoll uncles walked around ashen-faced. They looked as if they'd been up all night.

Losing one's house or barn is not that uncommon among the Amish. And Grandfather Stoll suffered no loss of face, even with his well-known trait of tangling with Amish bishops over mission issues—which could have produced whispers of God's judgment. If there were any such whispers, I never heard them.

The rebuilding efforts on a new house across the lane were begun at once. I've often wondered what part the fire played in the events that followed. Was Grandfather Stoll spurred on for change? Perhaps reminded of the passing nature of life? Driven to move where he might not have gone otherwise? I have no evidence, but I do know his movement into mission work soon followed. The talk, first of a children's home in northern Canada, which was followed by his focus shifting to the Central American country of Honduras. The Honduras possibility had come through an *Englisha* man Grandfather had met, a Dr. Youngberg, who had established a children's home in that country.

Dad, on the other hand, had different motives for his interest in all the talk about Honduras. His pesky younger brother, Uncle Joseph Eicher, for one, wouldn't leave him alone to work in peace. Also motivating Dad was an upcoming *ordnung* change that would ban all Amish construction work in Aylmer.

Uncle Joseph had always been a favorite at home apparently, and as a grown man he held Bishop Pete's ear close. For whatever the reasons, Uncle Joseph and Dad had a vibrant sibling rivalry going on. It could have had something to do with the fact Dad was prospering in his business and well-liked, while that wasn't always true of Uncle Joseph.

As Dad's business continued to grow, suspicions were being aroused that Dad was using methods against the *ordnung* to earn his money. I don't know who the source of these rumors was, but more than likely it was Uncle Joseph. At the very least, he fed them.

Once Dad showed me his building contracts from those years—$13,000 to $14,000 per home. It seems like a small amount now compared to the current $200,000 to $300,000 dollar contracts. But back then it was considered a large sum—or enough at least that some of the men in the Amish community of Aylmer were motivated to take action.

In a culture where hard work is prized, Uncle Joseph seemed to have had plenty of idle time on his hands, which he used to look into Dad's affairs. Uncle Joseph would often drive past Dad's worksites in Aylmer to look for electric tools or any signs of their use. Electrical tools were strictly forbidden by the church *ordnung*, and they were on the list of reported offenses Dad was supposedly committing.

Knowing Dad, I doubt he was innocent in the matter. There are many ways one can circumvent such laws, at least until a person is caught. Many Amish brains are kept limber not by higher studies but by inventing creative solutions to their restricted lifestyles, especially by the ones who plan to stay in the community. And Dad planned to stay—at least at the present time.

The truth was that Dad's crew kept a full complement of electric tools, which were run by a generator. All of them legally in someone else's name. A Realtor at this particular time. A man cheerfully complicit in the Amish church games.

I'm sure the crew had many a good belly laugh over the situation, all while keeping a wary eye out, watching for Uncle Joseph's buggy to turn in from the main road. They probably kept their gas skill saws nearby, ready to be fired up. Ready for the wild scramble to hide the electric cords and shut down the generator before Uncle Joseph got close enough to get a good look or listen. They were always secure in the knowledge that none of them owned the equipment even though they had paid for it.

Uncle Joseph was tireless in his pursuit, even though he never found any electric tools that I know of. He did finally hit pay dirt. It occurred to him one day to check the phone book for Dad's name. How this thought came to him, I have no idea. Perhaps he thought Dad had a phone hidden in our barn. How else, after all, could Dad be making all those lucrative home-building connections? Whatever the reason, Uncle Joseph checked and found a phone listing under Dad's name. He had found the loose chink in Dad's armor. Uncle Joseph must have nearly lost his hat running to Bishop Pete. And much wool soon hit the fan. This was a violation that couldn't be easily explained away.

Dad was indeed keeping a phone, but not in the barn. It was in the little storage shed he kept behind his building sites. He had the phone so the Realtor could call and set up appointments and for ordering materials. Why Dad didn't think to have the phone listed in the Realtor's name, I don't know. Perhaps this was one bridge too far for the longsuffering Realtor, even with the healthy income Dad was making for him in sales commissions.

By the time the dust settled, a new *ordnung* rule was in effect. No more Amish construction work was allowed within the town limits of Aylmer, Ontario, Canada—a rule still in effect to this day. A rule that if questioned now would be considered liberal drift, a wandering into the world, a loss of holy things.

The result was that Dad would soon be making threats to leave the Amish and join the Beachys, a fairly conservative Mennonite group, although I don't think there were any Beachys in the area at the time. Mom was adamantly opposed to that idea. She would not leave the Amish under any circumstances.

During all this, Mom had Grandfather's ear, and I'm sure he heard about the threats. How much this played into his plans for a new Amish community on foreign soil, I don't know. But I wouldn't be surprised if they hastened them. Grandfather had yet to lose one of his children to a more liberal Anabaptist church, and I'm sure he didn't want Mom to be the first casualty.

So with the *ordnung* change, the Realtor had to be told the news, along with explanations as to why his best contractor could no longer work in town. To his credit, he must not have laid blame on Dad's doorstep because the two remained steadfast friends.

A move to a foreign country might seem a little radical in response to all this, but that's how things shook down. I was a boy, so I couldn't have cared less back then about these matters. Or perhaps I blocked out the trauma portion of that time. I really remember nothing of the move. It's as if I awoke one morning and found myself in a valley outside of Guaimaca, Honduras.

Chapter 6

Nothing happens in Amish land without ministers, and Grandfather Stoll needed ministerial help for his mission venture to Honduras to succeed. And a new minister can't be made without an existing bishop's aid. So finding a bishop who would support the venture was the first order of business. And finding one would take a miracle. Bishop Pete, owner of the small store in our community, was having nothing to do with the wild plans floating around in Grandfather's head. Though in a testament to Grandfather's character, Bishop Pete didn't forbid the venture, which would have doomed it.

Grandfather didn't get his miracle immediately, but he got second best—two ministers who were willing to move with him. How he found even one, let alone two, I don't know. But he did—Richard Hochstetler and Vernon Schmucker. Both were ordained Amish ministers from the sprawling Old Order Amish communities of Northern Indiana.

And how Grandfather located and chose the valley outside of Guaimaca, I don't know. Perhaps Dr. Youngberg took him on a tour of the country. However it was done, Grandfather purchased the 550-acre farm called Finca Sanson and moved there in 1968, along with his wife, Anna, my Aunts Mary and Sarah, Uncles Abner and Mark, and Grandfather's foster child, David Fehr.

After arriving in Honduras and settling in, Grandfather wrote letters home singing the praises of the land and begging others to follow him. They could divide the property or purchase more, he said. There was plenty of land and opportunity. The mango and orange plantations were close by. All we needed to do was make the 3000-mile trip. Oh, and learn to speak Spanish. But that would all be fun, he said.

The men back in Aylmer talked, and weighed the options, and looked at maps. Dad was not involved in these deliberations. He'd made up his mind by other methods and for other reasons. The upshot of it was that by January of 1969, three of the men took the bait and set out on an exploratory trip. "To spy out the lay of the land," they said. The three men were my Uncle Joe Stoll, Monroe Hochstetler, and my dad.

On that first bouncy, curvy, dusty, four-hour bus trip between the Honduras capital city of Tegucigalpa and Guaimaca, Dad vowed he would never move to Honduras. But when he arrived at Grandfather's farm, he quickly changed his mind. The place had that kind of charm—an almost otherworldly feel.

Soon after they arrived, Grandfather gave them a tour of the farm. The elevation rose to just below 3000 feet and lay at the foot of a mountain called Mt. Misoco, that rose to approximately 3500 feet. Indigenous pines that whispered in the wind grew plentifully on the knolls surrounding Guaimaca. From everywhere the beautiful, broad sweep of the mountain range to the north could be seen. In the weeks before the dry season ended, the locals burned the pastures, turning the hillsides into creeping fires that at night seemed to encircle one with what looked like a thousand lights twinkling like evil stars fallen to the earth. A sight, I suspect, the three visitors were spared in January.

Being an honest man, Grandfather told the men about the ongoing war between Honduras and San Salvador. A small affair really, and Grandfather assured everyone there was no cause for concern. The border dispute had arisen from a long-simmering conflict over land lying between the two countries. The current action consisted of a few Salvadorian soldiers rushing into Honduras and then rushing back while being pursued by Hondurans. Shots were fired at each other without injury, and a stalemate developed.

Before the Amish scouts from Canada arrived, a little incident had occurred. Emboldened one dark night to acts of valor, the Salvadorian

Air Force rose into the air flying cast-off planes donated by the US military. They set out to see what could be bombed. In such a land, blackouts weren't even dreamed of. Wood fires in barrels don't produce much light anyway. Besides, who believed the enemy would come this far inland? Even with the home fires burning in Guaimaca, the Salvadorians missed the place by three kilometers; instead the bomb threw up sawdust at a local sawmill. They had no greater success at Talanga, a town an hour closer to the capital. They missed by a kilometer and bombed an empty field.

Sawmill in Guaimaca.

As Grandfather Stoll told them the story, there were nervous chuckles, but no one changed any plans. There clearly wasn't enough oomph in this place to blow up much of anything.

Eventually the talk turned to farming, particularly how it was done differently here than either in the States or Canada. Since the locals used no modern machinery and the horses were all scrawny and unusable for farming, they plowed with oxen. That is, what plowing was done. The plow consisted of little more than a blade—often wooden— that scratched the ground. It was pulled by oxen strapped together by a yoke and driven by tapping them with a stick and loudly hollering at them. A simple enough affair, but it horrified the visitors' Amish souls.

No, that would not do for these seasoned Amish farmers. They would need Belgian or Percheron horses. *Large* ones. So the men made plans to ship in Belgians, the Amish dream horse. The idea seemed right enough at the time. They would fly them in, and the problem would be solved. The locals might even learn a thing or two. And with good breeding stock on the ground, there would be plenty of horses for years to come. And that's what happened. The flying in part, at least. And the breeding plan worked reasonably well. But the result wasn't what they expected. For reasons not known at the time, the Belgians couldn't take the climate. The horses overheated, and not many years passed until there were few left. Eventually the Amish abandoned the plan, chalking it up to a lesson learned the hard way.

Fertilizer was unknown to the locals. The soil along the river bottom was black and rich though, and hopes among the three visitors soared. Weather-wise, there was the rainy season that lasted six months or so. This period bled gradually into the dry season, leaving only four months of rainless skies. Eventually the Amish would learn to grow two crops a year, trenching their land to irrigate the crops during the dry season.

The one drawback to the place was the aforementioned road, which the visitors had already experienced. That and the distance from Canada. But the road was the real abomination. Stories would long be told of its atrocities. Everyone had a nightmare of being scrunched in the seat of the local bus next to some smelly mountain man or of bouncing around like a jack-in-the-box on the hard vinyl seats while the bus driver dodged potholes. And all usually with a local resident's squealing pig strapped on top.

And there was the speed of the buses—or rather the lack thereof. Usually anything from fifteen miles per hour steadily with occasional thirty-miles-per-hour spurts. Visitors counted the curves and argued with the local Amish boys over the number. I don't remember the count, but it came in somewhere around a thousand. I would learn to know them as a sickening twist in my stomach. Dad used to take us into Tegucigalpa, the capital city, to McDonald's for hamburgers. For years afterward, even when we'd moved back stateside, I couldn't eat a McDonald's hamburger without feeling my stomach shift.

The three scouts took everything under consideration. Next up was a tour of the nearby town of Guaimaca, which consisted of colorful adobe huts. Not a paved road or street was in sight. Stores with wooden shutters faced the streets. The merchandise of local baked sweets and packaged products hung over the side of the windows. Familiar soft drinks were close at hand, including Pepsi, and served in glass bottles. Naked children stood in the doorways, staring at them. Pigs in the yards lifted their snouts to witness their passing, looking as if they were wondering why white faces had suddenly taken shape within their vision.

Seeing the immense physical and spiritual needs of the country stirred the Amish men's souls. I suppose they saw the potential of what needed to be done and what could be done. The realization had yet to grip them that here in poverty-stricken Honduras, they would be the rich in the land, no longer pitied as backward as they were up north.

The Hondurans in this little village existed on so little—basically beans and flour tortillas, a little rice, and produce perhaps. Three times a day with little variation that's what they ate. The scouts figured it shouldn't take much to improve such a life. Just a little work with a little energy applied.

So the three scouts returned home sober-faced but eager for the task. Why should their religion be locked away in Canada? they reasoned. Why should they have such limited influence on their culture when so much could be done on foreign soil? They looked the questions in the face and answered the "Why?" with a "Why not?" They would go. They would work with what they had. And in going, they would make the world a better place.

I don't imagine Dad was quite thinking those thoughts. He probably dreamed no higher than using an electric skill saw without his pesky brother driving up the street to try to catch him in a transgression.

Chapter 7

We were one of the first families to leave Canada for Honduras, arriving in August of 1969. I remember nothing of the trip down. My first recollections are darkness and driving onto a long gravel lane that ended up at a boxy two-story house. It wasn't until the morning that I saw the colorfulness of the white house with its line of tall coconut trees in the front yard and the immense orchard of oranges and mangos surrounding the backyard. We had arrived in another world. Strange and different yet populated by faces I knew. We moved in with Grandfather Stoll for three weeks while our living quarters back toward the main road were being prepared. I don't know how Grandfather managed with all of us crammed into only two upstairs bedrooms in that

Our first cottage in Honduras.

boxy house, but somehow we survived by sleeping in the basement and in corners here and there.

Grandfather took it upon himself to teach me the Spanish numbers in those early days. I remember sitting with him on the couch saying, *"Uno, dos, tres,"* and liking the sound of the words.

Dad threw together a wooden-framed building in three weeks. An enlarged cottage, actually, set on running boards instead of a foundation. It served its purpose. A well driller was eventually found in Tegucigalpa, and when he finished, water was hooked up to Mom's sink. That was as far as the plumbing went though.

We would use the outhouse for the four years we stayed in that house. It was a stinky place set up in the backyard just before the land dropped off in a gentle slope. A place that holds no fond memories for me. I also became acquainted with chamber pots at this time, what we simply called "the pot." To empty one in the morning was an intensely vile experience. Once we moved into the new house a few years later and returned to the blessed existence of indoor plumbing, none of us had the slightest desire to repeat the bathroom experiences in the cottage.

Most of the locals had neither outhouses nor chamber pots. And they toted the water they needed from the abundant streams in the area. Their washing was also done there if they lived close enough. Otherwise

Laundry day in Honduras.

they set up a washboard outside their shack and slammed their clothes against it or hammered the clothes clean with a rock on the spot.

The Amish brought along gas-powered washing machines in the crates they'd shipped into the country. When our crate arrived, Mom had her Maytag set up in an overhang behind the shop which, by then, Dad had finished, along with our small well-house.

Sometime later, a chicken house was built below the outhouse. I believe it was on stilts to give the chickens some protection from predators and some shade. All around the community in those days buildings were popping up like tents as more people moved in. Most of them were designed to be future pigpens and chicken houses, but for the time being they would serve as temporary people housing. All were built by energetic and enthused Amish builders.

Being in a foreign land, no one thought to ask the locals why they built with adobe instead of wood. I suppose the Amish assumed the reason was poverty—an assumption later proved wrong. The locals did build with adobe because it was cheap, but mainly they did so because of termites. All the early Amish buildings were built completely out of wood—and untreated wood at that. No Amish knew yet about the termites or, if they did, that the insects could and would fly to the houses. And fly they did. And quickly. The termites ended up everywhere and began eating at once.

Later efforts would be made to treat the termite-infested houses but with little success. I have recent pictures of those first buildings that are now crumbled to the ground. In some places there are only bare concrete slabs bearing mute testimony to what had once been. Today the *gringos* are much wiser and build with concrete blocks and use treated wood when wood is absolutely necessary.

There were other lessons to be learned. Some of them learned a little quicker. One of the first lessons was that this was a land of scams. Men would bump into a person on the streets, and the small glass bottle they'd been carrying would shatter on the ground. Wails would ensue, along with loud cries for help. Dramatic protestations were made over the great loss. This had been the only medicine the household could afford, a man would say. His child lay home sick, near death's door, and the doctor had said this was the only hope. Now the last lempira had been spent. And as God was their witness, they had no place to turn. Could the gracious *gringo* please have compassion?

As this tale was told and retold in the community, the Amish became wise to such schemes. When it happened to Uncle Mark, he continued marching down the street after the bottle shattered on the street. Not content with only foiling the scam, Uncle Mark stopped at the corner to peer back at the hapless fellow. Perhaps he was suffering from momentary doubt. What if this fellow really was in need? Had the suffering perhaps been real this time? But as Uncle Mark watched, the man stood there studying his broken medicine splattered on the sidewalk. After long moments, the man shook his head in disgust and reached into his coat pocket. Out came another bottle. And down the street he went, looking around for his next victim.

Such stories didn't stop the Amish's compassion, but it did drive home the need to distinguish between the real and the pretend. And, sadly, the real existed in great quantities.

⌒⌒

By October of that year, Uncle Joe and Uncle Stephen had arrived, as well as others of the Stoll family.

Our small parcel of land lay near the middle of the Sanson farm. The buildings were set along the lane that serviced the main house where Grandfather Stoll lived. Uncle Joe and Uncle Stephen, being farmers, took larger portions of land to the south of us. Uncle Joe set up on the east, and Uncle Stephen to the west.

North of us, near where the lane turned west toward his place, Grandfather Stoll would lay out the grounds for his children's home, a place where children could get support, clothes, food, and a safe place to sleep if they needed it. This was situated at the foot of what we called "the hill"—a small knoll stuck in the middle of things. By now Grandfather Stoll had adopted two local children, Conchita and Inez. At least those were their names for the years we lived in Honduras. Years later, in Canada, they changed their names to Esther and Jonathon. These two were the beginnings of Grandfather's dream of rescuing local children.

Years later, in the 1990s, my brother John would return to this same spot with his wife, Ruth, and their two small children. By then the children's home buildings had been rebuilt, and John eventually had his own two-story house raised at the foot of the hill. They served in the Honduras Amish community for more than thirteen years before returning stateside in 2008. One of our ministers said he'd never met anyone other than his own father who had such a heart for missions as did John. I could have told him John received the gift from his grandfather.

By fall, Dad had his machine shop up and running. It was a larger version of what he'd had in Aylmer. This one was complete with a full complement of welders, metal cutters, drill presses, and eventually a high-quality lathe. He could now repair or replicate the basic sawmill machinery and truck parts made of metal.

Business wasn't that great at first, so Dad set his entrepreneurial spirit to work by making hay wagons. Not one to aim low, we had wagon frames sitting everywhere in the shop yard. Dad quickly flooded the local market. He resorted to selling at a steep discount, eventually moving all of them.

Dad used a Ford 2701 diesel truck engine to run his new generator. Quite a step up from running concealed generators in storage sheds at Aylmer. Now nothing had to be hidden. The engine ran with a mighty roar and could be heard almost back to Grandfather Stoll's place. I don't know why generators were now allowed. Somewhere it had been decided in the *ordnung*, I suppose. Or perhaps it just happened, as many such things seemed to. At last my Amish dad was set up with his fully electrified machine shop. By the time we left Honduras, he would put over 18,000 hours on his beloved diesel engine.

The tale is often told of how the men from the young Amish community were having a meeting one evening. They were gathered on top of the knoll within sight of our place. The church house had been built there. The meeting was to explore business ideas for the many newcomers to the community. As the evening progressed, it became evident that new industries were difficult to execute in this foreign environment.

The conversation dragged into the late-evening hours. Then off in the distance the sound of Dad's diesel motor fired up, filling the night

Dad's shop in Honduras.

air with its roar. Dad had become bored and left, stopping in at the shop to work awhile before retiring. Amused, the men looked at each other and dismissed the meeting.

"That's our answer," one of them is quoted as having said. "Enough of this talk. It's time to get busy like Sammy Eicher."

Grandfather Stoll was already ahead of the others in getting busy. He'd knocked together a store building out by the main road. He sold everything having to do with grocery items—at least those that existed in the area. He also sold some local produce from the community, although the real market for that was in Tegucigalpa.

My Uncle Abner ran a route into Tegucigalpa twice a week. He would leave early in the morning, well before any of us were up, with the sideboards raised high on a flatbed truck, and the bed loaded to the top with fresh vegetables of all sorts, plus sour cream and eggs. Almost anything that could be raised would sell in the capital.

As for me, being too young for steady work, I wandered around the community after school and on weekends, visiting Grandfather Stoll's store often—mostly to drink Pepsi. Real Honduras Pepsi that was much better than what was sold stateside. Many are the theories why this is still true—from the use of glass bottles to the difference in sugar content. The latter sounds the most plausible to me—but who knows?

Chapter 8

The first Amish school was held that winter in Grandfather Stoll's basement. Aunt Sarah was our teacher. We only had a few books and bits and pieces of curriculum someone brought with them from Canada. It passed for my third-grade education. I sat at my little desk in the small room and looked out through the screens at the towering palm trees. We scribbled in our books, but my mind was mostly elsewhere. Already I roamed Grandfather's orchard with abandon, exploring through the mango and orange trees, occasionally walking all the way to the back fields where the creek ran in a deep ravine. Uncle Mark, who was part of the community from the beginning, took some of us children there the first time. To me it was like the edge of a great jungle. He led us on a trail to the dam. It was an overgrown path, through which little sunlight filtered, beginning where the mango orchard ended and following the rushing little creek. We arrived eventually at the concrete dam an amateur builder had poured across the creek— a rough-hewn model of architecture but beautiful to our young eyes.

Here lay the deepest swimming hole around at the time, filled with cool, refreshing water and hidden below a leafy canopy. You could do a decent dive, just not too deep. I went as often as I could find someone to go with me. Going way back there, even I didn't travel alone.

We walked everywhere at first. Back and forth between our place and Grandfather's house mostly. No one seemed to mind. Walking was a pleasure, and everything was close at hand. Grandfather's place lay to the north of us, with Uncle Joe and Uncle Stephen's places to the south. The other farm, La Granja, which would soon be purchased, adjoined Sanson to the east. All were within a handy walking distance, and hardly worth the effort of hitching up a horse to travel. Dad did eventually modify one of his wagons for our transportation. A sort of flatbed with the center lowered for seating, pulled by Molly, one of the Belgians that had been flown in.

To the south of the community's two farms lay the town of Guaimaca. Many Amish residents walked that far too. That is, the vigorous ones, mostly those from La Granja. They'd come from Amish communities in Northern Indiana and were a little strange to us. They had a more vigorous step than did the Stoll clan. It was as if they carried a more optimistic view on life.

I didn't go to Guaimaca in those early days, preferring to stay close around the home place. But once I was older and had my own horse, going to Guaimaca was a weekly or better affair. I took a twisty back trail through the woods at a steady trot and an occasional gallop. Out to the main road, past Grandfather's store, and up a small incline between the first two foothills, dashing through the wooded river sections, splashing across the streams, imagining giants and ancient warriors chasing after me. Then a turn to the left and I would be cutting across people's backyards, sending chickens flying, until I burst onto the main street of town. No one ever seemed to mind.

My first horse fit my dreamy view of life in those days, appearing as if by magic one day. I was standing in front of our wooden cottage looking toward the south at nothing in particular when a man appeared leading a gangly little steed. I turned my gaze in wonder upon such an object, my heart pounding harder.

Oh, for a horse to ride! It seemed completely impossible. Dad hadn't made any promises about buying a horse, and I had no hope that he would. I just knew the ugly thing was beautiful to my eyes. I asked the man if he was selling the animal. I used the Spanish I had acquired by then to finesse the conversation. He said he was, and I raced to find Dad.

When Dad came back with me, I breathlessly followed their talk.

Yes, the man said, he wished to sell the horse. And yes, he would take American dollars. In fact, he would only take American dollars. A fact I'm sure the seller made up on the spot, but it sounded like a decent bargaining tool.

Dad did a perfunctory check of the offered animal. Not looking very hard, I don't think. And neither did I. I wanted a horse, and this one could obviously be ridden. That was all that mattered.

"Fifty-five dollars," the man said, closing in on his sale.

Back then that was double in the local currency—110 lempiras. Dad hesitated but made the purchase. I couldn't believe my good fortune! I led the horse to the wooden fence and climbed on bareback.

I didn't know a thing about riding horses, never having been on one before. So I suppose it was by divine grace I didn't have a fire-breathing stallion for my first horse. At least I didn't break any legs or arms falling off its back.

I loved that horse. I never gave him a name that I can remember. I'm not sure why, but none of the reasons had anything to do with lack of affection. Under my care, and with good food and plenty of rest, this one fattened up some. I wasn't yet into traveling to the mountain, so he was only used around the farm and for errands into Guaimaca. I would soon know the back trail to town by heart.

⟳

Grandfather received his bishop miracle. I never heard or read how the contact was made, but a New Order Amish bishop by the name of Wallace Byler appeared in the community for a visit. Apparently he hit it off with Grandfather because he would return to provide the vital church leadership any new Amish community needs. Ministers had to be ordained, communion services had to be conducted, and eventually a local bishop set in place.

In the meantime, Amish families kept arriving, filling the available land on both Finca Sanson and La Granja. Our hopes rose high, and our spirits were comforted. Many took courage as all the signs pointed toward the Amish experiment on foreign soil working out for the best interest of all parties. I was approaching nine years of age, and I honestly didn't care about the logistics and community workings—other than the excitement of having other Amish people around. I was enjoying life on my own terms, which was not always for the best. Sadly, stealing and lying soon became a regular part of my life. Not a major part, I suppose, but little spots on the apple. And I remember having absolutely no troubled conscience about my devious activities. Depravity seemed to rise unbidden and remained unrebuked by me. But I did know right from wrong because I was careful to hide my erring ways from everyone around me.

One tale from that era can only be retold with shame. Grandfather Stoll had taken on another of his charity projects, a boy from over the mountain. Neil, I believe, was his name. There were no plans for adoption, but Grandfather's heart went out to the lad because of his hard-luck story. His father had abandoned the family—a common enough story in that area—and the mother had taken up with another man. The boy wasn't wanted.

In Neil's eyes, nothing fit the bill for a new start quite like taking up with an Amish family. We were *gringos* in the eyes of all the locals, and we were rich beyond most of their wildest imaginations. We lived a way of life they could only dream of. Neil was no doubt attracted by the lifestyle, but he also loved Grandfather's kindness, something he had known little of.

Grandfather Stoll wasn't totally into Neil staying long-term, so repeated efforts were made to take him back to his home. Trips were made over the mountain, and the boy was left with his family. But Neil kept coming back. And Grandfather's heart was too soft to force him out.

Enter me. For some reason I took a disliking to the boy. I have no idea why. He was older than I was and didn't encroach on my territory that I remember. But I figured out how to get rid of Neil when a large amount of money went missing. I was already slipping single lempiras from Grandfather's billfold when he sent me on errands, figuring they wouldn't be missed. So I knew about stealing, and I knew how much it was disliked.

I volunteered the information that I knew Neil had taken the missing money, that I'd seen him with it. It wasn't true. I had no idea who had really taken the money.

Vigorous denials followed from Neil. He had nothing to do with the theft, he said. He emptied out his pockets. He swore in the presence of God and the Holy Mother. But it was to no avail. Amish people don't like lying and stealing, but they like it even less if you don't confess once you're caught. And with me as the witness, Neil was guilty in their eyes. So Grandfather hardened his heart and Neil was gone. And I felt nothing but satisfaction in a job well done.

Soon my stealing expanded. I slipped small amounts of cash from the register at Grandfather's store on the days I helped him tend the counter. I used it to buy small snacks and the prized Pepsis I loved. Grandfather had too big a heart to ask Mom if she'd given me money. And Mom was generous anyway, so no doubt he assumed she had. I even stole from the aunt I loved the most—sweet, trusting Aunt Mary with her heart of gold. I did my dastardly deeds on the Saturdays when I rode along in the wagon with her into Guaimaca, where Aunt Mary ran a small route selling garden produce, butter, *mantiqea* [a local version of sour cream], and homemade ice cream. The drill was always the same. I kept small amounts of what I collected, buying food with it as we drove along even though Aunt Mary paid me at the end of each Saturday as a small gift for my time. Again, I had no qualms. It wasn't until years later, when I met goodness under the conviction of the Holy Spirit, that my conscience came alive. Then it didn't take anyone to teach me what evil was. I knew I was a living example.

Early that fall another evil came creeping into the community. We heard only whispers at first. Faint rumors that chilled our hearts as the men talked about it. And we knew it was true when the first of the animals became sick. The Venezuelan equine encephalitis virus—sleeping sickness, for short—was abroad in the land. A mosquito-spread disease that could even affect humans. I imagined the hungry mosquito coming in through our windows at night, settling on us children while we slept. Then soon would follow the shivering fever and the final falling asleep, never to awaken again. We trembled from fear and secured the screens the best we could.

Our horses were all at risk, we were told. And all around us reports came in of ranchers who were losing their animals. A general rush was made by the Amish to vaccinate the animals—a practice the locals didn't value very highly or couldn't afford. Those vaccinations ended up saving all but a few of the animals on our two farms.

We heard that Uncle Joe's horse was sick and went down to see. We didn't stay long, and when it became obvious after several days that nothing could be done, the horse was put down. An act to which I was not a witness. The telling of the tale was bad enough.

Also about this time, we heard the first whispers of thieves lifting items after dark. We responded by organizing a few amateur posses to sleep in the outbuildings. Unarmed, of course, and sleeping with flashlights at the ready. The situation wasn't something that couldn't be solved or controlled, the men reasoned. It could surely be solved by more careful locking of doors and windows and by a few scares from lights shone in the thieves' startled faces.

If they'd only known the truth, they would not have been so confident.

Chapter 9

Uncle Stephen's accident happened on one of those October afternoons we were all learning to enjoy so much. Eighty degrees, a slight breeze blowing, and no sight of rain from the puffy clouds overhead. Most of the community had gathered at the tall, two-story children's home, which had been hastily constructed by then to unload several heavy crates that had arrived from stateside.

Most of the families did this—shipped in their personal and business items in large packaged crates. These boxes sometimes wouldn't arrive until months after the family was already here. The arrival of a crate was a huge affair, both in the shared rejoicing that it had come and in unloading it. The children's home at the bottom of the hill was chosen as the unloading site because it was central to the community and this time at least one of the crates belonged to one of the single women who would be taking care of the children.

Several stout trees grew in the backyard. Oaks, I think, or at least a Honduras version of oak. The local truck hired to haul the crates from Tegucigalpa ended up backed under one of them. Block and tackle were brought out, and the unloading began. A strong limb was chosen, and the chains thrown over them. The adults discussed angle, limb strength, tonnage, and probable weight-bearing points. They decided to go with what they had, and the box was cranked into the air. When nothing happened to the limb, Uncle Stephen and Uncle Abner jumped on the truck bed surrounded by its tall sideboards.

The crack came without warning, like a shot from a large-caliber gun. It drew my instant attention from where I was standing near the children's home. Looking toward the truck, I saw Uncle Stephen trying to leave his perch on the sideboard. His body at chest level was still on top when the branch hit. It seemed to be in slow motion as the branch came down, squashing Uncle Stephen between the limb and the top of the sideboard. The impact bounce lifted the limb back up in the air, and Uncle Stephen's body flew out and onto the ground as the branch crashed down again on the sideboards without rising this time. Around us there was dead silence.

I ran closer as the men near Uncle Stephen rushed to his side. Behind me women poured out of the children's home. Through the forms of the men I saw Uncle Stephen's body crumpled, lying on its side, his face hidden from my view. No one said much.

A woman came rushing forward, Emil Helmuth's wife, Edna, I think. Someone had told her that Emil was the one lying on the ground. She quickly discovered the error, and Uncle Stephen's name was spoken. His wife, Katie, heard, unable to believe it. They helped her forward to kneel beside him. He was gasping for breath but still alive. When a sheet of plywood arrived—sent for by someone—they slid Uncle Stephen on it and carried him to the yard and surrounded his form with blankets.

That he was dying was the unspoken thought. We huddled around, our faces sober. Someone suggested sending for a doctor, and volunteers immediately surfaced. Daniel Hochstetler and Paul Schmucker, both young boys from La Granja offered their services. They wanted to borrow my horse, which I had tied to the fencerow a short distance away. They only had access to one horse—and that was for Daniel to ride. Paul needed a horse—mine. I should have said yes, but I said no instead. I wanted in on the excitement myself. "I'll come with you!" I told Daniel.

Daniel didn't look happy, but I suppose he knew this was not a moment for quibbling. So Paul remained behind, and Daniel and I mounted our horses and rode headlong into town, stopping only to spread the news to some Amish people we passed along the road. It was dark by the time we arrived and beat on the doctor's door. He wasn't home, we were told. So we rode over to another place Daniel knew of, where a nurse lived, I think, but with no greater success. Unbeknownst to us, another search party had left while Daniel was trying to secure my horse, caught a ride into town, and the doctor was already on the way back to the community.

By the time we arrived back at the children's home, the doctor had been there and left. A pickup truck and driver had also been found, and Uncle Stephen was on his way to the hospital in Tegucigalpa. Mom chewed me out for leaving the scene. She said I'd missed a very touching scene.

As Uncle Stephen lay there, thinking he was dying, he had gathered his family around him and given them his last words. Uncle Stephen's wife, Katie, and their children, had been in the inner circle, kneeling around the blanket. Others from the community had stood around them, many of them weeping. Mom said Stephen spoke tenderly to his family, telling them of his love and saying his goodbyes. He spoke of his concerns for the young church since he was the deacon. After he'd finished, Grandfather had led in prayer. And they had all sung *Gott ist de liebe* ["God is love"]. It was an old German song everyone knew by heart. They were fifty or so souls far from home, living in a strange land, and now facing a familiar foe—death. They sang as only those can to whom certain things are real. The German words came easily off their tongues as they'd sung the words many times before. But never quite like this.

It took the pickup truck bearing Uncle Stephen five hours to reach the hospital in the capital. He was, thankfully, still alive. We heard the first medical reports the next day. The doctors said he would make it. He would live. That was followed quickly enough by bad news as more injuries were discovered. Later, on a Sunday night, another crisis point was reached. Many of the uncles and their wives were called in and gathered around his hospital bed. Again they thought Uncle Stephen would be lost to the other side. They sang that night—an English song this time that was written by Aldine S. Kieffer in 1904:

> There's a city of light 'mid the stars, we are told,
> Where they know not a sorrow or care;

And the gates are of pearl and the streets are of gold,
And the buildings exceedingly fair.

Let us pray for each other, not faint by the way,
In this sad world of sorrow and care.
For that home is so bright, and is almost in sight,
And I trust in my heart you'll go there.

But Uncle Stephen rallied. He was home sometime later, recuperating from his wounds. Thinking he was dying in those first hours after the accident, he'd revealed much more than he intended, particularly about his fears for the church. Uncle Stephen was deeply concerned about the direction the fledgling Amish community was going. And as events would later prove, accurately so. I was never told what words he whispered that night about the church, but they're not difficult to guess.

Already some Amish were compromising on their shared beliefs, slowly but surely and driven by necessity as much as anything. Things that were anathema to Amish churches stateside occurred here. There, change, for whatever reason, was considered worse than dying, but here it was more accepted by some.

I would guess that Uncle Stephen saw the threat coming primarily from the two ministers from Nappanee, Indiana—Richard Hochstetler and Vernon Schmucker—who, along with him, served on the ministry team. The two came from Old Order communities and may not have been under suspicion at first. But opinion was changing. In little ways at first they failed in their dedication to upholding the *ordnung* rules. They saw no harm in moving the line, going beyond what Uncle Stephen was willing to tolerate.

And clearly—from the strict Amish perspective—the *ordnung* line needed holding. Some serious sandbagging was in order as the river of change was rising ever higher. Only a year into the experiment, and the floodwaters were breaking through. A person needed to look no further than Dad's extensive shop powered by his humongous electric generator for an example.

And then there was the choice of a bishop, the aforementioned Wallace Byler. He was from the New Order Amish. It was still Amish, but nevertheless was considered a compromise. The New Orders had formed their own conference following an outbreak of revival among the Amish in Holmes County, Ohio, in the mid-sixties or so. Tracts written by Billy Graham had fallen into the hands of several Amish ministers, who then invoked a renewed interest in teachings on the "new birth" and holding Sunday school classes on the in-between Sundays of church services. Neither of which the Old Orders thought necessary to emphasize and, in some places, stood in outright opposition.

I heard that the first minister who discovered the Billy Graham tract told his fellow minister, "If what it says here is true, then we are lost souls." Such input from evangelical sources was not appreciated by the established communities. No excommunication was threatened, but the two groups had parted ways. Preferably a bishop for our new community would have come from the Old Order, but the Old Orders were having nothing to do with Grandfather's great experiment in Honduras.

Up to this point, Bishop Pete in Aylmer had withheld condemnation but not his opinion. This foreign mission outreach would not work, he said. But he held his fire beyond that. Perhaps the Stolls attributed his attitude to the old animosity toward Grandfather, but it stopped any Old Order bishop from stepping forward. (Not that any expressed a willingness that I know of.) Even Northern Indiana hadn't offered a bishop, which seems suspect now. After all, Ministers Richard and Vernon came from there. And it's not like they had a shortage of bishops in that vast spread of Amish communities. Northern Indiana may have heard of Bishop Pete's objections, but I think it more likely their hesitation had to do with the home church's evaluation of Ministers Richard and Vernon. Something wasn't sitting right, and it didn't take a genius to figure it out. Certainly a Stoll could do so.

So Grandfather had settled for a New Order bishop. That Grandfather was open to a New Order bishop doesn't surprise me. That it caused heart palpitations in some of the others also isn't surprising.

The worst transgression though, was the church house—which was either already built on top of the hill at that time or in the planning stage. This was beyond the pale when it came to Amish beliefs.

I can't imagine how they dared do it. No stateside Amish man in his right mind would build a church house. The Amish *home* is the place around which all things revolve—birth, life, death, and church. Back in the States and Canada, the Amish held church in members' homes, rotating through the community on a Sunday by Sunday or month by month basis.

Perhaps the Amish adults didn't dare challenge the obvious that stared them in the face. That it made no sense to keep meeting in temporary storage sheds or even at the children's home, which also was intended for other purposes. Their homes were simply too small for church use. And to have built larger homes would have violated other principles, including not appearing as the rich of the land. They were already considered so simply by the color of their skin. How then could they adapt to this different environment as they wished to?

So just up the hill from where Uncle Stephen lay on his blanket, the foundation for the combination church and schoolhouse had been laid. They would have the first church service there in December of 1970, and everything that happens when a church family has a building, happened: the emphasis on growth, the delight in converts, the moving of the cultural heart from within the community family into a building, and, above all, the sense of unwanted progress, of moving forward into a world yet unknown. Uncle Stephen was not seeing a mirage. He saw clearly what was coming.

Chapter 10

The two side-by-side ranches, La Granja and Sanson, were by now humming with industry and activity. Along the river bottoms new trenches had been dug. These were filled with running water ahead of the dry season in preparation for a second crop of produce. Grandfather Stoll's orchard received its best treatment in years, with regular spraying for insects and vigorous pest control from Uncle Mark. The result was unblemished fruit hanging thick on every tree.

Crops were planted in the black soil, American style, with fertilizer and plenty of manual labor. The crops thrived, and the locals had never seen anything like it. They came to gaze in wonder as we harvested. The ripened produce was peddled in nearby towns along regularly scheduled routes, including Uncle Abner's twice-weekly run into Tegucigalpa.

The church house on the hilltop began to have its intended effect, pulling in local converts. They came at first for the meals served after the church service, I suspect. Our great spreads set out on picnic tables quickly gained a "don't miss it" reputation. The locals' eyes seemed to almost bug out because the people were used to eating flour tortillas and beans. One local reported his total satisfaction with his first Amish Sunday dinner. Especially when—much to his own surprise—he suffered no ill effects the next day from such bounty. "*Mama, mia!*" he exclaimed. "That was really something. Our women…they are nothing. All they know how to make is a little tortillas and beans. Around and around they go with the corn, and then they spread some rice on it and think they have made food. Now these are women. They have some weight to them. And you can tell just by looking they have eaten well all of their lives. And they make food. Hah...such food! Food that makes a man's stomach see a different day of the week every time he opens his mouth."

And word soon got around. So the locals let out their belt buckles another notch and came in droves.

◇

Along the main road, Grandfather Stoll continued to tend his store. He had a bout with heart trouble that December. He stayed in bed a few days, visited the doctor in the capital city, and continued on. Nothing much could be done, the doctor said, even though some heart damage was suspected.

Every morning the wooden flaps at his store were opened for another day of brisk trade. The place quickly became the bus stop for the community. The early buses into Tegucigalpa ran at three o'clock in the morning or so, bringing passengers into the capital in time to catch the stores soon after they opened. A later bus ran at four-thirty, and then the last around six o'clock.

For the industrious Amish, the three o'clock bus was the right one to take. Arriving in town at ten o'clock was not acceptable. Better to lose the sleep up front and get a running start at things. Besides, the first bus left Tegucigalpa for the trip back to Guaimaca at twelve, the late bus at two, putting a person back at the community just before dusk, tired and exhausted. A day trip into town was about all anyone wished to tackle. And staying overnight in the capital was done reluctantly.

Going into the capital was a ritual I grew to dislike intensely. Up at three, stumbling out to the main road in the dark, standing underneath Grandfather's store overhang while waiting for the bouncing lights of the bus to appear. Dad would run out to the road, hollering back for us to come if the right bus screeched to a halt.

The smell of the bus, with dust still rolling out from under the wheels in the brisk early morning air, hit you first. That mixture of body odor and smoke, which had been deposited from cooking over a thousand open fires in their kitchens, was tempered only by the undertones of roasted corn and fried beans. These odors were emanating from bodily externals or from the lunches few locals ventured forth without. The food was wrapped up in cloth and tucked amongst the clothing somewhere.

Riding the bus made for a full, miserable day. My insides were jerked around as I slid and bounced on the hard bus seats. Exhaust smoke and dust filled my nostrils. And the slow crawl of the bus, the motor roaring in my ears, going nowhere but toward the next spine-jarring pothole seemed never ending. The best drivers went slow to keep their bosses happy. The ones we liked went faster, which ended the agony sooner, but also often resulted in a broken bus axle and a fired bus driver. So all of them would go slow for awhile again.

The highlight of the day was stopping at the halfway point for breakfast at some little hut doubling as a restaurant, a colorful sign hanging out front and tables set up in the living room. We knew by then not to drink the water or eat the raw vegetables. The rest of the food we devoured with relish. Tortillas flavored by open fires on barrel tins. The beans, mostly boiled, but sometimes fried and laced with lard. Rice with fried vegetables. All quite delicious and wrapped in wood smoke until it arrived at your table.

By seven or so we arrived in town and rushed around all morning, going from store to store buying supplies. Sometimes, especially for us children, there was a stop at the dentist's office, an amenity we didn't have in Guaimaca. We hopped on and off the city buses as their bus boys hollered out the destination in a singsong chant. Newspaper boys were everywhere, waving about the morning's paper. Their cries of *"La Prenza...Tiempo...La Prenza!"* still ring in my ears.

With half of my face numb from the dentist office, I would make a mad rush to catch the noon bus back to Guaimaca. And then began the bounce home again on the four-hour trip. By the end of the day I would arrive back where I started, sick of life in general and of travel in particular. A trek indeed that was not for the weak of heart or stomach.

At his store, Grandfather Stoll established a clientele for the staples of life—corn and beans. But even that work tired him easily, and
the doctor advised a slower pace due to his heart trouble. Grandfather,
though, had things to do. He stayed in bed sometimes, but he was soon
up again, driving around in the cart pulled by his horse Silver.

Mom visited her parents frequently, walking up the lane to the
main house with us in tow. And not just because of Grandfather's illness, but also because she was lonesome for home. She never took well
to the foreign soil of Honduras.

In the midst of this, the Stoll children worried over Grandfather's
health. But what was there to do? Honduran medicine wasn't the most
advanced, and heart treatment, even stateside, wasn't that great back
then.

Aunt Mary left in the spring of 1971, headed back to Aylmer for her
wedding to David Luthy. The adults whispered behind their hands that
any real man would have come down and picked up his bride...per-
haps even holding the wedding in Honduras. But Luthy was having
nothing to do with the community. So they wrote it off to the eccen-
tricities of an *Englisha* man. I figured Aunt Mary loved him, and what
she loved couldn't turn out too bad.

Below us to the west and across a little ravine but still within sight,
Uncle Stephen built his house on a knoll with a walk-out basement, the
first such venture for the community. The hole was dug out of the hillside with a giant scoop hitched to the freshly arrived Belgians.

I went over to watch this experiment of basement-digging with
horses. Uncle Mark was in charge and determined. As the youngest boy
of the Stoll family, he didn't lack in grit or determination. An adven-
turous soul, Uncle Mark never seemed to carry the weight of the world
on his shoulders like his older brothers did. He was sure the basement
could be dug with his contraption, and he was not giving up.

The machine scraped back and forth, digging in deeper while the
Belgians strained in their harnesses. When the scoop was full, the

drivers brought it out of the ground and hung on to the handles while the Belgians headed for the hillside. There the handles were let go, and the scoop flipped over, depositing the load over the edge. And back they would go for another load.

I didn't stay for the whole thing, but Uncle Mark got far enough along with his scoop to finish easily by hand. No small feat to say the least, and one that Dad tried to duplicate a few years later without success. Our gentle sloping hillside turned out to be a layered rock slab, which the scoop couldn't dig through even with Uncle Mark's best efforts.

Uncle Stephen's family always stayed to themselves more than Uncle Joe's did. More like his dad, Uncle Stephen was introspective. His oldest boy was James, a husky lad with a mild stutter. He was the one who would marry Aunt Nancy Eicher in Aylmer once his family moved back.

Uncle Stephen's next two boys were twins. Thin little fellows and short in stature. They must have shared their growth cells between themselves, but they turned out cocky for their size and smart as whips. There was not a school lesson they couldn't get an "A" on.

My memory tells me one of them was the Stoll cousin from whom I copied the correct answer at the Aylmer schoolhouse. I would have been in the first grade, and they were always a year ahead of me in school, so it doesn't make sense why we were using the same books. Perhaps it was some subject that the two grades shared, which is common in Amish parochial schools. They never liked me, that much I know. But then I didn't exactly blame them.

The younger brother was Harold. A kind soul, he always seemed quiet. A misfit for the family for some reason, though I could never put my finger on why.

Nancy was the youngest. A girl finally, and valued highly in this family of boys.

A ridge ran from Uncle Stephen's house toward the north, then turned in a "U" shape back toward the west and south. On the opposite side, Uncle Stephen built his barn. From there you could see the river bottom containing some of the finest black soil in the community.

If you lifted the dirt with your hand, it ran freely through your fingers. It would grow anything in the rainy season and a second crop in the dry season when watered by the canal ditch that ran in from the north. Or, as Dad did later, with water from the river using irrigation pumps.

Further up there was a smaller strip of river bottom with the same characteristics. I don't think anyone tackled that section the first year. Not until Uncle John Martin settled there after having married Aunt Sarah. Their adopted boy named Louis, "Loo-wes" we called him, came from Belize. He would become my friend, though he didn't let anyone get too close to him. But neither did I, so we suited each other well. And he did know the local culture better than any of us ever did, which fit my wandering spirit.

Produce-raising in the community soon went into high gear. Fences were put up to keep out the locals' cattle, which were allowed to roam free. Cattle that were skin and bones, mostly. How the locals kept track of them, I never figured out. Perhaps they didn't care. Occasionally a stockowner outfitted his animal with a contraption tied to the cow's neck consisting of two sticks placed in a V shape over the neck and one crossbar on the bottom to hold it apart. Strapped together this made for clumpy walking, but it kept the animal from crossing most fences.

Dad's machine shop was also catching on and brought in more business. We soon had trucks roaring in from the main roads from early morning till dark each night. They came with busted springs and cracked truck rims. Sometimes if the job took longer than a day, the trucker would camp out under the trees beside the shop for the night. Phones were nonexistent in the countryside in those days, and likely his wife, living in a hut, didn't have another vehicle to pick him up with anyway.

Mom would take them supper sometimes, but not always. The truckers were highly impressed with a white woman. And it didn't matter really how she looked. They would watch Mom take each step with broad grins on their faces. They were a chauvinist lot and confident of their charming powers, but the Amish never feared assault on the Amish women by the local men. Though a few Amish girls did succumb to those charms in their *rumspringa* years, to the great chagrin of the community's elders.

Dad's shop.

At the shop Dad soon found his tools disappearing at a rapid pace. He took matters into his own hands by putting up signs that read, "Eyes Are Watching You." In Spanish, of course, with the words written beneath a pair of eyes that looked everywhere. Playing on guilt, I suppose. He had the biggest one placed on the open top of his big red toolbox on wheels. I don't think the thieving stopped completely, but it slowed things down even if most of the locals couldn't read. I guess the guilt thing worked along with the eyes staring at them. Most of them were nominally religious.

One thing was clear enough. Few of the locals could be trusted when we weren't looking. Taking what wasn't theirs was almost an honored tradition there. It went something like this: "What has no owner in sight must surely need one." Which they were more than willing to supply.

This rule excluded their own families, with even a few exceptions there if someone was corrupt enough. But for the average decent guy, taking something from those who had more than enough to supply the needs of those who didn't was considered a right of poverty.

Dad became an expert at amateur thieving prevention. He'd turn his rotary grinder with its long spray of sparks toward anyone who wandered too close to his toolbox. The sting of the fiery stream never harmed anyone, but the men would scurry out of the way while Dad grinned, safe in the knowledge his actions would be written off as accidental.

In the end, though, Dad learned to get along with things the way they were. The truckers always wanted to borrow tools. Losing hand tools was part of doing business in that part of the third world. Perhaps he calculated it into the fees he charged. Even checking carefully when they brought the tools back didn't always take care of the matter. I had a trucker gang once who treated me to sardines in the middle of a project—a rare treat for us in those days. This happened when I was working full-time in the shop. I ate the delicacy with my greasy fingers straight from the can. When the job was done, I opened and counted the returned ratchet set like I'd been taught. Everything was there. The men waved cheerfully on their way out the lane. Dad later informed me they had switched several of our good sockets with their cracked ones. Well, we lived and learned.

One man showed up at the shop on a Sunday afternoon and wanted work started on his vehicle right away, pleading great necessity. Dad refused even when the conversation descended into a theological discussion on whether the Sabbath started on Saturday or Sunday. From there it moved to whether it was from sundown or sunup. Dad held his ground, but he did get up that night at midnight to work, and the poor fellow was on the road early the next morning.

Chapter 11

The David Peachey family, a happy, cheerful bunch, came from Pennsylvania and settled in by spring. They built their house just above the children's home and church house complex, where the old lane turned west toward Grandfather Stoll's place. David and Miriam came with their five children, David Jr., the eldest, and Rebecca, the first girl. Joseph, the second boy, would become the closest thing I had to a friend besides Louis. Rhoda and Daniel filled out the rest of their family. Joseph epitomized the family's good nature and gracious kindness. I never met a person who didn't fall in love with the Peachey family. They needed this trait, I supposed, sandwiched as they were between the two Amish cultures from Aylmer and Northern Indiana. But in the end it didn't help. Even with their strong ties to both parties, nothing it seemed could bridge the gap between the two.

I wasn't old enough to get involved in the church *kafuffles*, but I had my own wars. At the center were two boys from the La Granja ranch, Daniel Hochstetler and Paul Schmucker. They were a year or so older than I was and a grade ahead of me in school. Paul was Minister Vernon Schmucker's son and a follower mostly. Daniel was the brains and leader of the duo.

That I was the gangly, stuttering, forceful boy that I was didn't help matters. They took delight in terrorizing my schooldays. Daniel's parents had stayed in Dad's chicken house for the first few months after their arrival in Honduras until their long, rambling house was built over in La Granja. During this time Daniel took or damaged some-thing of mine. I think it was a marking pen. He refused to right the wrong, so at school, during recess, I took matters into my own hands and took an equivalent item from his desk. Triumphantly I carried it back to my desk, a feat I made sure Daniel was fully aware of once school was back in session. I held up the item so he could see it. Dan-iel immediately raised his hand and reported what he called "a theft" to Aunt Sarah, who was teaching that year.

Aunt Sarah marched over and asked if I had indeed taken the item.

I tried to explain my side of the story, but with my stuttering it didn't come out right and took too long to say. I could tell the verdict was already decided in Aunt Sarah's eyes before I finished. No student of hers was going to lift another's property. Not for any reason.

Aunt Sarah returned the item to Daniel after an appropriate lecture for me. Daniel rubbed the conquest in by making gleeful faces as soon as her back was turned.

Beyond that, the two boys found small ways to make my life mis-erable, ganging up on me once on the long walk up the schoolhouse hill after recess. On one such day, Paul still had his mouth filled with water after taking a drink at the well pump. Daniel walked on the outer side of him, and as Paul came up next to me, Daniel hollered out my name. When I turned, Paul emptied the whole mouthful into my face.

I'd learned by then to leave the two alone. And who would have believed me anyway if I'd complained? They would have had some logical explanation to explain their innocence against which my stut-tered complaint didn't stand a chance. I suppose I was my worst enemy, doing little to counter the negative impressions I gave off. I bristled and fought at the slightest provocation, even with the Stoll relatives, most of whom had nothing against me.

Uncle Joe's oldest boy, Paul, once made some remark about me while the group of us schoolchildren were walking home. I have long forgotten what it was, but I took a swing at him, connecting with his head. The rest of the group looked at me in shocked horror, while Paul rubbed his injured body part. Fighting was strictly forbidden. No Amish boy was supposed to lash out. We continued on, and no one said anything until we arrived home. Then my transgression was immediately reported to Mom. She made a beeline out to the shop, coming back with Dad in tow. I could talk well enough at home to explain myself, and I repeated what Paul had said. Apparently it was bad enough that some sympathy was evoked because I wasn't thrashed. Instead it was decreed that I should go down at once to Uncle Joe's and apologize for my reaction.

I refused. Not because I was opposed to apologizing, but because of the horror that I knew lay ahead. I would end up on Uncle's Joe's front porch unable to utter a single coherent word with them staring at me.

Dad told me he would thrash me if didn't go. I managed to croak out that I couldn't talk in front of people. Mom must have had compassion on me because she said, "John can go with you. He can tell them what you want."

So with my brother John beside me, I walked up and down the slopes to where Uncle Joe's house lay. I stayed at the little wooden walk-through by the fence while John went on up to the house. When Paul arrived, I stammered out that I was sorry, and he graciously accepted the apology. I believe Uncle Joe's family really tried the hardest to break through whatever was bothering me, but I repeatedly rejected their advances. The world had become much safer for me when I stayed alone.

Some years later, during a ball game in the schoolyard, Uncle Joe's second boy, Peter, was moving in on a fly ball along with me. In the last mad dash, Peter accidentally pushed my glove aside. I ended up with a softball in my glasses, shattering them into a thousand pieces.

I had to go home from school that day so Dad could pick glass pieces from my eyes. There couldn't have been a boy more apologetic than Peter. He profusely said so in the schoolyard. And I knew he was. I never doubted his sincerity. But I wouldn't acknowledge it, even when Peter walked back up that evening for another round of apologies. I had closed up by then, and except for Joseph Peachey and Louis, I kept largely to myself.

Uncle Joe lost three of his sows that spring of 1971, right around Easter. The family woke up to find them simply gone. Not a sound or disturbance had been heard the night before, which puzzled the Stoll clan immensely. They liked mysteries, but not mysteries that couldn't be solved, and this one baffled their best efforts. How did someone sneak in and move three hogs without causing a racket? Usually a person only had to look at a sow to cause a terrible fuss. They talked about the matter at great length. They seemed more concerned with the mystery than with the loss of the pigs.

Uncle Mark came up with the most imaginative explanation. It was Easter time, and he noted that booze was plentiful among the townspeople. Some creative local had imbibed the sows, he claimed, and in their stupored state they had been led off without a sound.

A faint trail of hog tracks was found leading through the woods toward the main road, where the tracks vanished. This supported his theory, Uncle Mark claimed, because it showed the hogs had not been driven. If that had been the case, the tracks would then have been scattered helter-skelter. And if the hogs had been killed, there would have been drag marks and blood from where they'd been butchered. Instead, the tracks led forth in a nice straight trail that even a drunk sow could make if she were being led by a rope.

When some of the local help found out about the theft, they proclaimed Uncle Mark's theory totally plausible. The Stolls were satisfied the mystery had been satisfactorily explained.

In the meantime, other thieving continued in the community. Small things that were appropriate to the habits of the local population, it was decided. Nothing of grave concern. Better locks were purchased and installed, precautions unknown to us when we lived in Canada. Clearly this land was not like the one left behind, but we were all beginning to love it.

Chapter 12

With the church house functioning, Bishop Wallace Byler and his wife showed up for the first communion that year in June—an event looked forward to with great anticipation and hope. Communion in the Amish world is an important affair. This is when the state of unity is fully tested because there can be no communion if there isn't agreement on *all* matters. And this is more than simply agreeing to attend church together or tolerating each other's positions. One person must agree with another on a substantial level, giving consent to his opinion. It's a monumental task, and one of the reasons the Amish are often resistant to outsiders joining the faith. They have enough work cut out for themselves keeping those raised in the faith of one mind without bringing in someone who doesn't think like them.

Somehow the community had unity that year. And not only the unity to hold communion, but enough to also ordain another minister. There were two ministers already on the ground, Richard Hochstetler and Vernon Schmucker, plus the one deacon, Uncle Stephen. This was a sufficient number from which to ordain a bishop, and the option Bishop Byler wished to employ. An action that would release him from the necessity of further trips to Honduras. But there were objections. Another minister must be ordained before a bishop was chosen, they said. Objections to which I ascribe ulterior motives. Perhaps the Stolls were attempting to gain an equal voice on the ministers' bench. Or maybe they simply wanted another choice so they would be kept from having to vote on either Ministers Richard or Vernon.

Uncle Stephen, as the deacon, was never in running for the office of bishop. Some Amish communities include their deacons in the voting and others don't. My feelings are that Aylmer didn't. Or perhaps Uncle Stephen recused himself for personal reasons. In any case, they had only Ministers Richard and Vernon in the pool.

In the end, the ordination of a bishop was postponed. This decision apparently had its appeal for all concerned. And later Ministers Richard and Vernon would still have their opportunity at drawing the lot for bishop. Not much is diminished in a two man draw versus a three.

So Bishop Byler arrived with his wife, Mattie, flying into that primitive airport in Tegucigalpa. It's still one of the shortest runways in the world used by commercial aircraft. You come in tight over the hills, making the circle to land in one long swoop, with the landing craft nearly dragging the tile rooftops. Grandfather met Bishop Byler and his wife outside customs and escorted them home across those four dusty hours on the bus.

That Sunday we climbed the church house hill for our Amish service. No locals were invited, though if they came they weren't turned away. We had our German singing and then ministers Richard and Vernon went through the story of the Old Testament, speaking completely from memory. The first speaker took the story up to the time of Noah. The second, all the way to the end of the Old Testament.

At lunchtime we spilled out on the hillside. Families sat together eating their prepared lunches. Sandwiches, if I remember correctly, and a slice of pie for dessert, with water to drink from the spigot attached to the front of the schoolhouse. We spoke little, and then in soft tones. The women picked up the lunch leftovers, and everyone who needed to headed for the outhouses. These were down the hill a ways. The women's closer to the church house and the men's over the knoll. The line back inside started soon afterward. The afternoon service got underway by one-thirty or so.

Bishop Byler had the floor to himself for the afternoon sermon. He told the story of Christ, beginning at the time of His birth and concluding with His crucifixion. All was told in great detail without notes and took close to three hours. Then the bread and the wine were served, followed by foot washing and the votes for the bishop ordination. During the vote, a peculiar stillness fell over the room. However the vote went, a man and his wife's lives would be changed forever.

It took three votes to get into the running. A few minutes later we were told the news. Three men had made it: Uncle Joe, Monroe Hochstetler, and David Peachey. And on such a thin thread hung the future of our church. David Peachey was probably considered most likely to be a liberal minister because of his caring spirit. I think service to mankind would have been his guiding light. Some Amish principles might have been viewed as injurious if they stood in the way of the cause of reaching out to people in Christ and helping them.

Uncle Joe was the conservative candidate. He certainly would have held the line and stopped the drift that was going on. Likely his leadership would have split the church eventually, but he would have maintained the Amish heritage.

The kind of minister Monroe Hochstetler would make didn't have to be imagined because the piece of paper determining the outcome of the vote was found in his book. Bishop Byler took it out, stared at it for a moment, and then looked at Monroe. Sobs shook the candidate's shoulders before a word was spoken. The other two men rose and walked back to their seats, their brief moment on the historical cliff withdrawn. The people bowed their heads in submission to the will of God. Bishop Byler ordained the young man, charging him to preach the Word of God in season and out of season.

I would eventually grow to love Monroe Hochstetler as I have cared for few Amish ministers. Under his preaching years later God found me. I experienced His inexplicable love that defies understanding. I could have understood God's love directed toward many of those around me, but toward me? That was baffling.

Minister Monroe, later Bishop Monroe, didn't make a good Amish church leader though. Not because he was corrupt or ever left the faith. The man had a heart of gold. He just didn't have a clue regarding the politics of the leadership positions. He couldn't find his way through the maze of Amish church relationships to save his life. He would lose his church eventually, but he reached my soul. I wonder which he would have chosen if he'd been given the choice? I'm quite sure he'd pick the soul over the church. Monroe Hochstetler was that kind of a man.

Chapter 13

My youngest sister, Sarah Mae, was born September of 1971. The cutest of the bunch. So we were now nine souls in that little wooden cottage. Dad started talking of building a new house across the road.

Meanwhile Grandfather Stoll continued to regularly drive up and down the length of the Sanson ranch, bouncing by in his cart while his jolly face greeted one and all. The locals loved Grandfather. They apparently even loved him too much to steal his horse! But then one morning Silver turned up missing. Everyone was sure he was gone for good, taken as part of the petty thievery that occurred from time to time. Uncle Mark told us about the affair, shaking his head at Grandfather's loss. Things would never be the same without Grandfather's cart and Silver creeping along the ridge across from us while heading toward his store out by the main road.

The next morning Silver was back! Standing there, calmly chewing grass in the pasture. He had distinct saddle marks on his back. Someone had apparently borrowed Silver and decided to return him—an occurrence unheard of in that culture. Grandfather smiled even more the next day.

He continued to struggle with health problems. Everyone knew of his heart condition, but they assumed it was under control. Still, they said things like, "He's lost a percentage of his heart usage," "He has to take things easier," and "But he should be okay." Grandfather made frequent trips to see a doctor in Tegucigalpa, a Dr. Lazarus. And things were going as they should be, we were told.

I was ten years old on the morning he died. I remember little about it other than the usual daily events that transpired like so many had before them. We awakened with the dawn, dumped our dreaded chamber pot, and had breakfast.

We always were up by six o'clock. I don't remember anyone sleeping in. Honduras was that way. Mornings were not a time for staying in bed. The whole country awakens, bathed in the sensual stroking of the dawn. Smells drift through the open windows heavy with the scent of fruits and all things growing. Blackbirds make a terrible racket. The males hang around on the trees outside, their long plumage wrapped in the leaves. A thousand soft murmurings and the breathing of small insects are everywhere. And even on early mornings, a pair or two of the larger parrots could fly by in straight lines toward their destination. They croak, filling the air with sweet sounds that speak of mysterious sights in the mountains that our eyes have never beheld. Later, their smaller cousins would be out. Great flocks of them whirling in the sky. They were everywhere in those days, and a curse to the cornfields. But we reveled in the sight of their united flight. They could blanket the whole tops of trees if they chose to land. We boys would creep up with our Honduran slingshots and fire blindly into trees.

So it was in the midst of that regular morning that Mom disappeared around ten o'clock. Someone had arrived, had a short conversation, and she left. I can't remember her saying much to us children. She was just gone—on up to Grandfather's place. When she didn't return by lunchtime, I took it upon myself to investigate. I think I stopped in at the shop just to confirm with Dad where Mom was. Yes, he said. She'd gone to Grandfather's place. He didn't offer any further information. I walked across the fields, using the shortcut to Grandfather's house, walking on a little, winding pasture path.

I arrived at the two-story house to find a huddle of people standing near the outside stairs. Their faces were drawn, shock written on them. Mom appeared and whispered to me that Grandfather Stoll had passed away. This was information I couldn't quite absorb. He'd been well the last time I saw him. Mom led me upstairs and took me inside where more weeping people were standing and wiping their eyes with their handkerchiefs. No one said anything. Grandfather lay on the bed beside the window in the living room. He was on his back, his face blank. We stood there looking at him. Mom sobbed. "He just passed minutes ago," Mom told me. "If you'd come earlier, you would have been here. He died with '*Komm bald Herr Jesu*' [Come quickly, Lord Jesus] on his lips."

I felt no particular emotion about not being there earlier or, for that matter, about being there at that moment. It all seemed detached for some reason. As if this was something that wouldn't affect me. And yet it would. It would affect all of us deeply. Grandfather was the center pin that held the life of the community together. With him gone, nothing would ever be the same.

I found my way outside and down the stairs. My uncles walked around, not speaking to me. Young Joseph Peachey arrived on his horse, galloping down the lane on some unrelated errand. I told him what had happened, and he stayed on his horse, saying nothing. His mother was battling cancer by then. I remember wondering if he was thinking of her possible passing. His face revealed nothing.

I stood aside while Joseph sat on his horse and conversed in whispers with the adults. Moments later he wheeled his horse about and dashed off. No doubt sent on an errand to spread the news.

Uncle Alva came rushing in on the pasture path soon after Joseph Peachey left. He carried a small wrapped bottle under his arm. The alarm on his face changed to tears when they told him. He was too late, having been sent on a desperate errand to buy wine when Grandfather's attack had begun earlier in the day. I have no idea what medical value they considered the wine to have, but no doubt Uncle Joe believed it did. And now Uncle Alva slowly made his way upstairs with his shoulders heaving, his sorrow evident and made worse for not having been there in the last moments of his father's life.

Mom and I soon left for home. As was the custom, nonfamily members from the community would come in for the funeral preparations the next day. Mom must have been back and forth after we were in bed that night, helping where she could.

Telegrams were shot off to Aunt Mary in Canada, and phone calls were attempted. Everyone knew there was no way Aunt Mary could make it down in time for the funeral, even if they managed to place a call through to the phone in the Aylmer schoolhouse.

This was Honduras, and Grandfather must be buried within twenty-four hours, a task that fell on several unrelated young Amish boys. They began their grave-digging duties early the next morning. I remember seeing them still at it when the service began at nine. The hillside below the church house was made of shale rock, and the grave-diggers were making little progress. I heard later they finished a short time before the conclusion of the service and were forced to resort to axes for the final foot.

The little church house on the hill was filled to overflowing. Grand-father had made many friends among the locals. A great many of them came, pouring in to fill every nook and cranny of the building. I remember little of the actual service, but when we filed by to view the body, those images are etched in my memory. David Peachey was standing guard at the coffin, fanning Grandfather's face to keep away the flies in the warm weather.

Once through the viewing line, we spilled out on the hillside to wait, the grave down the grade finished now. The crowd swelled, moving with the simple wooden casket as it was carried out. I can't remember who said the last words at the graveside. I remember only the multitude of people spread out in all directions, pressing in to get closer. They buried him facing toward the east, toward Jerusalem from where the morning will come.

Death had come to claim its first victim in the community. And not a child, tragic as that would have been, or even Uncle Stephen when the tree fell on him. But Grandfather Stoll, the one we could least afford to lose. We bowed our heads and didn't question the will of God, the One who makes no mistakes.

Chapter 14

No story better captures for me the essence of what Grandfather Stoll was than my own experiences with him. The incident I have in mind began one Saturday afternoon. Mom was spending time at Grandfather's house like she often did. I was sent out with Grandfather to pick up fallen mangoes. We each carried a five-gallon bucket, filling them with the still-edible fruit that lay on the ground.

Parrots were ever-present pests, as well as other birds, and if the fruit was too badly picked at, we left it. I remember Grandfather being withdrawn that afternoon—pensive—as we searched under the mango trees behind the house. I can't remember what I did wrong to irritate him, but I suspect my attention wandered rather quickly from mango gathering to any number of more-attractive activities for boys. There were birds everywhere. And my slingshot was present to practice with.

I remember him repeatedly snapping at me. It could have been for my selection of fruit or from my lack of progress in filling my bucket. I certainly didn't fear the man. I was more puzzled than anything because this wasn't his usual behavior. We muddled through the afternoon somehow and returned to the house. I thought no more about it, returning home with Mom when she was ready. Before we left I didn't hear Grandfather complaining about me. Nor did I mention the incident on the way home. It just was what it was.

The next morning we awoke and dressed for Sunday services, walking up the lane toward the church house. Reaching the bottom of

the hill, we headed up. To my great surprise, Grandfather was waiting outside of the church house, his face sober. Some grave thing had
happened, I figured, and he would be speaking with Mom and Dad.
Instead he motioned for me to step aside.

I listened in shocked astonishment as he apologized for his behavior the afternoon before.

"I shouldn't have acted like that," he told me. "I'm sorry."

I nodded my head in acceptance, hoping to bring a quick end to
the conversation. It seemed so out of place. My grandfather, the man
we all looked up to, the man who talked with bishops, taking the time
to tell me he was sorry? But that was how Grandfather was, a man of
passions but always trying to become more like his Savior. I remember
that day, not because I had my heart broken, but because when that day
came I had seen a man I loved who cared. And because of that, I would
be able to look on those who had injured me and continue believing
that good people existed in this world. Would I be able to do that had
I not seen the evidence with my own eyes? I'm not sure.

Another story that illustrates my grandfather's life is somewhat of
an Amish parable. As it was told to me, there was once a gentleman
who needed to hire a coachman for his frequent drives in his carriage.
When the gentleman advertised for the job, three applicants showed
up. After interviewing all three and looking at their references, there
seemed to be little difference between them. The gentleman was at a
loss as to what he should do.

He soon stumbled on a plan. He would take each of the applicants
with him in the coach. They would harness all six horses for the test
drive, and how the applicants handled themselves driving the horses
would settle the matter.

The gentleman explained the plan to the three and showed them
the lay of the land. Behind his house was a wicked hill with a very sharp
curve. Here the test would be conducted. He would personally see how
each man handled that turn on the hillside.

The first driver got in the seat and followed the directions he was
given. As he approached the hill, the driver sized up the grade and
decided this was his chance to show his skill. Taking the carriage out

close to the edge of the cliff, the driver expertly handled the horses so that everything stayed under control with the carriage wheels passing a mere two feet from the edge. Complimenting himself, the driver finished the test and, smiling all the while, handed over the reins to the second. His deed would not be easily topped, he figured.

Grasping the reins the second driver took the seat, letting out the reins for a fast takeoff. They approached the dangerous curve again, with the second driver thinking the same thoughts as the first one had. He would need to make the most of this opportunity to demonstrate his skills. The face of the second driver fell at the sight of the carriage wheel marks laid out a mere two feet from the cliff's edge. This was not going to be easy. With his heart pounding, the second driver took the carriage even closer, to within a foot of the edge, the dashing horse's hooves throwing rocks over the cliff.

The second driver smiled smugly to himself. His skill could not be matched, he figured.

The third driver climbed in the seat and they set off again. Arriving at the curve, the driver noticed the wheel marks plainly and wondered how he was to top such excellent driving.

"This is hopeless," he said to himself. "We might as well get this over with and go back." So he slapped the reins, and plowed ahead, staying clear away from the cliff's edge, far from the previous drivers' wheel tracks.

With a rattle of wheels they arrived back at the starting point, and the third driver brought the team to a halt with a long face.

Now the gentleman stuck his head out the window of the carriage and looked up at the third driver. "You're hired there, my good man."

Whereupon all the drivers looked at each other with astonishment.

"What…what did he do?" the second driver stammered. "He couldn't have driven any closer than I did."

"I didn't want him to drive any closer," the gentleman said. "I wanted all of you to stay away from that cliff's edge."

The moral of the story in Amish country wasn't that hard to figure out. You stayed away from anything questionable. And Grandfather Stoll always did try to drive well away from the edge of the cliff.

Even with his passion for mission outreach and his hand in founding an Amish settlement on foreign soil, he believed both to lie well within the will and protection of God. And if he had lived he might have kept things from running over the edge.

After Grandfather's death, life was soon back to normal—surprisingly soon. The chicken thieves hardly missed a beat, their fingers becoming increasingly busy. No lock or device seemed to slow them down. In the dead of night, the chicken houses would be cleaned out, the occupants presumably carted off in burlap bags.

We had a chicken house sitting high on stilts below the shack, the grounds fenced in around it. I can't remember Dad losing any chickens, but he was adept at preventing such things. Plus we lived in a place with roads on either side of it. Stealing chickens where people could easily walk by might have been a hazard not worth taking, at least when there were easier targets available.

We would hear of certain chicken owners who took to sleeping in or near their chicken houses but to no avail. On the night they finally couldn't stand the stench any longer and retreated to the house, the thieves would strike. The thieves were highly coordinated in this way, which cast suspicions on the local help. Nothing could be proven though. Unless we caught someone with a stolen chicken in their hands, the locals were the most innocent people ever to walk the earth. And even caught with a bag of chickens, the offender would swear by heaven and earth that these had been raised from birth in his mother's kitchen, where they had eaten tortilla scraps dropped from the barrel top and pecked for bugs in the grass behind the house.

How the chicken became so fat on such sparse fare or how he climbed into the bag were matters they didn't worry about explaining. Being innocent of the theft, such things didn't need explaining.

⌘

That November, tropical storm Laura passed by the northern shores of Honduras, churning warm waters before slamming into British Honduras. The high winds and rain dissipated toward the center of Guatemala and never reached us in full strength. Enough did reach us to give us a foretaste of what was to come later. Honduras sits exposed to the ocean for the full length on one side, and it is a magnet for the hurricanes that wander the Atlantic each year. There was little in the way of early warning systems back in those days.

The highlight for me that winter was the arrival of the Gascho family from Canada. The group was led by Uncle Johnny, Mom's older sister Martha's husband, still known to me as Maple Syrup Johnny. They came overland by bus through Mexico. How that went, I don't know. The occasional four-hour trip into Tegucigalpa was all I needed or wanted of third-world buses. To travel for days on end in those conditions with the whole family along was another matter entirely.

I didn't see the family arrive. I found out they were in the community when several of the Gascho girls showed up at the schoolhouse, led by the eldest girl, Lois. She was a bubbly, outgoing girl, as were all her sisters. Lois's laugh was open and infectious. I don't think she ever had a dark thought in her life. I'd never seen a family where all the females were so outgoing and all the males so meek and mild. Usually the personalities get mixed up a bit at least. So that afternoon the hillside in Honduras rang with their laugher, and I experienced one of my few pangs of homesickness.

We all went up to Grandfather Stoll's place that first afternoon to meet the visitors, arriving before dark to sit out under the palm trees where picnic tables and benches had been set up. There we made our full reacquaintance with the Gascho family, none of whom looked worse for wear after their long trip.

Their eldest boy, Luke, had been a close friend in Aylmer, and we now chatted, catching up on the news. I couldn't wait to show him our mountain. It was cloudy that afternoon, so it was useless to walk away from the orchard for a better view or we would have. I described everything with sweeping throws of my hands, already having taken in some of the local customs, including gesturing while speaking, which also helped me with my stuttering, I think. He listened with that droopy Gascho smile of his. Luke told me he'd seen the mountain on the way in. He didn't seem as excited about it as I was, so I guess you grow to love things with perhaps a love that others can't always see at first sight.

We ate supper there, thoroughly enjoying ourselves before leaving for home soon after dark. The family would stay around for six weeks or so before heading back the way they'd come. I don't remember anything spectacular happening other than just hanging around together whenever we had a chance after school and on weekends. The Gaschos took in the local culture and traveled to town, but they never uttered a word about moving down, which was something we all hoped might grow out of the visit. I guessed Uncle Johnny was staying where the maple syrup trees grew.

Sometime after they left that winter, my strange childhood sickness began. I remember walking back toward our boys' bedroom after supper, and having Mom stop me and feel my flushed forehead.

"It's just a passing flu," she assured me.

I felt confident I would feel better in the morning. But I didn't, and I stayed home from school. When I stayed in bed the next day, and the next, Mom became worried. By the week's end, we headed for the hospital in Tegucigalpa, looking for a doctor who specialized in childhood diseases.

If I didn't hate the bus ride already, I hated it by the time we arrived in town. Bouncing around in the dust-chocked air for four hours while burning up with a high fever is not a picnic.

I was admitted at once and the examinations begun. X-rays were taken, and a puzzled doctor stood at my bedside. He didn't know what was wrong. I really didn't care one way or the other. I was too sick to care. The only emotion I could muster was irritation at the bumbling conclusions.

My lungs were infected with something, the doctor said. But just what, he wasn't sure. Perhaps tuberculosis (TB), he ventured. The doctor kept asking me why I constantly cleared my throat, but I had no answer. I tried to tell him without saying too many words. Nothing seemed to satisfy him. Mom offered that I had always spent a lot of time clearing my throat, mostly at regular intervals. The doctor wrinkled his brow and left. He came back again later. He seemed fascinated by my throat clearing.

Even after more X-rays, after weeks went by, and more hospital trips, the doctor still focused on that one point. "It must be TB with that throat clearing," he said. "Even though the other symptoms don't exactly fit."

I didn't know anything about TB, but it sounded serious enough. People die from the stuff, but no one told me I was dying. They just kept asking why I was clearing my throat.

So I was sent home with a full regimen of medicine to treat TB. I lay in bed at home, took the stuff, and bared my behind for the daily injection of whatever I was given. There was no nurse around, and Uncle Joe couldn't come up every day, so Mom took the task in hand. She was a good mother, but she didn't know beans about plunging needles into the backsides of boys.

Being bored I guess, she even invited people in for the show.

And what was I supposed to do?

"Hey, come in and watch Jerry get his shot."

Even ten-year-old boys have their modesty...or pride. Especially when you invite in boys they don't like.

A local boy named Porfideo was such a person. His father kept the house that had come with the Sanson farm and rested on the hill behind us. We didn't fight, Porfideo and I. We just had an intense dislike for each other. I should have had a heart of compassion for him, I suppose, considering that we often witnessed his severe thrashings at the hand of his mother.

Loud screams and cries would drift across the countryside, coming from the little hut on the hill. If one looked in that direction, Porfideo would soon come dashing out of the grove of trees surrounding the place pursued by his mother, who was applying whatever implement she had in her hand to his backside and screaming at the top of her voice.

Anyway, one day Mom invited him in to watch the proceedings. On that morning I thought only of my own humiliation and not his as I bared my backside for the world to see while Mom plunged in the needle.

All this humiliation and trauma didn't do any good. I clearly wasn't getting better. Mom became more and more desperate as the months went by. No diagnosis would be made by the Tegucigalpa doctor other than TB.

I was missing school, and I made no attempt to catch up at home. I was too sick for that. I have clear visions of those days. I'm sitting in the outhouse behind the house in the middle of the day, knowing something was very wrong but having no idea what it was. Often a sick child will be brought what is known as a "Sunshine Box" put together by their fellow classmates or, if they're older, by their own age group. Portions of the box are to be opened daily to prolong the pleasure.

I had only one deep longing during those months. I wanted a Sunshine Box. I waited for weeks, sure that one was coming just as it did when my peers were seriously sick. When one didn't come, I figured maybe it didn't happen as often as I thought. On the other hand, I considered that this was also my own doing. One must be a good child to receive a Sunshine Box, and I wasn't exactly anyone's version of a good child.

Months stretched on, and Mom brought in a foot massager, which was the latest Amish treatment going around for all things that ail you. A middle-aged woman came to visit. She rubbed pencil erasers into points on my foot. These spots were the nerves bundles, she explained to me, which stimulated healing in the attached body part. Debris and other body residue from the attached organ settled into the nerve ending in the foot, which was being dispersed by the rubbing.

It sounded logical to me, and my feet tingled during the treatment. A pleasant enough experience overall. But whatever good it did, it didn't affect my illness.

In the end, I simply got better on my own after four months or so. I weakly made my way back to school again. Years later, another doctor in Tegucigalpa, and at the same hospital, looked at my X-rays during some other treatment I was undergoing and threw a royal fit. I had been diagnosed incorrectly, he told us. And unnecessarily so even if, as he claimed, this lung disease I had endured was often mistaken for TB.

The doctor told us the disease I'd contracted came from breathing in bat or chicken manure. We cast about in our minds for a time when bats might have roosted in an attic above our heads and came up empty-handed. And we didn't sleep under the chicken coop, so we didn't consider the chickens possible culprits. Not even the poorest of the local poor were driven to such extremes.

Eventually we did find the answer. We children had spent hours playing under our elevated chicken house in the midst of chicken droppings and air filled with plenty of drifting particles from the active chickens above us. *Histoplasmosis,* I think the disease is called—a fungus that can be fatal in acute cases. Somehow I recovered on my own.

From then on there was no more playing under the chicken house, which didn't do me any good. As it was, for years afterward I had lung trouble, coughing often and experiencing deep chest spasms at random intervals. And when I went swimming, I couldn't hold my breath for any length of time. There were plenty of other things for me to do though. Fishing, floating, exploring, and camping—our place in Honduras became the center of many happy childhood hours.

Chapter 15

While my sickness was going on, the community continued to grow and prosper. Bishop Byler flew back in with Bishop Levi Troyer in tow this time. They had come to ordain a bishop for us. I wasn't at the ordination and heard no talk beforehand of a preference between the three ministers: Richard, Vernon, and Monroe.

Uncle Stephen was either not talking to the other Stolls about the liberal tendencies he was seeing in Ministers Richard and Vernon or he didn't see them. My guess would be the former. Uncle Stephen was a man of high moral principles, and he didn't run his mouth easily, even when he feared the worst...as he may have in this case.

And Minister Monroe in the past year had done a good job of soothing any jittery Stoll nerves. They would have wished to know more about the leanings of the young minister. Was he liberal or conservative? I don't know what Minister Monroe told them, but everyone loved the man, so he couldn't have expressed anything but support for the Amish way of life.

The community scheduled the communion service, and toward the end of the day, all the members whispered their choices to Bishop Byler and Bishop Troyer. Again Uncle Stephen was either not eligible or had recused himself.

After the voting was finished, all three ministers had the required three votes needed and were included in the lot. Songbooks were placed on a bench in front of the church house, with one of them containing a slip of paper that would determine the new bishop. The names of Ministers Vernon, Richard, and Monroe were called out in the order from the oldest to the youngest, measured in length of ordination time as a minister.

A short silence followed. I believe Minister Vernon went first and chose his book. Minister Richard would have gone next, and Minister Monroe took the book the other two ministers had left.

Once Minister Monroe was seated, the books were opened, beginning again with Minister Vernon. His was empty. Next went Minister Richard. His book didn't have the telling slip of paper either. By the time Bishop Byler opened Minister Monroe's book, he would have known Monroe Hochstetler was to be the bishop.

The die was cast.

Contrary to many Amish ministers, Bishop Monroe was never shy about stating his call from God. Not his qualifications, of course, as no one was considered qualified, but he was certain of his calling.

I'm hard-pressed to remember the words to any of his sermons, other than one in particular. I can still see Bishop Monroe standing behind that wooden pulpit, the shutters half-closed behind him, the bright streams of sunlight falling all around him. His face always looked peaceful. Speaking out of the first chapters of Revelation, where the Lord addresses the angels of the churches, Bishop Monroe said, "Just as it says here that these men were the angels placed in charge of the churches, so the Lord has placed me as the angel in charge of this church."

We understood he didn't think he was a real angel, just a man placed in a holy calling. And Bishop Monroe took to his duties like a natural. He was a young man then, still in his early thirties. He hadn't been schooled in the ways of preachers, yet he seemed to take his place with ease. Broad-shouldered and of average height, he had a soft heart for people. They instantly felt comfortable with him. People opened their hearts to him, and the road to his house was soon well traveled.

The trail to Bishop Monroe's place went east from the church house. We would cross old Turk Road, go past Emil Helmuth's place, then over the ravine on a long, wooden trestle bridge without any side-boards. The little affair was only wide enough for people traffic. When driving horses or vehicles, we went further north and crossed on a con-crete bridge.

Even the locals took to stopping by, and Bishop Monroe put a lot of effort into learning Spanish. He got the accent closer than some of the others did. There were those who fought hard with the roll of the R's, some with more success than the others. Mom's Cousin Ira was among the worst. I don't think the poor man ever got it right, though he tried his best. Bishop Monroe could soon converse at length about Scripture and spiritual matters in the Spanish tongue. And preach, of course, which produced another problem. How much of the services should be in Spanish instead of the usual German?

Bishop Monroe looked out over the crowded church house on Sun-day mornings, and more often than not found reasons to preach in Spanish. Ministers Richard and Vernon followed his example. It was the natural pull of things, a result that had been warned against by the Amish bishops up north. They'd said we couldn't resist the pull of the culture once we began to evangelize.

In Bishop Monroe's conversations with the locals, a subject much in demand was the matter of nonresistance, especially with all the petty thievery going on. The locals shook their heads at the "stupidity" of these Amish folks who didn't believe in shooting people. Why not just use the guns some of the Amish have stacked in their closets for hunt-ing? the locals asked. Wouldn't a few shots fired in the air during the nighttime do much to discourage the chicken thieves? Not to mention a few threats dropped discreetly in town.

One of the locals broached the subject with Bishop Monroe one evening. I wasn't there, but I was told about the conversation.

"So why is it that you Amish people let people steal from you?" the man asked.

I can see Bishop Monroe putting on his patient look. "We don't let people steal from us. That's in God's hands. We trust in Him, and take what measures we can. See over there? I lock my barn where the tools are, and at night we lock the house. It's not right for people to steal, and we would be encouraging theft by leaving everything open. But we cannot kill anyone for stealing from us. Killing belongs only to God."

"But a little bullet here and there does much to help without hurting them," the man replied. "I know because I have lived here for a long time, and that's the way it is. Our people grow up like this. Our fathers and our mothers, they all steal when they can. Only from family we don't steal. The uneducated mountain people who know nothing, they steal from their families. But we will steal from the others if there is opportunity and we will not get hurt. Why not take it? That is what my father said."

Bishop Monroe would have kept his patient look as he tried to explain. "This is, of course, all wrong, even if your father said it. We should not steal from each other. Not even if they are not family."

"Well, of course you say so," the man shot back. "You are rich. We are poor and have to live by stealing."

"There have been times in my life when I have been poor," Bishop Monroe would have assured him. "And it's not that I'm that rich now. But I have found nothing is gained by stealing. Stealing teaches the wrong lessons about life. It teaches us to leave God out of our everyday needs. God wants us to earn our money and possessions by working. It takes faith in God when men or women look to work as their hope for improving their life. Maybe it may not seem to you like it does, but it does."

The man probably looked stunned in the face of such a startling doctrine.

Bishop Monroe continued. "If you look to stealing as your hope for improvement, that takes no faith at all. Just a chance to steal. And you are never sure if that will come or not. If it does come, you're still not sure whether you can pull it off. Work, on the other hand, takes faith in yourself and in God. Men and women with such a faith expect to improve their life by working. They look around for something to do at which they excel. Come rain or shine, cold or hot, they get the work done."

"Bah!" the man exclaimed. "Who believes that kind of stuff?"

"I do," Bishop Monroe assured him.

"So what if I told you that I would shoot you for your money? Would you just stand there and let me do it?"

"If you would shoot me, I wouldn't stop you," Bishop Monroe told him, sober-faced now. "Because I believe that Jesus is the Son of God, and that He came down to earth and died for me. As a follower of His, I would rather follow His example and lay down my life than protect it by killing someone. I believe that following the example of Jesus results in much greater good than shooting would."

"Well, you are a strange people," the man said. "I have never heard of such things. So I think you had all better go back to the United States or Canada where you came from. Such strange people will not make it down here."

"I believe we will make it," Bishop Monroe said. "And God will work many great things in this country."

"You are *loco*," the man told him. "If I owned a gun I would never let anyone shoot me." With that the man crossed himself, bid Bishop Monroe good night, and headed back to town.

To the south of Bishop Monroe's place, a little knoll tucked itself in the lower corner of the La Granja ranch. Nothing big compared to the foothills that stood in the background, but tall enough that it took a few minutes to climb.

On this knoll Bishop Monroe often went to pray after his ordination. Not too many people on either farm were aware of this. And if someone saw him, he would have appeared to be out on an early morning walk. Such a thing was acceptable in the community, but the idea of an Amish bishop out on a hillside praying might not have sat well with many in the congregation. Not that prayer was an objection, but doing it up on a hillside instead of in your closet smacked of liberalism. Up high like that, you lifted yourself above the others, as if you were closer to God, an impression Bishop Monroe wouldn't have intended. Perhaps that's why he kept his activity a secret.

In the meantime, the church house filled on Sundays with locals seeking fellowship. The inevitable conflict with the Spanish language grew worse. "It's simply unrealistic," some said, "that we expect these converts to learn English, let alone German. The sermons will have to be preached in Spanish at least part of the time so the converts and other locals can be fed spiritually. How else can they be expected to mature without good, solid spiritual food spoken in their own tongue?" So the argument went. And Bishop Monroe's sympathies lay clearly on the Spanish-speaking side.

In rebuttal, the conservative side made the point that the locals were being converted without a lot of Spanish preaching. "They came to us while we sang German songs and preached German messages. Why is that not good enough still?" Hence the converted locals could get along quite well as things were, the logic went.

And then too there was the issue of the Amish culture being lost. This was of primary importance.

Bishop Monroe nodded, smiled, and proposed a compromise. "We will preach the opening message and other comments in German," he announced. "But the main message will be done either with an interpreter or in Spanish."

This worked fine for a few months, but that's not how it stayed. The issue of Spanish preaching was never really settled, even though eventually the services were conducted almost entirely in Spanish.

I cared little about the arguments. I could understand both languages just fine, thank you. There were a lot of other things more important to me. Chief among them was having to move back stateside if the adults didn't stop fighting with each other.

No one was saying the words yet, but I sensed danger on the horizon.

Chapter 16

Soon after Bishop Monroe's ordination, the Amish discovered their cash crop: potatoes. Potatoes were better moneymakers than chickens, certainly better than produce, and better than most anything else they tried. So the race was on to get as much of the rich river-bottom land planted in potatoes as possible. Farming tools were modified to form the mounded middles, and long lines of green potato plants were soon growing.

The local thieves followed suit, abandoning chicken stealing for the much more profitable potatoes. It didn't take much effort to slip down to the potato patch dragging sacks. They'd dig up all they could carry. It also didn't take the Amish long to figure out that something had to be done as harvesttime approached. Morning after morning revealed rows of dug up potatoes. Precious income vanishing into pockets unknown.

Uncle Mark and Cousin Ira took it upon themselves to remedy the matter. Scaring off the thieves wouldn't violate any nonresistant principles, they reasoned. Why not camp out for the night in the potato patch, and let any thief who showed up know he wasn't alone? The locals were obviously stealing, but so far no one had confronted them. It was time to do so—without making threats of bodily harm.

On the designated night, the two men set out with their heavy flashlights that were capable of casting beams a hundred yards into the darkness. With sleeping bags in hand, they set up camp on the edge of the potato field. After the expected last-minute jitters, as darkness fell they dropped off to sleep.

One of them woke the other in the dead of night, motioning toward the rows of potatoes in the dim darkness. Raising their heads they looked, at first seeing nothing through the mist that had drifted up from the river. But clearly someone was there. They could hear the soft sound of a shovel going in and out of the ground, the thud of dirt being turned over. And then what sounded like a bag being pulled at intervals, rustling as it brushed the potato vines.

"It's him," one of them whispered. "But what's that other sound?"

They listened, hearing what sounded like leather squeaking on a saddle spaced at regular intervals.

"It's his shoes," the other whispered back.

"Get ready then. Let's go," the first one decided.

Together they came out of their sleeping bags and over the top of the potato plants with flashlights blazing. They swept the field of potatoes from the left to the right, and then back again. On the third pass they caught the man in the crossbeams. Both fixed their lights on the stooped figure.

I have no idea what they expected to happen. Probably a scampering of feet across the potato plants, followed by a hasty dive into the brush of the riverbank. Instead, the thief left his bag and calmly walked away, taking his time before disappearing into the overgrowth.

Uncle Mark and Cousin Ira turned their flashlights on the bag left behind and walked up to study the contents more closely. One of them laughed, picking up the half-filled bag.

"At least we don't have to dig these up," he joked.

Moments later the laughter stopped. The thief had popped back up from the riverbank, his own flashlight out now, sweeping across the field. Unable to reach cover among the trees in time, Uncle Mark and Cousin Ira dove between the rows of potato plants.

"Should we make a run for it?" one of them whispered.

"No!" the answer came back. "He seems to mean business."

The man kept coming, his light playing over the field. The sharp slap of his pants hitting on the potato plants could be heard. Clearly the time for flight was past even if they had dared. The man was getting much too close to their hiding place for comfort.

"What do you want?" one of them finally asked, still keeping his head down.

The slapping steps stopped, followed by silence. Then a soft click came, followed by six shots, one after the other in quick succession. Soft pops in the dirt landing all around them. His gun empty, the man ran off.

Uncle Mark and Cousin Ira waited for the pain to burn in their own bodies. When it didn't, they wondered about the other. Was he still alive? Neither of them moved for the longest time. Slowly one stuck his foot across the potato rows until he made contact with a leg. When he got a kick back, they knew the other was still okay.

When all remained quiet they got to their feet, leaving in the opposite direction the thief had taken. The bag of half-filled potatoes stayed where it was. They used no lights until they arrived back at the house, running by memory over the landscape and through the fences. In the morning they told their story and went to look for the gunnysack but it was gone.

Needless to say, there were no more attempts made at catching potato thieves. Let them have what they wanted. I don't think the story was told that widely even among the community people. Being shot at was not something to be proud of. But getting into such a situation would have been the hardest part to explain.

I heard them tell the story in the privacy of the Stoll family, and the terror of the thieves began growing in our hearts. Not full-blown yet, but growing. The first rumblings of the approaching thunderstorm had sounded.

⁓

With Grandfather Stoll gone, the store out by the main road was taken over by Emil Helmuth. I didn't hear any explanation of why that venture didn't last long, but Emil soon handed over the ownership to Bishop Monroe and his boys. Under their guidance, the store flourished for the rest of our time in Honduras.

We loved making trips down to the store for whatever items Mom wanted. Between that and trips into town on my horse, I was on the road often. My memory tells me we also had a pony and a cart in those days, but the reflections aren't pleasant ones. I think we overturned the flimsy thing a few times, which shows, I suppose, how recklessly we drove. There was also always someone wanting a ride on the cart. I preferred a solitary ride with a saddle creaking under me.

It was during this time that brother John and I took it upon ourselves to raise peanuts. We planted a piece of ground and roasted the harvest in drums over an open fire. I think Dad made some contraption for us out by the shop. It worked fairly well, and the peanuts were edible. Enough so that we hitched up the pony cart, setting off to sell our wares in Guaimaca.

Riding alone on my horse, I would have taken the short way through the trail in the thickets. But with a cart we had to take the circular way around. John was driving, and the bags of peanuts were strapped under the cart seat in a large gunny bag. We were in business. I hawked our wares to passersby at twenty-five centavos a bag. Each offering contained enough peanuts for a decent appetizer. Our sales were also helped along by a few free samples and the fact the peanuts could easily be husked by hand.

We had brisk sales while driving along the dusty streets of town. Flocks of children followed us. The adults bought enough that we were soon sold out. I remember having no problem talking under those circumstances, but perhaps I simply wasn't aware of my speech during those moments. Uncle Luthy would tell me in later years that it was a trial having to elicit information from me. And that was referring to the time before we moved to Honduras, a time in which I have no recollection of experiencing trouble speaking.

On the days when I was sent to Bishop Monroe's store, Mom always gave me extra money for my beloved Pepsi. I'm thinking the cost was low—thirty centavos or so. I always purchased my Pepsi and drank it in the shade of the overhanging porch at the store.

I've spoken of my great love for Bishop Monroe, but it didn't start that way. I don't know if he did it to all the children or just me, but he took upon himself the burden of correcting my faults. His worst com-plaint was my excessive Pepsi drinking. He may even have complained to Mom, but I don't think so. Mostly I got to listen to his lectures on the great dangers involved in drinking too much sugar. As far as I was concerned, I didn't care about sugar content. The storekeeper was sell-ing a product, and he was getting paid for his product. And there was nothing in this world coming between me and my Pepsi—at least on my part.

Strangely enough—or perhaps not so strangely—I did turn out to have a problem that was aggravated by sugar: *hypoglycemia*. This prob-lem tormented my teenage years and remained undiagnosed until I was in my early twenties. I guess we should listen to our elders even when they seem like meddling busybodies.

Bishop Monroe didn't stop with his Pepsi lectures. He tasked me one day with carrying a copy of *Family Life* to his place. Next to my Pepsi, I loved to read. And having a fresh copy of the Amish magazine of the day in hand, just arrived in Honduras, wasn't to be sneezed at. Bishop Monroe must have been aware of my love for reading. Or per-haps I asked if I could read the magazine. He told me I could if I didn't pass some visiting relatives of his on the way home who apparently weren't staying that long. If I did pass them, I was to give them the mag-azine to read first. He wanted them to read a section of the magazine before they left. I could have the magazine afterward.

So I set out with Bishop Monroe's copy of the latest issue of *Fam-ily Life* under my arm. I didn't see any visiting relatives. Well, I did, but you know what I mean. That night I devoured the magazine and deliv-ered it the next day, safe and sound, to the bishop's house. But Bishop Monroe didn't leave the matter alone.

"Didn't you pass my relatives?" he demanded. "You promised me you'd give them the paper. Now they're gone."

"I didn't see anyone," I blatantly lied. I figured he had no way of finding out, and my conscience didn't bother me in those days anyway.

A day or so later at the store, Bishop Monroe confronted me again.

"I spoke with my wife," he said. "And you did pass my relatives on the way. Why did you lie to me?"

I had nothing to say, and I probably couldn't have given a lengthy explanation if I'd wanted to. He lectured me again, and I left with my head hanging. But it didn't do much to change my ways. I just learned to be more careful with what I said.

Thieving was always a problem at Bishop Monroe's store. An affliction he and his workers rarely had success foiling. So when a success story came along, the tale was told far and wide. It was listened to with great interest by the community and written up as one small victory over the forces of darkness. I heard that Bishop Monroe's oldest boy, Glen, had come out early to carry the day's cash home from the store, a practice they maintained to lessen the chances of the last man being robbed on the way home.

While Glen waited and closing time approached, a small boy who had been hanging around for hours, approached the counter. He made a small purchase, handing over a 100 lempira bill to Bishop Monroe. Although not that uncommon, even in those days, Bishop Monroe still examined the offered paper with care. Everything seemed to be in order, and Bishop Monroe gave the boy his change, consisting of nearly the full value of the bill.

The boy climbed on his horse and set out riding into the falling dusk. Bishop Monroe finished closing up the shutters, and Glen added the bill to his stash and rode off in the other direction. Arriving home, Glen's brother Dan took the bag of money to count it. Moments later Dan rushed out to declare that he'd found a counterfeit hundred lempira bill in the bag.

Disbelief abounded. The bill was further examined under bright lights, and the conclusion confirmed. Some enterprising local had used some homegrown method to duplicate the original with reasonable success. A 100-lempira loss at the store was not something easily recovered from.

Incensed, Glen climbed back on his horse and galloped back to the store. There was no sign of the young boy on horseback. Still, he knew in which direction the rider had gone, and nothing would be lost by pursuing, he figured.

A hard gallop later, following the main road toward Tegucigalpa,

Glen spotted the boy ahead of him. He pulled up beside him and demanded his money back.

"I didn't do anything," the boy declared. "I'm just going home."

"Yes, you did take something."

"I'm not a thief!" the boy declared.

"Then what have you got in that bag?" Glen demanded. "I just saw you at our store where you gave my dad a counterfeit 100-lempira bill."

"You did not," the boy said. "I got these groceries in town. Just bought them an hour ago. And I've never seen you before."

Glen soon tired of this useless argument. He grabbed the boy's groceries and gave him back the counterfeit bill. The exchange was made peacefully enough, and the two galloped off in opposite directions.

Chapter 17

Sometime in the summer of 1972, Dad began construction on our new house across the road. The plan included a basement and greater square footage. The first order of business was digging the basement. Uncle Stephen had dug his using Uncle Mark's horse-drawn shovel and then finishing the work by hand. So the men came over to examine our hillside. They soon concluded that the layered shale made digging with the contraption unfeasible.

Uncle Mark still had to try his hand at it. Full of youthful optimism, he thought there was a chance he could figure out a way to do it. Arriving with two Belgians hitched to the giant shovel, they dragged the machine across the ground, hitting rock almost at once. The second try went no better, and Uncle Mark had to admit failure.

So what was to be done? Backhoes were out of the question since they didn't exist in Honduras. At least I never saw one in the eight years we lived there. They did later find a dozer for the pond digging, but I never heard that option discussed. Perhaps it was too expensive for such a small project.

Dad pondered the situation for a while until a local man, who must have heard about the problem, arrived with his proposed solution. He would dig the basement himself, he said. His brother, Pedro, and he would take care of it. His name was Fausto. He was a jolly man, always ready with a laugh. A man of medium height, he proclaimed the basement digging *no problema* and showed off the large biceps in his arm as evidence. The man clearly was used to hard work.

Still Dad was skeptical. They went down to the site, and Fausto took a few test whacks at the shale. The ground broke off easily under the point of the pick, which was smaller than Uncle Mark's wide shovel. It was still *no problema*.

Dad laughed and moved on to the next point. How much would this digging by hand cost? No doubt seeing Canadian manual labor prices dancing in his head, Fausto quoted a ridiculously low amount, like 200 or 300 lempiras for the whole project. No doubt an astronomic sum in his mind, but Dad was truly stunned.

"We'll be done in no time," Fausto proclaimed. "Me and my brother, Pedro."

"I don't know about that," Dad told him, not wanting to take unfair advantage of the situation. "How about we set up a weekly rate? I'll pay you at the end of each week until you're finished."

The two sized each other up for a few moments.

Fausto stood there, the young man who had only recently taken on a young wife and whose first child, a daughter, had been born the prior year, being about the same age as my sister Sarah Mae. While on this job search, he had left both his wife and daughter behind at his parents' place, or rather his parents' hut, more than two hours away by bus.

Dad was the Amish man with seven children. He ran a prosperous machine shop, living in tight quarters across the road by our standards. But the place had more rooms than any three local huts, and now he was building a yet larger house across the road.

I cannot fathom such contrasts, even in looking back. But it illustrates the problems faced by the Amish in a third-world culture. Their norms were completely upended, and they hardly knew where to begin setting them upright again. Stateside, few people from the *Englisha* wanted to be Amish. They admired them, perhaps, but from afar. There the Amish were the poor living among the rich. In Honduras, the Amish were rich beyond all local comprehension. What Fausto was thinking while he made his deal with Dad, I don't know. But I got to know him well afterward. He would stay on as our worker all the years we remained in Honduras. I can guess his thoughts.

An honest man he was, open-faced and trustworthy to a fault. The

man couldn't read or write, and he had no desire to learn. It wasn't necessary for the life he wanted to live. So I think Fausto saw more than just a
basement needing to be dug that morning. Here in front of him was the
life he wanted to live: working for a rich man from the States. A person
whose business wouldn't fail next year. Someone who wouldn't disappear on him next week. A person who wouldn't be out of money when
payday arrived. Fausto saw all of this, or at least a glimpse of it, I'm sure.

"Twenty lempiras a week," Fausto said, his face breaking into a
broad grin. "For me and my brother Pedro."

Why not? Dad thought. Ten dollars in American money. There
was nothing to lose. And he wouldn't be cheating the man with a pitiful contract price.

"Okay," Dad said. "Twenty lempiras a week. When can you start?"

"Right now," Fausto said. "Where is the wheelbarrow?"

The needed tools were produced, and the digging began. Digging
that would go on for long weeks, and all done cheerfully. The two men
worked hard all day, from seven in the morning until four in the afternoon. And each Friday Fausto collected his twenty lempiras, gave eight
of them to Pedro, and disappeared for a weekend visit with his wife. On
Monday, the two were back again, digging away. They dug all week, the
one man for six dollars American and the other for four.

That scene is a permanent fixture in my mind. The great dig, going
on and on. Never a week missed that I can remember. Not for sickness,
or heat, or storms. It took them over four months, if I remember correctly. The shovels were worn into half-moon circles by the time they
were done.

Dad kept the tools as mementos for years, dragging them with him
when we moved stateside, and bringing them out to show visitors. He
would tell the story of the two locals who dug his basement by hand
through shale rock.

When the hole was completed, Dad hired Fausto on full-time for
eighteen lempiras a week. That would be nine US dollars. And Dad
built a small one-room shack for Fausto set up a few hundred yards
north of our house. There Fausto brought his wife, Elsa, and daughter, Maria, to live.

It was while the great dig was going on that I had my one-and-only true fist fight. I showed up bloody and bruised at the dig one afternoon to display my battle wounds. Neither Fausto nor Pedro seemed that impressed, which greatly deflated my high.

The altercation had begun in Grandfather's mango orchard after lunch. The local boys had nicknamed me *pata sopae* months earlier. Local slang for "buzzard feet," I think. Not that I objected; it was true after all. I was tall, skinny, gangly, and consisted mostly of feet. I resembled, I suspected, the ugly black carrion-eating birds who are a constant presence in any Honduras landscape.

But such designations do bear down on the soul, however bravely born. So when the fistfight was proposed between me and one of the local boys, I was honored by the attention more than anything else. I was glad to be considered a worthy opponent. Winning wasn't exactly something I expected. What I thought would happen, I'm not sure. Things were kind of hazy in my mind. I was clearly doing something forbidden and well knew it. Amish boys didn't fight. But this wasn't really the kind of fighting the adults talked about, I reasoned. We weren't angry with each other.

So I agreed, and much excitement ensued. A few of the locals bowed out at once, much to my surprise. But a boy was finally found as the designated fighter to stand against me. We lined up, facing each other. We were just on the other side of the little wooden footbridge that spanned the canal in the mango orchard. We moved closer to each other, and he got a few licks in on my chest and face that cut and stung for awhile. I really didn't know what to do; I didn't have a clue. Finally seeing an opening, I took a swing and then another one. I put everything I had into them.

The result was pure amazement on my part and on the part of the boys standing around me. The fellow was lifted literally off his feet and thrown onto his back. He lay there stunned for long moments while I stared down at him.

Cheers and wild exclamations broke out, whereupon the boy on the ground leaped to his feet. He took one look around before racing off through the mango orchard. I felt pure joy rush through my veins.

From the power of the blow. From the cheers around me. From the raw admiration. I had never felt such a thing in my life.

"Let's put someone else up against him," the other boys proclaimed at once. But no one could be found. I was the victor of the day. And they chattered in great detail about every move of the fight, which really hadn't lasted that long. For my part, I made my way back to the digging of the basement and presented myself for more accolades. I shut up about the matter after being deflated by Fausto and Pedro's bored reaction.

The following day I learn that fame carries a high price. A person becomes the target that must be dethroned. A local boy—a *really large* local boy—and much older than I, worked on Grandfather's place. He hadn't been there on the day of the fight. He was now ready for the proposed rematch. The others encouraged him, and he grinned with glee at their urgings. He was clearly taking upon himself the challenge of lowering me down a notch or two.

I knew and he knew that he could whop me—and do it easily. So I said no, I wasn't going to fight him. That wasn't an acceptable answer. He hounded me for days. He dogged my steps, insisting on setting up a time for the great challenge. But I always said no. Finally we passed him on the trail out in the open fields on the way to Grandfather's place. Brother John was with me that day. The boy challenged me again. I again refused; whereupon he came up and slapped me in the face. Hard. That produced the result he wanted. I flew into him, fists flying. The fight lasted less time than the other one had. He was on top of me, pounding my face.

"I'm sorry, I'm sorry," I muttered repeatedly.

Sorry for what, I didn't know. For winning, I guess. It seemed the appropriate thing to say groveling in the face of a bully. And it produced the result I wanted. The beating stopped.

He got up, brushed himself off, and strutted on down the trail.

"You should have beat him on his back with the wooden end of your slingshot," I told John, trying to salvage a little of my bruised pride.

"I should have," John agreed.

We both knew it would have been useless. The outcome had been preordained. And John would have been beaten up for his efforts.

I gathered myself together and stayed out of fistfights from then on. Even Mom never found out. Or if she did, she kindly didn't broach the subject with me.

Chapter 18

Two events would conspire to stop the great dig while it was ongoing, but neither succeeded. One was when word swept through the community that the new road from Tegucigalpa would pass through the lower part of Sanson, cutting the farm in half and greatly reducing its value to anyone. A low-flying plane was even seen passing over, allegedly marking off the new road.

Should the community consider moving before such devaluation took place? And if moving was in the works, Dad sure didn't want another house on his property to dispose of.

Fausto and his brother, Pedro, scoffed at such a thing. "It will never come," they said. "Who has that much money to spend on a road?"

But the Amish had a vested interest in the subject, so Dad went in to talk with the officials in Guaimaca. They counseled remaining calm, not wanting to lose such valuable contributors to the local economy. Surely land prices would actually increase with a paved road, or perhaps this paved road would never happen.

Not that any of us wouldn't have welcomed a paved road running from the capital to the community and then on out east to Olancho. The problem was believing the road would happen in the first place, and second, when, in this land of *mañana*. After more consideration, Dad ignored the talk and the basement digging never halted.

The road did end up coming through, exactly where the people had said it would. Only it was *years* after we'd left. I never heard of anyone losing property value in the process.

The other event wasn't so easily shaken off. Fausto and Pedro didn't scoff this time. They shook their heads and said little. We sat out on the wooden fence beside the old cottage for hours that morning, feeling the shock in the air. Three of the David Peachey children came down to talk to us children about it—Rhoda, Daniel, and Joseph.

I don't know what they thought they could do. Comfort us perhaps. Share in our shock since the robbers had also been at their place last night. On top of that, their mother was dying of cancer, a fact well-known in the community by then. But that's how that family was, always kindhearted and thinking of others.

I'd slept through the whole thing, but my two oldest sisters, Susanna and Miriam, had awakened and peeked out of their bedroom, only to flee back at Mom's orders to hide. They hid shivering under the covers until the robbers left.

The evening before, up at Grandfather's place, Uncle Abner was loading the truck around nine o'clock for his usual produce run into Tegucigalpa. Uncle Mark and Cousin Ira were helping, along with the driver of the truck. They were just finishing up, working by the light of the vehicle and gas lanterns, which they'd hung around. It wasn't a small task, packing in all the vegetables, butter, sour cream, and other goods. They had to be packed well enough to survive the rough, bouncing, four-hour ride the next morning.

Things were far enough along that Cousin Ira decided to leave. He walked up the dark path between Grandfather's place and where he and his newlywed wife lived along the creek. Near the irrigation canal he was jumped by four men with guns. They ordered him to lead the way back to the produce truck.

He did, of course, what with guns stuck in his ribs and all. When they arrived at the produce truck, a mad rush was made into the light and guns were flourished. Uncle Abner, Uncle Mark, and the driver were quickly secured, and the four men searched the premises, taking whatever they wanted. The loot was gathered outside on the ground.

Grandmother was alone with them upstairs while they searched that part of the house, but she suffered no physical harm at their hands, other than being frightened out of her wits.

Quickly it became apparent that the four robbers were operating under the command of a fifth man. This man lurked in the shadows during the whole night's episode. Never visible but always consulted when the time came for important decisions. Now there was such a decision. The men could find only one gun in their search of the house, and there were supposed to be two. The fifth man said so.

Uncle Abner admitted that, yes, Grandfather had kept two guns in the house while he was alive. But that one had been borrowed by his nephew Paul, Uncle Joe's oldest boy, that very afternoon for bird hunting. Much grumbling ensued, but what could be done about it? The gun wasn't present.

"Then we must go to Joe Stoll's place and find the gun," the order came from the lurking fifth man. So the march began with two hostages—Uncle Abner and Cousin Ira—in tow. Uncle Mark and the driver were left behind with instructions to stay put for the night.

The impression at the beginning was that decisions were being made by the robbers on the fly. But now I question that. The event fell together too neatly to not have been planned in some detail. First, it wasn't necessary to go past our place to arrive at Uncle Joe's. They could have gone on the other side of the ravine on the trail that lay between us and Uncle Stephen's. Going over the gully would eventually lead them past the children's home at the turn, which would have put the robbers in sight of another likely target if the thing had been unplanned. And there would have had to be lights on at the children's home because the Northern Indiana Amish never retired until late.

Either way, the trek with the hostages leading the way went past our place. The robbers decided to stop in. The four men proceeded to beat on the front door, which didn't induce Dad to open it. He believed in nonresistance, but he wasn't going to willingly open a door in the night to strange men who beat on it. This problem was quickly overcome by orders from the four robbers to the hostages. "Speak to them in your language." With gun barrels at their backs, Uncle Abner and Cousin Ira obeyed.

"It's us, Abner and Ira," they hollered in German. "Open the door." Dad finally did, turning the lock on the door. He was nearly knocked to the floor by the force of the gun barrels thrust into his ribs. The marks were there for days afterward. Mom was in her nightgown, and in no condition to receive visitors, but there was no choice in the matter. That was also about the time my two sisters stuck their heads out of the bedroom. Mom shooed them back in with quick orders to hide.

Mom never did learn to speak Spanish for reasons of her own, but that night she understood when the men asked, "*Muchachas?*" [girls] after seeing the retreating forms of my sisters.

"No," Mom lied, fearing the worst. "*Muchachos*" [boys].

I doubt if they were fooled. They simply had other things on their minds: guns and money. Dad had been planning to leave for a trip to the capital in the morning to restock supplies, so he had plenty of money around. The robbers made off with a big haul, around 3000 lempiras. And they took the last of our guns. This fact pained me the most as I was consigned for the rest of my time in Honduras to a pellet gun. (Which may not have been that bad an idea, come to think of it.)

Leaving our house, the little party proceeded into the darkness, taking Dad with them as a third hostage. Hands tied behind their backs, the men went with orders not to make a noise unless told to. Somewhere between Uncle Joe's place and ours, among the gently rolling slopes, the hostages were ordered to kneel on the ground. Consultations were taken with the shadowy commander. The three thought they were going to be shot because their usefulness was over. I had only to look at Dad's face the next morning to know he'd been fully convinced of that. He carried about him the shadow of death.

For reasons unknown, they were ordered back on their feet and on to Uncle Joe's place. Twice more that night that ritual would be played out. Whether for terror purposes or because their captors really did plan to shoot them and were persuaded otherwise, no one would ever know.

Arriving at Uncle Joe's, the procedure was repeated. Only this time, Aunt Laura opened the door because Uncle Joe was tending to a sick baby. The robbers rushed in and caught the poor man in the bedroom without his pants. I've had many bad dreams of having to cross a crowded room and being unable to find my pants. Of running and running and never arriving. But I have never had pistols prodding my ribs while I was trying to put my pants on. I doubt that Uncle Joe found the situation amusing in the least.

When it became clear the house had been thoroughly searched for guns and money, the men made ready to leave. They left Uncle Joe behind with strict orders not to leave the house, saying they were leaving someone outside to guard the place, which turned out to be untrue.

From there the party backtracked past our place, ending up at David Peachey's house, and using the same routine there. They seemed to become less violent with the gun punching as the night proceeded. Perhaps they realized we really were peace-loving people.

Forcing the hostages to carry the bags of loot, the robbers continued on over to La Granja, crossed Turk Road, and hit Emil Helmuth and Minister Vernon's places before calling it a night. The robbers made their last threats to the hostages, warning them to never report this to anyone, let alone the police, or they would be shot. With those words hanging in the air, they vanished toward the mountains and into the early morning mist.

Back at the house, Mom hadn't slept a wink, tormented all night and certain she would never see Dad's face again. She was too scared to set her foot outside the house before daylight. I can imagine the greeting Dad received when he arrived home.

And so we sat on the wooden fence the next morning and repeated the tidbits of the tale we knew with the Peachey children, hardly comprehending that such a thing had happened while we slept.

Long discussions were held by the adults that day at the church house. Was Honduras livable any longer? Could they go on with the community when such threats hung over their heads?

At home, Dad asked, "Should the basement digging continue?" Fausto and Pedro were sober-faced and had no ready answer this time. But they never stopped digging.

The driver of Uncle Abner's produce truck did notify the police, and they came out to investigate. But with the magnitude of the assault, they said, the matter must be referred to higher authorities.

So the Honduras version of the FBI soon arrived, "the DIN," and began their questioning. They arrived quickly at conclusions of their own, largely unsupported by the evidence. A notorious criminal had done this, they said. Someone just released from jail.

A few days later the man was brought out on the back of a truck and driven around the community tied down like an animal on display. The police were hoping one of the hostages could finger him, but no one could.

So he must be the fifth man, the DIN decided. The one you never saw. And that was about the extent of the investigation.

Chapter 19

Soon after the ruckus from the armed robbery, Fausto and Pedro finished the basement. They were flushed with excitement from their accomplishment. The hole extended for a great length along the side of the hill, coming down the slope for a walkout basement the full length of the backside.

Fausto, for his part, had sealed his place in our hearts. His ready laugh and fun-loving ways are prominent among my childhood memories. Whatever farmwork I helped with, such as clearing the land with machetes and later planting and harvesting potatoes, Fausto was always there.

Pedro was the youngest of the brothers, and more lighthearted than his older brother, but he still had a touch of a serious side. Their older brother, Beto, came by occasionally and would eventually find work in the community. Pedro did too.

Beto was the most serious of the brothers. As in *really* serious. He would laugh sometimes with the others, but always at their instigation. On one point, the three were alike. They carried themselves with dignity and valued their own personhood. Unlike many of the locals, they didn't seek to gain position with the Amish by attending their church. I never saw any of the three brothers at the services. Deeply religious though, they spoke often of Mother Mary, who lived "up there." *La Virgen,* they said, watched over them.

I never saw Beto or Pedro participate in making eyes at the

community's women or the girls who often passed by. Ogling was a national pastime for the locals, done openly and without shame. Grown men would stand staring with broad grins on their faces as their eyes followed every step of the Amish girls and women.

"Wow!" they would gush. "Two weeks with her in the mountains. Now that would be something."

Fausto did have his faults though, such as taking up an occasional affair with a local woman. And he wasn't that bashful about it either. The weakness of man was simply a fact of life to him, and he didn't make any excuses for it.

Now that the basement was dug and his position as our worker firmly established, Fausto had brought Elsa, and his daughter, Maria, to live in the shack Dad built on the northern edge of our property, just off the path from the cattle guard.

Elsa was a slim beauty, shy, and soft-spoken. Fausto had met her while he worked a short stint on one of the neighboring ranches called El Mansion. He struck up a romance with her—as most locals did— by meeting secretly along the riverbanks. Elsa's father, as was also common, fiercely opposed the union. Why, I have no idea, but it seemed the usual practice. The fierce father trying to keep the girl from sneaking off, and the two sweethearts still accomplishing the feat by hook or crook. Fausto claimed he snuck up to the creek while Elsa was washing clothes. It may have been a tall tale, but Fausto told it with a straight face.

Once the romance had heated sufficiently, Elsa ran off with him one night—also a common occurrence. They went to Fausto's parents' house—likely a place that didn't have more than two bedrooms and was already crowded. Having grown up in a house with plenty of bedrooms and just as much room besides, I have no idea how all that worked.

Now Fausto had been without a job and had a wife to support. Not that they were legally married. That would have been too expensive. Living together sufficed, which was also the local custom. The running away date served as the beginning of the common-law marriage.

So with his wife living at his father's place and at odds with her parents, Fausto had showed up with his offer to dig our basement. And having succeeded beyond even his expectations, he now had his own place to live with his wife and child. It was no wonder he settled in with a broad grin.

I spent many happy hours sitting outside their little one-room shack with a covered kitchen shed off to the side. Elsa had a baked mud oven covered with a barrel top that puffed smoke out through the roof. I sat there and ate the delicious food Elsa prepared. Tortillas from corn pounded out with a stone, formed into patties, and thrown onto the barrel top. All of it eaten amid the smell of wood smoke and surrounded by the open air.

For a delicacy, Elsa would replace the regular round beans inside the tortilla with *frijoles fritos*. That translates into *fried beans,* but this was much more. I never thought to ask how she made them. And in only a few authentic Mexican restaurants stateside have I tasted anything remotely similar. It's made by mixing in fat, I think, and other similarly unhealthy ingredients. But the mixture is awesome to eat. It must have cost more on their meager salaries than I could have imagined. I never thought to wonder why Elsa went to the expense. I didn't see myself as the rich white kid that I was, with my dad as the boss of the farm. I was simply a boy caught up in the charm of their simple lifestyle.

The kitchen also served as their living room, spilling into the outdoors without a door. The one enclosed room, its door opening directly to the outside, was the bedroom. There was no raised wooden bed inside like I was used to sleeping on, simply a mattress on the floor and blankets for the baby. The wooden slat siding let in the sunlight and the starlight as well. Rain though, was somehow kept outside.

Periodically Fausto would have one of his affairs. He was, he told me with a bemused look on his face, *mucho enamorado,* much in love. The first we would hear of these escapades would be the specter of Elsa packing up her meager things in a wrapped bundle and preparing to leave.

"I'm leaving," she would tell me when I wandered by to show my sympathy. "Fausto isn't coming home evenings any longer. He's staying in town all night."

The funny thing was it usually involved an older woman. They seemed to be Fausto's weakness. I guess he already had his young wife.

Guaimaca was a good trek on foot and not undertaken lightly. But Fausto always showed up for work on time in the mornings, staying away from the little shack all day while the current affair was going on. Dad always chose not to get involved.

I got into the middle of things.

"Where are you going?" I would ask Elsa.

"I'm not telling you," she'd say. "Because you'll tell Fausto."

I didn't argue with that logic because I probably would have if Fausto asked me. Fausto never did though, taking care of his own problems in his own way. In the course of a few weeks, Fausto would get tired of the woman in town and figure out where Elsa had gone. How, I don't know; probably through family is my guess. But there were also only so many places she could be. And on some Sunday afternoon they would be back, Fausto having made his amends that weekend. His wandering spirit settled for a time.

Pedro was still young and didn't have either a wife or a girlfriend that I knew of. He was the best looking of the three, and would have been a prime candidate to pursue one of the Amish girls—by legal means, of course, as he could have converted to the faith. This was what several of the locals were attempting already—seeing marriage to a white girl as the highest achievement they could possibly attain.

Pedro turned his nose up at such ventures. I picked up disdain from both of the brothers whenever they mentioned the names of the amorous locals suddenly sprouting Amish suspenders and broad fall pants.

Years later, on one of my trips back, I asked Pedro—who had by then married a local girl—why he'd never pursued a white woman.

"It's doesn't work," he told me, waving his arms around. "She would always be pushing me. She'd want a refrigerator, and then I'd have to work harder and always harder. And then she'd want a bigger house, and I'd have to go work in the States and never come back here." But I guess going to the States with a white wife wasn't considered all that bad a deal for the others. Numerous Amish and, later, Mennonite girls would end up marrying locals.

Beto though, the sorrowful brother, ended up making the biggest mess of all. He never tried to join the Amish church like some did. Rather, he stuck with the local customs, blending them with the Amish *rumspringa* and coming up with a truly explosive mixture. The event involving him didn't happen until we'd left, but it helped scatter the remaining Amish stateside. *Rumspringa,* Honduras style, turned out to be more than the Amish could handle. Beto was working for a family in La Granja by then, and he fell in love with the eldest daughter.

"He had it bad," Pedro told me later, claiming that Beto had never been in love before. That may or may not have been true. Most local boys had girlfriends at one time or the other. Be that as it may, there was no question that Beto had fallen hard for the Amish girl.

How Beto persuaded her to elope with him, I have no idea. But on one of those deep, dark Honduras nights, she slipped out of the house with him.

They met at the prearranged place, the young woman likely changing into local clothing that Beto brought along. An Amish girl traveling with a man at night would have aroused suspicion.

Reaching the main road, they flagged a ride or caught one of the early buses going toward Tegucigalpa, although that would have entailed considerable risk, taking the chance other Amish might have been aboard.

They arrived well before daylight north of Talanga at his father's place—the same house Fausto had taken Elsa, and where Pedro would take his girlfriend to later.

So in the local custom they were hitched. At least Beto thought so. To the Amish girl, it was all for fun, I assume.

Back at home, morning brought consternation and panic as the girl's empty bed was discovered. Disbelief at first soon set into reality as a further search was made, and the girl wasn't found. Beto was surely involved, the other workers informed the father when Beto didn't show up for work. He would have taken her to his father's home, they said.

The father set off at once, following the directions he was given. I doubt if Beto expected that from the father. Local fathers didn't pursue their daughters when they ran off, but he hadn't bargained for an Amish father.

Arriving at the home, the father made his presence known, asking the girl to return with him at once. I doubt if the argument was that difficult to win. The thought of another night spent in a Honduras shack with the parents snoring through wooden slats on the other side of the wall would have taken much of the fun out of the jaunt by then. The girl chose to return, and Beto was heartbroken. I don't know what he was thinking.

Even with the girl back, the shock went throughout the Amish community like a man hit in the stomach with a full frontal blow. This was a ghost from the depths of Amish depravity come to haunt them on foreign soil. Not only had they fallen, but fallen lower than what some of them had left behind. It wasn't hard for them to imagine what would be said stateside.

"So you think you're better than the rest of us? You people always thought you were so spiritual. How do you feel now? All your complaining about the young people from some of our communities, as if any of us could be perfect in this life. You didn't like the impure dating practices. What do you think now? Is this where your spirituality was taking you?"

Pedro told me later that Beto tried to marry the girl, the American way this time, and was rebuffed. Whatever the truth was, Beto never recovered from his love-stricken state. Though Beto wasn't given to drinking, he entered a bar one night and intoxicated himself. Afterward, he attacked the bartender with his machete. Naturally, the man defended himself, pulling a pistol and shooting Beto to death.

And contrary to local custom, none of the brothers sought revenge against the bartender.

"Beto had a death wish," Pedro told me, his face sober. "He wanted to go."

Chapter 20

My friend Joseph Peachey's mom, Miriam, continued to lose ground in her battle with cancer. The whole community waited, expecting the worst. Visitors—sisters, I think—came from the States to help out. I met them only briefly when I stopped by to visit Joseph. We were spending considerable time with each other by then, often hanging out at his place. The feed mill his father ran was a fascinating place. It was always filled with dust and the smell of ground flour.

We were playing in the basement of the house one afternoon, with no thought on my mind of Joseph's sick mother lying above us. One of the visitors appeared in the stairwell, telling us to quiet down. She sounded pretty upset—as she well had a right to be. I should have been told to go home, but I suppose their good manners didn't allow such a radical action.

I was told later that Miriam feared the growing cancer in her body greatly—as is understandable. But she especially feared the pain usually associated with its advance. And as the diagnosis became certain, Miriam prayed that she might be spared this agony in her body while living in a land that didn't offer morphine. Miriam had her prayer answered, dying relatively pain free. We buried her on the hillside above Grandfather Stoll's grave.

Perhaps it was the family nature of the Peacheys, but I never saw them openly mourn the death. Not like the Stolls, who expressed themselves freely. The Peacheys kept it inside, going on with life the best they could. And they did a good job of it. The family never showed any outward signs of trauma, hanging together quite well. Their home became a welcome center in the community, entertaining visitors from far and wide. I know. I spent many a wonderful hour there.

David Peachey made several efforts to remarry. First with a local Amish girl—a spinster who turned him down. We weren't told why, other than the supposed fact that she didn't get along with his children. That seemed like a weak excuse to me. We all got along quite well with the Peachey children.

The other attempt I was aware of began with writing letters to a widow back in Pennsylvania. I don't think David had met her in person until she came down for a visit. The attempt didn't go that well either, and again because of the children. So perhaps they weren't as nice to a prospective new mother as they were to the rest of us.

David Peachey was a driving force behind many of the church's financial outreach projects, promoting and broadcasting them in his letters in the Amish paper, *The Budget*. One of these projects began in the spring of 1972. It was called the Poor Ladies Project. In the proposed venture, widows or abandoned wives would obtain a regular stipend with which to support their families. That there was a need was not a question. Honduras abounded with abandoned wives and children. That is, if you counted their common-law way of living as marriage.

So a program was devised and put into action with the best of intentions. A weekly allowance of food and money would be supplied through Bishop Monroe's store. Applicants would be interviewed in person or at their residence in order to determine eligibility. Neighbors would be asked questions, and so forth. One of the rules stated that the woman had to be truly abandoned, without a man living in the house. Even male relatives would disqualify her. The Amish wanted to help only the truly needy.

So with this in mind a committee of men was formed. Why they didn't think to use women, I don't know. There would have been nothing in Amish tradition against such a thing that I know of. But then, there was nothing in Amish tradition about a Poor Ladies Fund either.

Applicants poured in and needed to be interviewed. And after they had been approved, they had to be reinterviewed on a periodic basis, just to make sure their situation hadn't changed—which the Amish had figured out by then did happen frequently due to the constantly shifting alliances of Honduras female and male relationships.

Dad got his turn on the board soon enough. He had to make trips into Guaimaca on Saturday afternoons with David Peachey and Emil Helmuth to visit homes and talk to the neighbors of the applicants. He didn't like the deal in the least, and not just because it took up his time. I never thought of Dad as a man astute in the romantic arts, but even he could see how this weekly activity in town might appear to the locals. Here you had three Amish men visiting single women on a regular basis. But then perhaps Mom was the one who educated him on the matter because Dad raised considerable objections to the project, although to little effect. The Poor Ladies Project stumbled on even with its obvious faults.

For one thing, the project held great appeal to Amish donors stateside. There aren't that many direct Amish charities outside of local tragedies for Amish folks to contribute to. And this one sounded good, even a little exciting—helping downtrodden women of the third world better their lives, all on a pittance of ten dollars a week. A sound investment indeed, which any thinking Amish man and his wife could see clearly. And it was run by honest Amish men who kept none of the proceeds for this charitable operation.

The problem was the downtrodden women of the third world were quite crafty. They had their own way of handling this influx of monies from the States. The first order of business was to take full advantage of the opportunity, making her application at Bishop Monroe's store, whether she had a man around the house or not.

From there they learned the routine quickly. First, you swore by the saints and the Holy Virgin that your husband had left you penniless and starving. Then, Bishop Monroe would smile and tell you when the first inspection would occur. An event easy enough to handle since you now knew when the *gringos* would be stopping by.

On that weekend you made sure your husband, live-in boyfriend, or whatever, wasn't present. And when the Amish became wise to your tricks and made surprise weekend inspections, you made sure that all your weekends were male free. During the week, of course, the Amish didn't do inspections. They were too busy working.

Worse perhaps was the local men's attitude. There were documented cases of men leaving their wives for younger women because they were depending on the Amish safety net to ensure the first wife wouldn't go hungry.

One hard case played out right on the Sanson ranch. A lady by the name of Rosa Sanchez and her children were given free housing on Amish land. A worthy project indeed, and over time Rosa became good friends with Aunt Sarah and others of the community's women. The problem was Rosa continued to bear children each year, when there was obviously no husband around. These continued pregnancies, while the woman was living right on their land, was the consternation of the Amish's charitable minds. But the Amish women loved her, and the men were unable to drive her out into the cold, hard world again. So Rosa stayed and raised her brood in plain sight of everyone.

The project received the occasional stimulus by actually helping a woman and her children who were in dire need. These were the real stories—eyewitness accounts of starving children with swollen stomachs living in squalor and filth that kept everyone encouraged and moving forward. At least they were helping *some* people, they told each other. And so the Poor Ladies Project was left to limp along, dodging around the mysteries of mankind that only God can solve.

∽

School began that fall—late as usual. Sometime in October, I think. And I entered the sixth grade. The church/schoolhouse building was a familiar fixture in our lives by then, sitting near the center of the community on the highest knoll around. Most of the people walked there on Sunday mornings, including the folks from La Granja, who lived the farthest away.

In the center of the building was the church auditorium, which faced south. On either side were the school wings, with the lower grades on the west and the upper grades on the east. I spent only one year on the west side, starting my second year on the east side. I don't remember who our teacher was. They kind of come and go in my mind.

We had wooden shutters made of slats built all along the side of the schoolhouse. They didn't swing sideways to open and shut, but folded in on top of each other, held in place by friction. These could be turned open in good weather and shut during bad weather. They were shut for overnight too.

Someone arrived early one morning to find Harlan, Emil Helmuth's oldest boy, hanging by the neck, suspended between the slats of the shutters. I hadn't arrived yet, so I didn't get to see the resuscitation efforts or the mad dash to bring his parents up to the school. But the news was on the lips of everyone when we arrived. Harlan was found hanging by his neck, but he would survive we were told.

Harlan had come early to school and, finding no teacher there and the door locked, he took it upon himself to climb in through the slats. Things went well until his hold slipped and he fell back, catching his chin on the collapsing shutters. From there it was all downhill because his legs didn't reach the ground. If someone hadn't arrived in time, there would no doubt have been another grave on the hillside only yards from where he would have died.

Sober warnings were given to us all that day, which were entirely unnecessary in my opinion. None of us had any plans to climb in through the wooden shutters anytime in the future.

Sometime during that school year, my agony with the fairer sex began. This was an attraction to which I vigorously objected—which, I suppose, only made matters worse. I should have talked to the girl or at least tried. Our school desks sat only a foot apart. It should have been easy, but I just couldn't. And I probably couldn't have even if I hadn't stuttered. My crush was severe and would remain so for years.

The girl was older than I was by a year or so, but we were in the same grade. Before this, I hadn't fantasized over girls or even dreamed of marriage. The whole thing caught me unaware. Surrounded by the constant talk of the Honduran men, I wasn't ignorant of the ways of love. I just hadn't expected this to happen to me. Strangely, I knew from the beginning I wouldn't marry her. It just wasn't to be. I never wavered or doubted about that. Yet there was no getting away from the torment. At home I could forget her. But at school was another matter.

In the community I was a loner, a scarecrow that stalked the land. The thought of her returning my feelings didn't even cross my mind. The whole thing was absurd. She was "up there," and I was "down here"—*way* down here. I was alone, awash in my emotions. So I did stupid things. I tore up a few sheets of blank paper that slid off her desk. I handed the papers back to her in pieces silently, without saying a word.

The other two girls in our class, who were seated around us, stared at me aghast. They comforted her at recess in whispered words. No doubt talking about the ogre who lived in their midst.

I don't think they had any idea the depth of my feelings and wouldn't have believed me if I'd told them. It's no wonder I had so few friends acting like I did. Yet looking back now, I think she understood. She never said an unkind word to me, even when I handed her the torn paper.

Perhaps she felt the same pain, the impossibility of everything, knowing what could never be for reasons neither of us could understand.

I know those memories are shrouded in the cloudy mist of youthful idealism. I also know that a man never forgets his first love. So although in many ways these memories are suspect, they have never left me. Life and living dull the senses and turn us into hardened skeptics. But in the beginning it isn't so. We believe in goodness, in virtue that has no flaw. We look beyond the doors of our hearts and are made better persons by the sight. We all have someone who catches a glimpse of us lying behind the ugly, beyond the brazen. Who see the beauty in us present from before our forebears ate the apples in the garden. And it is that shadow we ought not to forget. That fleeting moment when love first calls. For then we see as we really ought to see.

Chapter 21

With school in session that fall, thoughts of the armed robbery earlier that year faded from everyone's memory. I heard little talk about it at home, and we began to move about more freely after dark. Surely it had been only a onetime thing, we figured. And the petty thievery could be dealt with.

Uncle Stephen's family returned from an extended summer visit to Canada. He was a quiet man and not given to conflict. But his message delivered upon his arrival back in the community jarred many. It was spoken quietly to a few extended family members and was clear enough. His family would be returning to Canada once they sold their farm and set things in order.

Uncle Stephen turned out to be the "canary in the mine." But three years into the new settlement, no one quite knew how to handle it. Some thought his claims of liberalism in the community were simply preposterous. Bishop Monroe was, after all, well-loved, and he clearly had no intentions of leaving the Amish faith or leading anyone in that direction.

The arguments were clinical back then, not yet fleshed out for all to see. And Uncle Stephen talked mostly in terms of keeping the *ordnung*. Or rather, he spoke of the slippage he saw from the *ordnung* while in Aylmer. These were both things few wanted to hear, especially when it came to the subject of the Aylmer *ordnung*.

Plus there were more exciting things going on, such as saving souls and outreach—the throngs of locals who were interested in joining the church. Was that not what Christianity was about? And the reason we were here?

I don't know what could have been done if someone had really listened to Uncle Stephen. Perhaps that's why no one seemed to. The subject was difficult to address, let alone solve. How do you reconcile the preservation of the past with a vibrant Christian witness in the present?

Stateside, the matter has been satisfactorily solved by a sort of unwritten truce between the two cultures. The Amish preserve their heritage without trying to push their beliefs on the *Englisha* people. And their beliefs are such that the general culture doesn't attempt to emulate them anyway. Mostly those beliefs concern things of practical living, such as buggies, cape dresses, and nonviolence. All of these things are practiced while keeping the undergirding tenets of Protestant Christianity: faith in Christ, belief in the Trinity, and a multitude of similar doctrines that place a belief system firmly in the Christian family.

The whole arrangement hangs on the Amish not wanting to be *Englisha*, and the *Englisha* not wanting to be Amish. Sure, each side can be influenced by the other, and a certain admiration can even exist. But there is a line that isn't crossed. The Amish faith must always to some degree remain undesirable to the general culture or, if admired, be unattainable by the multitudes. On this hangs the balance.

In the third world, this arrangement is set on its head. Half the local countryside wanted to be Amish it seemed. And what was difficult stateside—joining the Amish church—was now the easiest thing in the world. If you joined the church, you instantly had access to three times the living space you had before. Your mud hut floor became concrete or at least wood. You moved from eating beans and rice to eating cakes and potato casserole. The sale was not that hard to make.

Even the black felt hats, which are staples of Amish piety and humility stateside, were now symbols of wealth and status in Honduras. The Amish had to abandon wearing them for that reason and, instead, switch to straw hats or no hats. Some did exactly that, including my family.

It was the end of 1972 by that time, and I was eleven years old. I didn't know what being Amish meant, nor would I have noticed the gradual changes occurring around me. Apparently neither did most of the adults.

All around us questions were being asked that would have been unthinkable at home. "What good, really, are suspenders?"

"Why wear hats at all?"

"Why make clothing by hand?"

Here the culture conspired to loosen the answers from their Amish traditional anchor. An anchor sunk in stateside religious dogma. Here it made no sense to wear suspenders to differentiate yourself from the world. The world stateside threatened us. Here the world didn't threaten us. It wanted to be like us.

And here a new convert could hardly afford his pants let alone a pair of suspenders. A pair of suspenders which, by the way, had to be imported from the north before it could be worn. And where would that money come from? So this added cost cast a whole new light on the issue of wearing suspenders.

Here also the arguments for hats fled away. Stateside, Amish theology has long traversed the tricky waters of 1 Corinthians 11 with caution, having to dodge the icebergs. Because they know the admonitions on a woman's head being covered are coupled with equal admonitions that a man's head be uncovered, the dodge is made by calling the hat a weather garment, so it lies outside the principles of the Scripture passage:

> Every man who prays or prophesies with his head covered dishonors his head. But every woman who prays or prophesies with her head uncovered dishonors her head...A man ought not to cover his head, since he is the image and glory of God; but woman is the glory of man...Judge for yourselves: Is it proper for a woman to pray to God with her head uncovered? Does not the very nature of things teach you that if a man has long hair, it is a disgrace to him, but

that if a woman has long hair, it is her glory? For long hair
is given to her as a covering (1 Corinthians 11:4-5, 7, 13-15).

In Honduras, there was no weather to speak of other than balmy,
pleasant conditions. So the hat wasn't needed for weather, leaving the
issue defenseless.

I suppose someone could have brought up the real reason why the
Amish men wear the hats stateside—as a method of cultural identifica-
tion and as a barrier against the prevailing culture. But they were a spiritual bunch, so I doubt if anyone would have wished to trot out that
argument. He would have been laughed out of the room if not openly
scorned. Besides, the argument wouldn't have worked. They already
had a problem with being too identified as Amish, and making the
matter worse by wearing hats wasn't solving anything.

Making clothing by hand soon became an even larger problem. No
one among the locals had sewing machines. In Honduras you had to
be rich to even have a floor in your shack. Where would money for a
sewing machine come from? Or where would it sit if you had one? In
the dirt? And with no lock on the door, how long would the thing stay
in your house? Even your relatives would be tempted to temporarily
change their convictions on stealing from family.

These Amish cultural questions were not raised stateside, and even
questioning them would be considered heresy there. Persecution over
many centuries had resulted in a buffer being put in place between the
Amish communities and the general culture. Here there were no walls,
no agreements, and no persecutions. The Honduran "world" loved us.
And we made contact with that world every day. Heresy couldn't be
far around the corner.

In the meantime, the weather was wonderful. The mountains
standing in the distance spoke of the majesty of the Lord. And the
church house on the hilltop was full each Sunday. Marriages were taking place. Even several older men found mates for the first time. The
place was alive with goodwill and enthusiasm. I doubt if anyone would
have listened even if Uncle Stephen had shouted his message.

But he didn't shout. He simply faded away.

⌒⌒

The dam project was begun that fall. An ambitious undertaking for that country, but so was most everything else going on in the community. To the west of the children's home lay a natural ravine that began just below David Peachey's place.

A dozer was hired. From where I have no idea, remembering that Dad had his basement dug by hand. But that was the contradiction of the country. Perhaps they couldn't persuade an operator to travel a long distance without a large job once he arrived. Uncle Joe and most of the other uncles bought into the project, contributing a set amount of monies for future usage of the pond. Fishing was on the mind of the adults, but we children thought of swimming.

The dozer arrived and set to work. When it was done, a dam had been thrown up spanning the ravine and running parallel to the mountain. Behind it lay an acre or so of potential water area. Not filled yet, it soon would be with the coming rainfall. A metal overflow pipe stuck out of the water, off the side of the dam a dozen feet or so. This proved adequate in the years to come. I never saw the dam overflow, even in hurricane weather.

There was now a new road to Grandfather's house that traveled across the ravine without having to walk through it, which opened up a quicker route for vehicles. The old road past David Peachey's mill was nearly abandoned.

I remember a lot of walking in those days, going to and from Grandfather's place and to other points on the Sanson farm, which seems strange now considering we had riding horses. Perhaps it took too much effort to catch a horse and throw on the saddle. I do know that I considered any place on the La Granja ranch a long distance and normally didn't walk there. Nowadays, when I visit, those distances don't appear quite so far.

My world revolved around the schoolhouse, walking to school on weekdays and to church on Sundays. In my off-hours, I was often riding horseback into Guaimaca on errands for Mom.

I'm not sure when the monkey arrived at our new house, but it was sometime soon after we moved in. We set the monkey up with a belt strapped around his middle, and attached to a long, thin chain that ran on a steel bar. He had free range where his chain reached on the ground and in the trees on both sides. Don Gilbert, an *Englisha* farmer living twenty minutes toward Tegucigalpa, gave him to us. Perhaps the monkey was a gift or maybe Dad purchased him. Either is possible since Don Gilbert was well liked by Dad and others of the community.

Our monkey couldn't do tricks or distinguish himself in any special way. He was just a monkey. He'd chatter at a high rate of speed when something startled him or when he was mad, which was often. Sitting on his haunches or hanging from his tail on a tree limb, he'd let the world know his displeasure.

We children all made friends with him. We had to give him food to start off the relationship. He'd grab it out of our hands and rush up the tree, hanging by his tail while he munched away. Eventually he'd allow us closer until we could cuddle up to him while he was on the ground. We'd sit beside him, breathing in his musty smell, his hairs tickling our arms and faces. Occasionally he'd lay his head down in our laps or wrap his long, spindly arms around our neck.

Brother John was the tease of the family, and he couldn't resist pulling the monkey's tail, as well as other tricks, such as yanking on the monkey's chain. Things got so bad the monkey ran up the tree and gave off long, chattering scoldings whenever John came within sight. John always eventually made up with him.

The monkey seemed to have flashes of bad memories. These arrived without warning in unprovoked moments. I'd be cuddled up to him, thinking the relationship was on solid ground, when he'd flare into a blinding rage, chattering and leaping away. As he grew older these took the form of occasional unprovoked bites, which we excused for awhile. But they grew increasingly worse, and one day he broke his chain and assaulted me viciously, leaving me bloody before Mom could pull him off. That was the end of the road, and our monkey was no more.

Chapter 22

Grandfather Stoll had given us a puppy when we first arrived in Honduras. I think its mother had been left on the place by the previous owner of Sanson. Clearly our puppy came from a source other than the standard local fare of mange-ridden dogs. We named her Jumper, and she developed into a highly intelligent and fiercely loyal animal.

At nighttime her bark would alert us to any caller arriving. We trusted her completely, and she rarely let us down, yapping up a storm when anyone approached. We would rush to the window if we weren't already in bed. After dark, Dad would use her barking as a signal to turn on the emergency lights he'd rigged up along our driveway.

Being an ingenious man, he'd run a starter wire from the engine in his shop to his bedside, a distance of 300 yards or so. With another wire, he could bring the huge engine to a stop. A throw switch inside the front door of the shop activated the wires at night, so they weren't turned on during the day.

I didn't know until later how un-Amish such a thing was. It was another of those things the community ignored, I guess. It certainly was a far cry from Dad's days in Aylmer, when his brother haunted his worksite trying to catch him using electric tools. Now the use of electricity was out in the open, and no one said much about it.

I did overhear a visitor from stateside exclaim one day, while looking over Dad's setup, "No wonder the Aylmer community keeps the *bann* on you fellows." The Aylmer community didn't keep the *bann* on anyone in Honduras, and at no time would they. The man was exaggerating. But it was a huge joke, and he and my dad bent over laughing. I stutteringly repeated the line to Uncle Stephen's boys sometime later, expecting the same reaction. Both of the twins stared at me like I'd just admitted being a witness to an awful crime. I promptly strangled my laughter and didn't repeat the matter again. Apparently some people took the opinions of Aylmer more seriously than Dad did.

Uncle Joe and Uncle Stephen's families were close at heart. Perhaps due to the fact the two Stoll brothers married sisters. But it went deeper than that, I think. The relationship was a bond, one I often wished I were a part of. I never succeeded in gaining entrance, and I'm sure my actions didn't always help either.

I once overheard the boys from the two families making plans for an all-day cattle drive to some ranch east of Guaimaca. A desire to participate seized me.

"Can I go too?" I asked one of them. "I have a horse and everything."

They knew I had a horse. That wasn't the problem. But they were too nice to elaborate. After long, silent looks between themselves, one of them said, "I guess you can if you're allowed to."

I was ecstatic. Now all I had to do was convince Mom. Surely that wouldn't be too hard. Why would there be objections? They were my cousins. But once I arrived home, I had no more than begun to explain when I saw by the look on Mom's face that this wasn't going to be as easy as I thought. She was not agreeing to this. Obviously she knew things about me and my cousins I wasn't willing to admit.

I begged and explained until she cut to the chase. "Did they invite you to go along?"

Her decision hung on my answer, and I was not about to pass up this chance.

"Of course," I lied. "Paul asked himself."

"Okay," she said. "Well, that's different."

I imagine Mom suspected I was lying. She wasn't thickheaded like I was when it came to personal relationships. She probably figured I needed a lesson. Or perhaps she felt sorry for me. I didn't have that many friends, and even an imagined invite from my cousins was worth pursuing.

I looked forward to the day with great anticipation. I would be riding with boys I looked up to, and doing so on an outing I would thoroughly enjoy. Plus we'd be traveling by horseback, and this for a whole day. I got up early that morning and headed out to where the rendezvous was to take place. My cousins were organized and efficient. It was soon obvious they had brought along enough people to do what needed doing. I was only along for the ride. An uncomfortable entity thrust unwillingly into their midst.

We went through Guaimaca driving the cattle and arrived at the ranch around noon. I was consumed by thirst by then, having failed in my excitement to bring along water. We headed toward home, and I thought I would die before we finally made it back, creeping along those last miles on our tired horses. We didn't arrive home until late afternoon, and I was experiencing raging thirst by then. Local tap water couldn't be drunk, I knew, nor could water from the rivers, even though we'd crossed several. And you couldn't buy water in those days. Besides, I didn't have any money along anyway—for water or Pepsi.

I didn't ask again to go along on any jaunts with the cousins. Or with anyone else. The searing memory of not belonging didn't go away quickly. Nor did the memory of burning with thirst. I made it my business to buy a plastic canteen from one of the stores in town, an item I would take on any extended horseback trip from then on.

No doubt my cousins' aversion to my company was not without basis. They didn't know everything I did in those days, but it couldn't have been hard to figure out that I was a walking menace. My worst escapade involved Rosa Sanchez, whose shack was just beyond the dam. She lived there with her brood of youngsters on Stoll generosity. All of her children were girls, I think. The only male around the place being the one we never saw.

I had no animosity toward Rosa, and she was well liked in the community. But I did bear a great grudge against her dog. He was a little critter in that land of long-legged, skinny, raw-ribbed dogs. Whenever I (or anyone else for that matter) went past Rosa Sanchez's place on horseback—or worse, on foot—the dog would pursue me, nipping at my heels.

Any dog of decent respect and deportment should know people were allowed to walk there. But this one seemed not to care about correct opinion. He would nip, and I would stop in and complain to Rosa.

"You're going to have to do something about that dog. It's biting me."

She would laugh heartily, throwing her head sideways in her mirth. "He's not hurting anyone. He's just a little thing."

And since I never had teeth marks to prove anything, things stayed as they were. I kept walking past, and the little animal always tried to take a chunk out of my leg. I had to find a stick each time I went by, and even then I didn't dare make liberal use of the weapon. Hondurans love their dogs. They love their children and their food, but nothing stirs their passion like their dogs. They can starve their dogs until they are nothing but skin and bone, turn them out to fend for themselves, but physically harming them is strictly *verboten*.

In this matter, the Honduran natives conduct their lives a little lower from even the peoples of India, who at least put platters of food out for their idols. Here a dog, being protected by heaven, was also expected to eat by the hand of heaven.

I knew if the dog was hit by my stick, there would be sharp yelps of pain followed by a mad dash toward the shack. Then Rosa would appear and yell, not at the dog but at me. From there, Aunt Sarah would hear the story and tell Mom. And then I would be in more trouble than even I wished to be.

So I endured the chases. But it was all getting to be a little too much. Clearly something had to be done, and it wasn't long before a plan occurred to me. The dog lived under the shack, which was set up on blocks. This left spaces in the crossbeams where he could hide, spots that ran for the whole length of the shack and were excellent positions from which to launch his attacks. He would flatten his body almost level with the dust, thrilling thoughts of the chase no doubt running through his mind while he waited for a victim.

When the plan came to me, it seemed simple enough and totally foolproof. I'm ashamed of the plan now, but back then it seemed a good option. I would take a patty of raw hamburger and fill it with poison. Then I'd leave it for the dog to eat. Presto! There would be no dog hiding under the floorboards of the house ever again. But from where would the poison come? I didn't possess sufficient money to buy such an expensive item. Nor would I have known a place that sold it. Then it came to me. The Stoll uncles constantly mixed chemicals to spray the fruit trees at the orchard. They handled the mixture carefully, like it was poisonous. Why wouldn't it kill a little dog? I calculated that it would if I mixed in enough.

So I placed a handful of pesticide from Dad's stock inside a hand-ful of hamburger I took from Mom's refrigerator. So armed, I set forth, walking past Rosa Sanchez's place. On the first try I got chased by the dog, but I continued on my way. On the way back, Rosa must have left for somewhere—perhaps a visit to Aunt Sarah—and the dog had tagged along as Honduras dogs were inclined to do.

Running quickly toward the shack, I threw the patty of hamburger under the crossbeams. The dog would smell the meat the first thing when he came back, I figured, and leave this world soon thereafter.

Heading home, I calculated the job done and felt no remorse.

The next day, though, the dog was still there. He chased me as vig-orously as before. So apparently he'd eaten the hamburger with no ill effects. At least that's what I thought. I soon learned the truth. My plan had indeed succeeded. Only not in the way I thought it would. Rosa Sanchez's flock of chickens had found the hamburger well before the dog arrived back from wherever it had been that day.

Aunt Sarah told Mom the story in horrified tones how Rosa had mysteriously lost her whole flock of chickens in one day, coming home to find them lying dead all over the backyard. And all for no discern-ible reason.

I was struck to my heart, but I kept my mouth shut. What could I say? I would have received a well-deserved thrashing and had my already rough reputation besmirched even further. I left the chemicals alone from then on.

Chapter 23

With the memory of that night when the armed robbers appeared drifting ever further from our minds, it now seemed unlikely such a thing could happen again. But events would soon conspire to drive any such illusion from our minds. Thieves and misfits lurked in the community after the setting of each day's sun. If we had paid more attention to the small incidents occurring around us, they might have served as fair warning.

One night Bishop Monroe had a visitor after dark. A man arrived, shouted about the house, and demanded they open the door. When Bishop Monroe refused, the man stomped around for awhile before firing off a shot into the night and disappearing. That didn't seem too threatening, we told ourselves. At least he didn't shoot into the house.

Uncle Joe, who lived in the first house coming in from the main road, had someone arrive in the middle of the night. A man whose voice they didn't recognize awakened them in the night demanding a flashlight and money. When they wouldn't comply, a long conversation occurred, but went nowhere.

"Give me money and a flashlight."

"No, we won't."

This was repeated back and forth several times.

Finally the man thrust something into the tilting glass windowpanes. Uncle Joe thought it was a machete. A common enough implement carried about by almost all Honduran males. The oldest boy, Paul, overcome by youthful vigor, grabbed a wooden pole they kept in the house and gave the protrusion in the window a mighty whack.

The result was a splaying of glass as several of the panes broke. Whether the man ended up with glass in his eyes or not, no one ever figured out. But he did leave after that ruckus without money or a flashlight.

We listened to the stories, smiled, and stayed inside after dark. During the daytime we pretty much went where we liked.

In my mind there are two defining events in the community's thieving history. One was the night of the "Great Robbery," when Dad had guns stuck in his ribs. Two was the day of the "Great Thievery." I am apparently unique in seeing this day as a watershed moment in the life of the community. There is no record of the event, at least that I could find, in two other books written about our years in Honduras, so I have only my memory to go on to piece together that day and what followed.

On that Sunday morning the day dawned bright and clear. By eight-thirty, the slight fog along the riverbank had lifted, and the sun was left by itself in the sky with only a few fast-moving clouds as company. All of the Amish from La Granja were on their way to church, walking either in pairs, singly, or in family groups. Even from the outskirts of La Granja they rarely used buggies.

Dressed in their white shirts and dark pants, the men cut straight figures beside the women in their long dresses and white headdresses. Before leaving for church, they all made sure everything was shut up as usual. Perhaps they would have checked better if they'd been able to see over the riverbank that ran along the eastern property line of the ranch. But it's doubtful this would have made much difference. With the condition the houses were in at that time, entry would not have been denied. Staying home would have been the only possible solution.

Unbeknownst to the Amish, eyes were peering at them, counting who was leaving and checking to make sure the only solution that would have stopped them wasn't in place. Perhaps they'd already been checking the Amish out for several Sundays, since, at times, sickness kept some members at home.

Sometime after nine, the watchers on top of the riverbank gave the all-clear signal. They poured out of their hiding places, gunny bags in hand. Keeping to the fencerows where possible, they scurried toward the homes of Leroy Hostetler and Minister Vernon. Leroy's house was the first target. Like the flying locusts that come in for a landing and eat everything that lies in sight, they picked up anything that looked usable—first from the barn, then from the shop, and then from the house. They probably couldn't believe their good fortune. The doors gave way easily to their crowbars. At Minister Vernon's place they kicked in a window and climbed in.

They moved quickly through each building. The gunny bags soon heavy with shop tools, housewares, saucers, kitchen knives, and any money they could find. The search for money turned every dresser into a mess of strewn clothes. Every closet was emptied. Some money was found in a jar on top of the refrigerator, which caused an intense search of the pantry for more jars.

When they were done, the group left, following the fence line again, to disappear over the riverbank with their gunny bags full. It must have then become obvious to them that they made quite a sight hauling their bags. If anyone saw them the person would instantly know they were up to no good. No one in the third world walked around on Sunday morning carrying gunny bags packed with loot.

I suspect they stayed holed up for the afternoon in the thickly wooded lower area of La Granja. Perhaps in the bamboo patch below Uncle Alva's place with a few sitting as guards while the rest meandered on home, trying to keep the grins off their faces and unable to fathom their good fortune.

At twelve-thirty the first of the Amish came back up the road, walking home from church. The open front door at Minister Vernon's place caused some curiosity, but they figured someone had forgotten to shut the door properly. The wind, they thought, must have blown it open in their absence.

When they walked in, the littered indoor landscape lay before them. Their first response was to have someone run across the field for help. Although what help could have been offered? Comfort was more likely the goal, a common instinct that runs deep in Amish blood.

The person sent forth with the news found Leroy Hostetler's place in a similar condition and the just-arriving Hostetler family in shock.

"It's happened here too?" the messenger from Minister Vernon ventured the obvious. "What do you think we should do?"

"Do you think we should go to the police?" someone asked. The police were a motley crew from town, hardly able to defend themselves. A fact everyone was aware of by now.

"We almost have to, don't you think?" someone else offered. "What will happen if we don't? Something so awful as this can't just be left to itself."

Word spread quickly of the event. Minister Vernon and Minister Richard thought of calling an emergency members' meeting at the church house but decided against it. They met instead that evening with only the family members affected, after their places had been restored to some semblance of order. It was a gathering full of long faces and sober talk.

"Who would have thought something like this would happen?"

"We were just starting to feel at home here."

"Will any of us be safe anymore?"

"What will life be like if we have to lock up everything we own?"

The talk went on until late. Then a consensus was reached. The police, however dysfunctional, would be contacted in the morning. Some weren't sure about that, but they gave in after the others were adamant in their arguments.

The objection to contacting the police came from strong Amish beliefs of peace and nonresistance that have been passed down for more than 400 years. But outside it was dark, and the memories of how their houses looked that afternoon were still fresh in their minds. Besides, they were far from home and alone in this strange world. Maybe if they had called the members' meeting, things would have turned out differently. But they didn't.

So without the meeting, the others in the community didn't get involved. In the Amish world, someone doesn't jump into others' affairs uninvited. Not unless the ministry invites the move. And in this case, two of the ministers were already involved. So for whatever reason, plans were made to contact the police about the break-ins.

In the morning, the local workers showed up for work as usual. Upon hearing the news, general expressions of consternation were made.

"*Que lastima!*" [What a shame!] "We cannot believe this happened to you. You're all good men. You've always been so good to us. But don't you watch your houses on Sundays?"

From the looks on the Amish faces, it was obvious no one had ever thought of that.

"Then we can do that," they said, nodding in unison.

"For you, we watch house on Sunday. We watch first two Sundays for free. No one else watch better than us."

They were thanked, but the offer was declined. "No, we will look after things ourselves. There will be no more easy pickings. Now we'll place protection on the windows and doors and lock things up well."

The workers nodded. "This is a good plan. We will help you do this. Put locks on doors. Better protection on windows. No more will anyone break into your houses."

So the Amish headed for town that morning and the police station, which lay off the center square in Guaimaca, a plain-looking building with a white stucco front. Inside the door, the front office consisted of a low countertop for the transaction of business. A room immediately to the left was the jail, with iron bars across its full-height door. The cells looked dirtier than many a horse stable.

A lone officer in military uniform usually stood guard, lounging about. He would have greeted the arriving Americans, shaking their hands. "Is there a problem that you have?"

"Yes. Our homes were broken into yesterday, and we would like to report it."

"I will tell my boss then, and we will go out with you and look at the situation."

The Amish men agreed with the arrangement and returned to La Granja.

"We would like to speak with the workers that you have," was the first request once the police arrived.

"With our workers? But they work for us. They had nothing to do with this."

"We still would like to speak with them."

And so the workers were informed. They shrugged their shoulders, gathered up their tools, and took them along for the questioning.

At the house, the officers were waiting. They asked to speak with the workers alone. Animated conversation ensued, with much waving of arms and gesturing, ending with the police handcuffing everyone and throwing them into the back of the pickup trucks.

The Amish demanded answers.

They would have been told, "These men are the ones who robbed you on Sunday."

"Robbed us on Sunday? That's not possible. We trust them to take care of the place. It couldn't be them."

And the police would have smiled. "You are ignorant of some things. You trust people too much. Here in Honduras, you don't trust anybody. These men and their families are the ones who robbed your homes on Sunday."

"How do you know that these are the ones who robbed us?"

The smiles would have broadened. "Come. We will show you. Follow us to their houses. Trust us. We know who did this."

Arriving at the workers' homes, a small complex of houses beyond the store and hidden behind one of the knolls a mile or so off the main road, they pulled up to several huts. The officers jumped out and motioned for the Amish men to join them. They left the handcuffed men sitting in the back of the police vehicles.

As they prepared to enter the houses, the women of the houses appeared and protested. "Please, señor. Why are you coming to our house? Why are our husbands handcuffed in the backs of your vehicles?"

"We will search your houses, señora, for stolen goods. These *gringos*, their homes were broken into yesterday. And we have reason to believe the items are here."

"This is simply not true. Our husbands would never steal anything."

"Please, señoras, step aside. We will search the house."

Weapons were flourished, and the women pushed aside breaking into loud wails. A quick search was made first, and then the Amish men were asked to come in afterward. The group was led across the dirt floor to a room in the back.

Tortillas would still have been warming on the lid of the fifty-gallon drum from the morning's preparation of food. Outside the open window the chickens would have flown off into the yard with a mighty fluttering of wings. Pushing aside the cloth curtain that served as the door, the officers led the way into the room. Stacked from the floor to the ceiling was American merchandise: tools, hoes, rakes, kitchen utensils, and gunny bags of things still unpacked.

The officers turned to the Amish men. "Is this all yours?"

The men could only look at each other as they nodded. "Yes," someone finally said.

Consternation ensued once the report was taken back home.

"You mean to tell us that it really was our workers who robbed us on Sunday?"

"*Yah,* we saw the stolen goods ourselves."

"But how could they have robbed us? They were such nice people. Look at how hard they worked around the place. There was nothing they would not do for us."

Parties were sent to bring the others up-to-date on the news. And from there the news spread through the community.

By the afternoon the stolen goods were safely back home, with a high ranking officer from the police station coming along.

"You have a reward posted for the return of your goods. Is this not true?"

"Uh, no, not really," the Amish men informed him. "But we're glad that the things are back."

"My officers told me this morning when you came to report this crime that there was a large money reward for the return of your stolen items."

Continued denials from the Amish men followed. But the officer didn't give up.

"This has been a great favor done for you—that your things have been found so soon. And there were many things lost. I believe if you look, you will find everything there except for some minor items, maybe. And we got a full confession out of these thieves. They are really small-time people. They do not know how to steal things well. This is why we catch them so easy. With a little persuasion they have told us everything, and where they have hidden more of the things. My officers went back to the thieves' homes to search again and also in the hills behind their house. We believe everything will be found eventually. If not, then when more things are found these will also be returned."

"This thing of the money," one of the Amish men ventured, "we certainly are grateful to you and to your officers for finding our things. And I suppose we can give a reward for their return. We have just not spoken of it yet, but I will speak with the others about it."

The officer smiled. "I will be expecting your decision then in several days. Yes. In the meantime the thieves remain in the prison for a long time. Your large reward will ensure that they stay there for a very, very, long time—maybe a year, maybe two years. Our prisons are very good—with hard ground to sleep on. We keep our prisoners from wanting to come back too soon. We do not feed them, so you do not have to worry about an extra expense. Unless the family feeds them, they not eat. They all get very thin in prison. A year is a long time to be in prison here. Your reward for the stolen goods will help these men not steal again. Yes, I am looking forward to the time when you come in with the reward. We will speak then of how long the sentence will be for these thieves."

With that the sergeant left, and more meetings were called that night in the Amish homes. What lay behind this request for a reward? And what should be done with the men in jail? Obviously they would not be treated lightly by the authorities. Did they wish to cause such suffering? And what about their nonresistance stance? How could that be reconciled with throwing men in jail?

Then there would have been talk from the perspective of how things were done stateside.

"This is simply wrong, making us pay for something the police should be doing anyway."

"These police are corrupt, that's all there is to it."

"They must have planned this all from the start."

"It's all about the money, that's what it is."

"Makes me think now that they knew who did this before we ever reported it."

"Did the workers have some kind of deal with the police?"

"It sure looks like it. And if that's true, the police must have double-crossed them when we walked in this morning. Probably thought we had more money."

"Must be this rich *gringo* mentality they have down here. Everyone who is white is considered rich."

"What do we do then? Keep our mouths shut and just take it? This is awful."

"I'm afraid something in that order is all we can do. If we accuse the police of this, it could just make things worse and still not solve our problem."

"Okay, so the police want money. But how can we ethically pay what amounts to a bribe?"

And someone would have said, "If you had just listened to me from the start and not gone to the police, we would not be in this predicament now. Our people have always had a deep distrust of the police. This just goes to show why this has always been so."

And they would have been right. Stateside, the police had become quite easy to work with, even when the Amish questioned the wisdom of it.

Their beliefs on peace still ran deep though. God's people never depended on the secular authorities for their physical protection. They trusted in God. The stories had been told and retold. Not just the teachings of Jesus, but Old Testament stories. Of the time Ezra made the trip from Babylon to Jerusalem when the returning Jews had miles of territory to cross with their possessions and carrying large quantities of silver and gold the king gave them for rebuilding. They traveled through territory full of robbers, thieves, and killers, yet Ezra and his men were ashamed to ask the king for soldiers to protect them. Hadn't they just told the king how great their God was? So instead they fasted and prayed for several days and made the journey without any of the king's soldiers. They arrived safely in the land of Israel without any loss of life or property.

Finally a solution to the mess was suggested.

"We can go to the police and tell them we are sorry that we started this whole thing and offer to pay bail for the arrested thieves. That would free the workers without any prison sentence. It would also give the police some money, which seems to be what they are after."

Throats would have been cleared and hands wrung, but no better answer was found. So in the morning they arrived back at the police station to be greeted by a very happy officer.

"Yes, you have come to pay the reward. You are glad that my men have returned your things to you. This is good. Now both of us are very happy. You because all of your things are back. Me because you will pay a good reward. So how much will the reward be?"

"We have not come to pay a reward," one of the men would have said.

"You have not come to pay a reward? How can this be?"

"We will not pay the reward, but we will pay the bail for these men so that they can come out of jail."

"Ah." The face lit up again. "You will pay money then. And you want the men to come out of jail. Then you will deal with them on your own. Psst...psst. But you must not tell me about this. The bail money will be enough."

"Nothing will happen to the men," the sergeant was assured. "We just don't want to be responsible for their incarceration."

The officer looked puzzled, but he understood the sight of the money they placed on the counter. And the jailed men were soon out on the street, expressing their profuse thanks to the Amish men.

Chapter 24

The news spread like wildfire into every nook and cranny of the Honduran world, it seemed. *Gringos* have paid the bail for the men who robbed them. The thieves had been let off scot-free. Dad was beside himself. He was a firm believer in nonresistance, and he would never have taken up a weapon to defend himself. "This is the stupidest thing I've heard in a long time," he said. To broadcast the matter, and in a country like Honduras. "We might as well put out a welcome sign to one and all. Come rob us," he told Emil at the shop. "Take what you want. We will do you no harm."

Dad never laid claims to being a prophet. He was just a practical man, seeing things that others often missed. And on this point, he couldn't have been more right. I make no claims to know what the correct method of introducing the peace doctrine into a third-world culture would have been. I only know what I saw. And what I saw were Amish people scrambling to deal with the problem without resorting to violence as the locals now descended upon them after dark to pick up the easy loot.

I was there and felt the fear. The trembling inside closed doors at night. The clank of the wooden bar across our front door each night at six-thirty. The starting at the slightest unusual sound. The awakening when the dogs burst into barking fits. The dry mouth that comes from sheer panic. And the absolute terror of darkness lying anywhere outside our four walls.

Things were soon pushed to the edge of foolishness. But that's said from a stateside perspective, where people are surrounded by a competent police force who looks out for citizens whether they desire it or not.

One incident occurred after we'd spent an evening at David Peachey's place eating an enjoyable supper and socializing afterward. On the way home in our flatbed spring wagon pulled by Molly, the Belgian, Dad stopped short of the cattle guard still some distance from the house.

"There are lights in front of our house," he said, his voice hushed.

All of us children stared openmouthed into the darkness, not uttering a sound.

"You didn't leave anything on in the house, did you?" Mom asked him.

"No, I checked before we left," Dad replied.

They consulted further in hushed tones.

"There are men moving about," Mom finally said. "I can see them."

We looked, and there were indeed several men moving about between the house and the driveway. Light came from flashlight beams bouncing on the side of the house. Low voices could now be heard.

Dad had enough. Without a word he wheeled Molly around on the dirt road. And away we went, tearing back toward David Peachey's place. Molly broke into a gallop, lashed on by Dad's thrashing of the reins. I hung onto the side of the wagon, the night wind rushing across my face. The faster we went, the more noise we made. The thudding of Molly's hooves, the bouncing of the wagon wheels across the ruts in the road, the wild clanging of harness chains against the steel wagon shafts. One of my sisters claimed only recently that her knees were knocking together that night from sheer terror.

We raced past the children's home, never slowing down. Dashing up the slope we must have sounded like a rolling nightmare ever drawing nearer to the Peacheys. David Peachey came out on the porch with his gas lantern, an astonished look on his face.

Dad brought old Molly to a stop by their wooden fence and her sides were heaving.

"Is there a problem?" David asked.

"There were people in front of our house with lights," Dad said.

"Do you think they were robbers?"

"We don't know," Dad said. "And neither do I want to find out."

David seemed to understand, making no effort to persuade Dad otherwise. He opened his home to us for the night. Molly was unhitched and turned into the field. Where everyone slept, I can't remember, but I ended up in the basement thankful just to be alive.

In the morning, once the sun was shining, Dad went to investigate, leaving us at the Peacheys. He came back to report that nothing seemed to be amiss. We figured we had escaped the robbers by the skin of our teeth.

Thanking David, we loaded up and went home. Later in the day we found out that our night visitors had been Uncle Abner on the way home from his produce route. Seems he wanted to drop off some unsold items for our use.

We should have been embarrassed, I suppose. But I never heard anyone mention anything to that effect. Nor did Uncle Abner do any laughing at our expense. He knew—as they all knew—what it was to be afraid. There had also been gun barrels stuck in Uncle Abner's ribs on the night of the Great Robbery, and he had not forgotten.

Fausto took pity on us when we told him the tale, and set out the next weekend to purchase a gun on the theory that nothing had happened, but something was surely bound to happen eventually.

"Just call me when there's trouble again," he told us. "And I'll shoot in the air."

His shack was well within shouting distance of the house, so the plan was workable. I waited for Dad to object on religious grounds, but he said nothing. He never used the plan either, so he might have remained silent so as not to offend Fausto.

Mom and I, though, had no such compunctions. We were quite willing to use whatever methods were at our disposal. But again it was largely an exercise in foolishness. Sometime during those years, Mom awoke me in the middle of night. Dad was gone on an overnight trip into Tegucigalpa, and she obviously didn't want to face the situation alone.

"There are men at the door," she whispered as I came out of a deep sleep.

We still lived in the basement of the new house at the time, and I could hear them outside our bedroom window walking about, hammering on the door, shouting for us to open up.

"We have to do something," Mom whispered.

But there was nothing to do while the men were outside our house. So we waited and listened to the stomping feet.

Great terror produces a great need for bathroom facilities—and quickly. I held it in as the minutes ticked by. By the time things fell silent outside, I was near the explosion point. I snuck quietly into the bathroom. Mom had her head by the window when I came back.

"We still have to do something," she told me. "They're now over at Uncle Stephen's place."

I didn't question her word. If she said they were at Uncle Stephen's, I believed her. Besides there were faint sounds of shouting still hanging in the air.

"We have to call for Fausto's help," Mom informed me.

I rolled the matter over in my mind and came up with no objections to calling for help. Clearly something had to be done before the men came back.

We crept upstairs, each move an exercise in moving muscles frozen with fear. When I arrived at the open window above the stair door, I leaned close to the screen and hollered, "*Fausto! Ladrones! Ayúdenos!*"

Silence fell after my voice shrieked into the darkness. I shivered, hardly able to move but needing the bathroom again.

When nothing happened, I repeated the call. "*Fausto! Thieves! Help us!*"

"Come! It's not working," Mom said, pulling on my arm. She was probably afraid we would get caught in front of the open window by the returning men.

We were moving toward the basement stairs when two shots tore into the night air. A thrill ran through me. Fausto had heard! He was trying to help. We were not without a friend. We made our way into the basement again, hearing nothing more from either the men or Fausto. Sometime in the early hours I fell asleep.

The next morning Uncle Joe arrived, very worried. "We heard shots fired near your place. Are you okay?"

"*Yah*," Mom said, telling him the rest of the story.

Uncle Joe didn't leave the matter there though. He headed down toward Uncle Stephen's place for further questions. He came back to report that Uncle Stephen had opened their door after the men identified themselves as police officers. They were looking for somebody, they said. Some escaped criminal. As to why he would have been in the area, I have no idea.

They were still at Stephen's place when Fausto fired his shots, Uncle Joe said, and almost came back looking for the source, thinking it was the man they sought. Uncle Stephen persuaded them otherwise. And Fausto was spared from bearing the brunt of our mistake. Not a small matter when dealing with the police force of that country. They don't exactly read Miranda rights before the questioning begins.

But even with the foolishness we fell into, real thieving was taking place all over the community. Minister Vernon was hit again, as was the children's home. Many of the community lost valuable items in their outbuildings. People came out in the morning to find most of their windowpanes gone.

I guess the thieves figured there was more profit in taking the glass out than in breaking them. That way the owner wouldn't be inspired to replace the windows with some new style less amenable to breaking in.

But they had never dealt with Amish ingenuity before either. Several of the community men showed up at Dad's shop to talk about what could be done. And they soon struck on a solution. Not that original, I suppose, but workable. Making bars to place over the windows and doors.

A booming business quickly developed at the shop, though I doubt Dad charged much. I was lassoed in to help on my free time after school hours. I couldn't weld yet, but I could run the metal cutting machine. A repetitive job, but one easily grasped by a youngster.

The bar design was a simple affair made to fit the rectangular shape of the window, with a steel frame around the edges consisting of a quarter inch by one inch metal turned on edge. This rectangular outline was then filled with the same size metal, creating crossbars running horizontal and vertical through the frame. What was left were small spaces through which no one could crawl, and one could barely reach inside.

Some of the people chose the squares evenly stacked. But most chose a random design. Dad even tried a version in which the spaces were larger with a tapered piece of metal sticking up in the middle. That design had too much of a prison look and didn't catch on.

After completing the frame in the design chosen, four side legs were attached on each corner with flares on them. Through this, carriage bolts were run. They extended completely through the exterior wall and into the inside where the nut was fastened.

This practice of putting bars across the windows and, in many cases, across the doors of the houses, was unknown stateside. It would always remain a great vexation to the consciences of those who had to resort to such a measure.

Not to be outdone by bars on the windows, the thieves now kicked

Our new house in Honduras. Notice the window protection.

in the doors. When those were replaced with solid wood frames, they bored around the locks in circular patterns until the piece fell out. Then they reached inside to open the lock or remove the bar if one was placed across the door.

The Amish soon learned to place solid steel plates around the door lock. A plate wide enough and tall enough so that no hand could reach the knob or bar inside after drilling through the still-exposed wood. In this the locals manifested energy and ingenuity, but apparently drilling around a large steel plate in small hole increments was too much for even their enthusiasm.

Before the steel plates were placed on the doors, some of boys took to sleeping out in the buildings where the worst break-ins were happening. Most of these were businesses. I'm sure the soft sound of a wood bit going around and around in the door above your sleeping bag was guaranteed to cause tense moments. After waking up and nudging each other, the boys conferred in whispers as to the proper response. All the brave and bold recourses planned the day before failed them—actions that had been schemed when the sun was shining and no pieces of wood shaving were falling on their heads.

In the end, they settled for simply yelling. The yells were enough for the drill smith to cease his work. After the running footsteps faded away, the boys checked their watches with flashlights covered in cupped hands. Then they managed to get some sleep for the rest of the night. The next day their fathers put things on emergency status and had steel plates installed.

Uncle Mark found great mirth in this story—but then he wasn't one of those sleeping inside.

Emil Helmuth had his own complaints about the thieving. He kept showing up at the shop to tell Dad about the racket out by his barn. Not that it happened every night, but often enough to keep Emil from getting sleep. He would check the next morning, but no one had succeeded in breaking in that Emil could tell.

Emil worked full-time at the shop, and so he had full access to bars and steel. His place was well protected. But the racket was getting to be a nuisance. Emil's dog would raise a fuss. And sounds would follow that would require Emil getting up and shining his flashlight about the barn area to quiet things down.

Finally Emil had enough of this. The next night when the dog got going, he snuck out the back door with his revolver. A revolver that no one but his wife knew he possessed. Hoping that Bishop Monroe wouldn't hear him, he fired it twice into the air. There was a pause in which everything was still. It was followed by a thrashing from the bushes behind the barn. The sound receded in the direction of Turk Road. Silence fell once again.

Emil smiled to himself and went back to bed. He told the story next morning to Dad with far more pleasure than any Amish man should show in such a situation. They regaled each other with their imaginations of the frightened fellow running through the bushes and tearing himself up in his haste. Though it could well have been a four-legged prowler for all any of us knew.

Dad always managed to stay ahead of the thieving curve. Other than the night of the Great Robbery, we never suffered much loss. This was in part because of Dad's generator, which he used to run his lights. When the dogs barked, one of us pushed the button by Dad's bed, the generator in the shop fired up, and the yard was flooded with light. The roar of the diesel could be heard almost to Grandfather's place and halfway into La Granja. In defense of Dad, I suppose his method had merit. Didn't the Scriptures say that evil deeds were done in the darkness? What better way of thwarting them than by throwing light on the subject.

To top things off, Dad mounted a siren above the rafters in the engine room of the shop. This maneuver required the placement of a third switch in the bedroom. But the wail of that siren on a quiet Honduran night was one of the sweetest sounds I heard in my growing-up years. It was like a voice lifted in agony toward the very heavens, and I felt certain it was heard by God Himself.

With his lights, the roar of his diesel, and the wail of his siren, Dad kept his shop from being broken into. His efforts also had the effect of throwing a cordon of safety for a quarter of a mile on each side of us. Outside of that, you were on your own. Dad believed in praying for protection, but he also believed that a person should turn on the lights when it lay in his power to do so—a lesson I have not forgotten.

In the midst of all this, Dad's business was increasing. The sawmill managers had learned the value of his services—that Dad could do keyways in metal, lathe work that baffled the mind, and most any work associated with metal.

We counted our blessings by day and were thankful to wake again as each morning dawned.

Chapter 25

Sometime during the school year of 1972, while we still lived in the old cottage, my clumsy attempts at practical jokes made their first appearance. The whole affair was quite innocent, even amusing, at least from my point of view. But others had a different opinion.

It all began at the schoolhouse where Glen Hochstetler was teaching the upper grades and Dora Miller the lower grades. I think Glen was only there that year for a month or two. But it was long enough for several of us boys to get into our heads that a romance must surely be going on between the two teachers.

We whispered and laughed amongst ourselves. The two did act sweet enough when they were together, although I suspect now that it was professional courtesy. They never dated each other in later life or expressed romantic interest in each other that I know of. But shorn of this future knowledge, we boys were not deterred in our surmising.

There was love in the air. We were certain of it.

I don't recall why Joseph and his younger brother, Daniel, were along that day or even what the reason was we were all at the schoolhouse. But my brother John and I found ourselves there after hours along with the two brothers.

The conversation quickly turned to the perceived romance between Glen and Dora. We shared our recent observations of a quick look or smile between the two. All of us agreed the two teachers were growing closer to each other.

The other three would have left things there, but not me. I had to take action.

"Let's leave a note," I suggested.

The others looked at me, puzzled. Chuckling about the matter was one thing, but leaving an announcement of our presence was quite another thing.

"Glen loves Dora," I said, mulling the matter over in my mind. I could see the look on Dora's face when she saw the words. Then she could express her love openly.

"Where would you put it?" one of them asked, warming to the idea.

"We'd put 'Dora loves Glen,' in his desk, and 'Glen loves Dora,' in her desk!" I announced.

Their faces glowed with excitement. It was the perfect plan. No one would ever know who had left the notes. If things went well, the romance would be greatly enhanced. Each might think the other was sending a secret message.

I seized pen and paper and wrote out the words. I should have noticed no one was helping. They all stood there with wide smiles on their faces, enjoying the fun, but not touching anything. I opened the drawers of the desks sitting in front of each room and dropped in the notes.

No one said anything more as we left. I heard nothing the next day at school. Both Dora and Glen acted like they always did. Apparently no romance had been enhanced, and the plan had failed. I soon forgot about the matter. That is, until I was roused from a deep sleep late one night. I was sleeping on one of the upper bunks in the room I shared with my brothers, when Mom nearly hauled me down to the floor. I was told to slip on my pants and shirt. I followed her out to the living room.

Dad was standing there waiting, but Mom clearly had the floor. They had been at a school board meeting that evening, I vaguely remembered. Apparently something had happened.

"A terrible thing has been discovered at school," Mom said. "There were love notes found in each of the teachers' desks."

She didn't repeat what the notes contained, preferring to leave the horrible matter hanging in the air. It's an amazing thing how different a subject looks when viewed during the nighttime. Especially when you've just been awakened from sleep, and your parents are staring at you with horrified looks on their faces.

"Did you have anything to do with this?" Mom asked.

I could have lied, I suppose. I often did. But I chose not to that night. Perhaps some scrap of dignity exerted itself, and I didn't wish to join this jury in its unanimous condemnation of my prank.

"I did," I said.

Mom didn't look surprised, the poor woman. But she'd obviously not told anyone of her fears at the school board meeting. Looking back, I suspect the community had already guessed correctly, perhaps giving her and Dad sideways glances while the matter was discussed in hushed tones. Why else would she have hauled me out of bed with such certainty?

"You will go and apologize to the teachers," Mom decreed, obviously thinking she was letting me off easy.

Or perhaps she knew the truth. That this public humiliation would be worse than a thrashing. I dreaded having to initiate a conversation where each word came out only with great effort and was accompanied by wild static in my head.

I returned to bed with the ax hanging over my head. This was on a Friday night, so there would be no school in the morning, which was a good thing. On a school day there would have been students around as witnesses to my humiliation. This way I had the weekend to settle the affair in private.

I can't remember where I sought Dora out. Their family lived in the upper reaches of La Granja. I can't imagine traveling over on a Saturday to speak with her. But Dora wasn't the problem. She was a sweet woman with a kind face and heart. She would have been most understanding and the task easy enough. No, Glen was the problem. And my solution was to approach him after the services that Sunday, seizing my chance when he was alone somewhere between the church house door and the men's john down the hillside.

"I need to speak with you," I whispered, walking aside for a distance.

He followed, his face frozen. I was a worm, I knew, crawling into his world with my awful deed. I offered no explanation, accepting fully the wickedness of my act. Clearly my value system was misaligned with the world I lived in, and I needed to adjust. How? I didn't have a clue. But for now the words of apology needed saying.

I kept the words short—to a bare minimum.

Stuttering is a physical defect that shatters the ego. It leaves you a pariah, a misfit for which there is no remedy. Men have sympathy for illness, even for disfigurement. But they are at a loss around the sound of a stammerer's words.

Communication is one of the essentials of human survival, and speaking our primary means. With it we transmit a thousand signals we're not even aware of. And stammering-speak has lost all of that. The subtleness. The inflection of tone. The movement of the eyes. The gestures of the face and hands. It's all swamped by the horrible sounds that come out of the mouth.

"I was the one who left the notes," I finally managed. "I'm sorry."

He nodded, saying nothing.

We left it at that and parted company. Nothing more was ever said about the matter.

But lest you think ill of the man for being so cold, let me hasten to add a postscript. One which shouldn't have surprised me, but it did. Glen taught full-time in my eighth year of school—the grade in which I first tried my hand at writing fiction. Our class had been given a research assignment on the care of an orchard. We were to write a short introduction on the subject, followed by a lengthy outline. The next assignment was on stars. Both of my works were graded "B." Most of the errors circled were for spelling. (I don't find that surprising. It was a subject I didn't appreciate in school and so ignored it as much as possible.)

The new assignment was on hog farming. I did my normal research, reading up on the subject from our encyclopedias that sat on the book rack in the back of the schoolroom. I then visited two of my uncles, Abner and Alva Stoll. Both of them were hog farmers.

For the introduction piece, an idea occurred to me. Why not write it in story form? I consulted no one for advice, simply plunged forward, driven more by boredom with research papers than anything else. I had no idea back then what a risk I was taking, or how unconventional this was. Glen could easily have disallowed the whole effort, forcing me to rewrite the piece. Instead he read my assignment with a big smile spreading across his face. He loved it, he said. This was good.

I glowed on the inside.

Glen then went a step further, not just mentioning the matter in our eighth-grade class of three girls and two boys. He got up in front of the entire school and praised the piece. I can't remember if he read it out loud, but it's possible. That would have been in character with him.

He marked my paper with an "A," adding a *"Very Good!"*

None of this was necessary on his part. I wasn't popular in school, so he had nothing to gain by calling attention to me. Yet he did what he did. Here's my report, written when I was around thirteen.

Hog Farming

Willie the pig had only been born yesterday. He lay in his pen with his four brothers and sisters. He was still young and did not know that his owner, whose name was Dick, was going to sell him to a butcher.

Dick always gave him a lot of separated milk which was very important to him, and made him grow like a weed. Every morning Dick checked carefully to see if Willie had any sicknesses. Willie's mother needed a lot of water. Water was more important to her than feed.

Days went by and Willie grew. Dick sold him to a man who was fattening hogs to butcher. His name was Fred. Fred gave Willie a clean place to sleep and play, along with nine other pigs. He chased them all into one pen. He always gave Willie and his companions a lot of separated milk, which helped make them fat. Milk is high in protein and very good for pigs.

It is easier to buy small pigs and fatten them because for fattening pigs you can put them all into one pen. While for raising little pigs you have to have a separate pen for every mother pig.

One day Fred's boy, Bob, came out in the middle of the day and let the pigs out. The sun was shining very brightly. Bob didn't think he was harming the pigs. They were out in the sun for two hours before Fred noticed it.

Fred then hurried to chase them back in, but Willie was not too willing to go back in. He decided to run away. It was another half an hour before Fred got them back in. The next morning both Willie and his nine companions were very sick. Fred quickly went to town to buy medicine. It was two weeks before Willie had recovered. He had lost thirty pounds, but as time went on Willie regained his strength.

When Willie weighed two hundred and forty pounds Fred butchered him and sent him to Tegucigalpa. He sold him for ninety-five centavos a pound, and that was the end of Willie the Pig.

Both Fred and Dick enjoy this job.

Source of information—Abner Stoll and Alva Stoll.

Chapter 26

Our family developed an evening routine that continued throughout my growing-up years in Honduras. Dad shut down the shop by five or six every afternoon, and we were all inside the house for supper by six-thirty. The door was locked and the bar dropped. Steel bars covered our windows and doors.

Across the field in his little hut, Fausto and his family shut down about the same time. Fausto had nothing to steal, so he had no need for bars. He did have his machete and now his gun, neither of which any locals took lightly. While the gun stayed home, Fausto carried his machete at all times, as did most of the local men. And they were experts at handling the huge knives.

Hardly a year went by without stories of fights in town with at least one of the combatants sustaining fatal injuries. Usually this happened over the Christmas holidays.

Fausto told me the story of someone he knew who found himself defending his honor. Not long into the fight, the man was cut badly. However, the sight and smell of his own blood had the opposite effect from what his opponent expected.

"The more he bled, *lo mas el brinco*" [the more he jumped], Fausto told me, grinning from ear to ear. So energized, the cut man's opponent was soon vanquished.

In the case of such a death, there was never an inquiry into who had done what. The one who killed was always at fault, and it behooved him to flee for a time…usually for a few years at least. Not just from the arm of the law necessarily, but from angry relatives. The killer would flee to another town a sufficient distance away so as to discourage pursuit or he would go to our mountain, La Montaña.

During Christmastime we often heard shots fired around us at nighttime, most of them coming from the direction of Guaimaca or somewhere in the foothills west of town. For the most part, we ignored them.

Fausto claimed two rich men were shot one Christmas. They had drunk too much whiskey. Usually a woman was involved, but Fausto said this time it was about money. Probably gambling. They pulled their pistols, Fausto claimed, and fired at the same time. Both died.

At least Fausto said so, and I believed him.

I believed most of what Fausto told me. Even when he had me in terror for a few days. He once told me that hearing the whistling of some rare local bird, the name of which I have now forgotten, brought death within days. But when I kept waking up days after hearing the bird's call, I assumed Fausto mistaken.

Against all the violence and altercations we retreated inside and locked the doors. Supper was served at six-thirty and was over by seven. That left an hour until bedtime at eight. So what did we do with an hour of evening time with no television? No music. No computers. No appliances running in the house. Just silence.

My siblings have memories of eating popcorn, but as for me, I remember books. Dad puttered around with his office work and Mom with the housework. We children sat on the couches with our noses in books. Our choices weren't many. The ones available we cherished and passed around. Copies of the Pathway Papers—three of them: *The Family Life*, *The Young Companion*, and *Blackboard Bulletin*. All were devoured with relish when they arrived after traveling slowly down from Canada, usually a month or so after they were published.

From somewhere I obtained a copy of *Anne of Green Gables*. I quickly became lost in the story of the young orphaned girl. For years I thought I'd dreamed the story because I was unable to find the book again.

In my reading I fell in love with stories and, of all things, political news. I have no idea why Dad approved it, but I ordered a year's subscription to *Time* magazine. I was hooked from the first issue, which of course arrived weeks after it was issued, but I didn't care. I sat on the couch with our gas lantern hissing above my head and read things I didn't understand. But I was mesmerized nonetheless.

I think I was the only one in the community who followed the Watergate scandal. At least no one else talked about it, and neither did I, for that matter. Instead I read pages and pages of fine print about break-ins and cover-ups, about political outrage over something I couldn't understand accompanied by wild denunciations.

And then came President Nixon's resignation. I thought he must have killed someone. That was the worst sin I could think of. But *Time* didn't write about a killing. The writers were just angry, really angry.

I didn't know what to believe. I doubted half of the stuff I read. It's hard to explain the surreal experience of reading news that has no supporting structure in your environment. I didn't even approach Uncle Joe about the matter; rather, I pondered these things on my own. Not until we returned to the States in my teens did I discover the context and begin to make sense out of what I'd read years earlier.

Political news wasn't the only thing I devoured. Mom had an old copy of a children's Bible storybook around the house. This storybook taught me Old Testament history. I read and reread the stories. Beginning at Genesis, I'd stop just after Solomon. For some reason I always got lost in all those kings of Israel and Judah, the men who reigned after the two great ones, David and his son Solomon.

But no story so gripped me like the account of Joseph that begins in Genesis, chapter 37. Joseph was the boy whose jealous brothers sold him as a slave to a passing caravan. I think I cried every time I arrived at the place where Joseph revealed who he was to his brothers during the famine, when the brothers had to go to Egypt for food and unknowingly encountered their brother all grown up and in charge. There were pictures that went along with the stories, but the pictures painted in my heart were the ones that endured.

I could see Joseph living in his father's tent surrounded by the desert and the sheep. I could see the coat of many colors his dad had given him. And I could see the family gatherings where Joseph announced his dreams while wrapped up in his innocence of how the world worked.

At the end of Joseph's harrowing story, goodness wins. We should still tell stories like that. And we should still believe them! That's the important thing.

Chapter 27

Early that winter of 1973, a wedding was announced at church. We were all invited. Bishop Monroe's eldest daughter, Iva, had been wooed and won over by an Amish boy from stateside. Joseph Wagler was his name. He'd stalked through the community a few times. He was a quiet man of grim countenance. Iva didn't talk much either, unlike her younger sisters, who could chatter away at a mile a minute. Apparently enough conversation ensued between Joseph and Iva to suffice. Their wedding was one of several the community put on during our time in Honduras. Weddings were events of great importance and excitement even in the midst of our already-interesting lives.

To the locals, weddings were mega events. My suspicions are that many people went to them, whether invited or not. The slightest connection to the family was reason enough to show up.

We gathered at nine o'clock in the morning, the usual time for services. The ceremony began, the happy couple seated up front, their backs outlined against the slatted shutters. The church house was filled to the max, with the women and smaller children on one side and the men on the other.

We still sang the slow German at that time, our voices filling the rafters above. We were a sight to behold, I'm sure. I wouldn't have thought it back then, being in the midst of it all, but it must have been so, with us wearing our hats, our suspenders, our long-sleeved plain shirts, and our women in their long dresses.

Some of the families still kept the rule from the Aylmer *ordnung*, that men and boys could only have three buttons on their Sunday shirts. All of them near the top, of course. Not that I would have noticed one way or the other. I wore whatever Mom gave me. But I overheard Uncle Joe holding forth on the issue with Mom and Dad. Uncle Joe had apparently spotted a visiting Amish man who came from a community with buttons allowed all the way down the shirt. Uncle Joe maintained he was influencing our members, though perhaps unconsciously, to allow or make the change.

"His shirt was bent open between the buttons!" Uncle Joe recounted in horror. "Right outside the church house. And you could see his chest hair hanging out."

The adults were silent at this news. The reasons for the three-button rule was finally fully explained to me.

"I guess we can see now why Aylmer only allows three buttons on the men's shirts," Joe added for good measure.

I didn't have any hair on my chest yet, so I didn't care. But I did understand that forces were at work to change things. Changes from which no good could come. And *that* I cared about.

But such undercurrents were laid aside on a wedding day. We were all one happy family rejoicing to see another young couple in love and marrying.

After the vows had been exchanged in German and repeated in Spanish for the benefit of the attending locals, we poured out onto the hillside. The sky was a lovely blue above us. The day a balmy mideighties even in February. Strangely it never rained, not during any of the weddings we held on that hilltop. Not even in the rainy season. I have no idea why, as the rains certainly didn't always respect the other public functions we held.

On wedding days, tables appeared from somewhere. Men and women mingled with the locals as the food was laid out. The spread was a bountiful affair consisting of meat loaf, casseroles, cakes, and pies. We ate well, even for Amish people. For the local people raised on tortillas and beans, the feast was heaven on earth. They loaded up their plates because the meal was served cafeteria style. Many went back later for seconds. Laughter was everywhere. Even the mountain smiled in the background, and the two graves on the eastern slope couldn't dampen the joy.

I overheard one of the local men while eating his second plate of food tell the Amish fellows, "*No he comido para días, esperando este momento.*"

"I haven't eaten for days, waiting for this moment," someone repeated for the benefit of the stateside visitors who didn't understand Spanish.

I joined in the laughter as the local fellow laid aside his plate and symbolically loosened another notch in his belt. He didn't look that thin, so I doubt he really hadn't eaten for days. But he'd made his point.

We never had an evening service after a wedding—something that had been a solid tradition stateside. Another change in custom was the civil ceremony required the day before. The Honduran government didn't recognize church weddings or give ministers the authority to grant marriage licenses to couples. The papers had to be signed in front of a judge.

So the day prior, the couple made the short trek into Guaimaca, dutifully answering the questions and signing their names. Mostly it was about leaving behind the proper fee, as it is for most government functions the world over. Now legally married, the couple always waited until the church wedding before spending the night together.

After the wedding, Joseph Wagler stayed a few days at his bride's family's home. After that the two said their goodbyes to Bishop Monroe's family and left for stateside.

Chapter 28

I believe it must have been sometime that winter that Fausto referred me to a friend he knew. A friend who could tell me where grapes grew on the mountain slopes. The friend would take me himself, if I wished to go, Fausto said. I accepted, happy for the chance to explore the mountain. The search for grapes was only an added incentive.

I'd recently obtained the horse I would ride for the rest of my time in Honduras—a beautiful, dusty-white animal. I'd gone down to pick him out from a group of horses Uncle Mark had for sale. They were grazing behind the pond near the water's edge. I looked them over, and it didn't take long to make my choice. I snapped a rope on his halter and led him home. Lightfoot, I called him.

So Fausto's friend and I made our plans and set out early one morning mounted on our horses. With creaking leather, we rode up Turk Road and turned right, going around the upper edges of La Mansion, a very large ranch. As we rode in the foothills, I gazed in awe at the open, cultivated fields of La Mansion that were interspersed with their grasslands. We didn't have this kind of acreage on either of the two Amish farms.

As we climbed higher, the vista below turned into splotches of farmland with the town of Guaimaca off in the distance. If I hadn't been in love with Honduras before, I would have fallen in love that morning.

Our horses heaved and sweated as we climbed higher into the chilly morning air. The trail led around the edges of ever higher hills and into the clouds. I soon lost sight of the peak, hidden now by the nearness of the mountain itself. We passed the first hut clinging to the hillside and then others. No one paid us any mind. Busy with their own lives, I guess. Cornfields hung on the sides of the slope, planted and harvested by men possessed with the agility of goats. Lazy smoke drifted downward, swirling to mix in with the clouds.

We stopped to water our horses beside a rocky stream glittering with the glint of gold. I climbed down to dip my hand in the cool water and run the sand through my fingers. My hand sparkled.

My guide grinned. *"No es oro,"* he said.

"Come on," I replied. "It's looks like gold." I'd read of fool's gold, but I hadn't known it looked so real. And a riverbed full of it, beckoning and drawing me in. What if it really was real? The thought dazzled me. Riches unimaginable ready for picking.

We rode on, ever higher to the slopes where the grapes grew. And they really did. Wild and free for anyone who wished to take the trouble. We filled our bags and draped them across the back of our saddles. The clouds had lifted away by then, and I was more entranced with the view than with our bags of grapes. From here it took my breath away. Honduras in all its wildness and wonder spread out like a feast for the eyes. I lingered for long moments, taking it all in. My guide didn't seem impressed, but he'd obviously been here before. Yet for me, I decided it would never grow old, no matter how many times I returned. That day *La Montaña* truly became *my* mountain. My personal playground to which I would return as often as allowed. Here the air was always fresh, the currents always shifting, the clouds washing the land and touching the people living in their huts. All of it fashioned by patterns hundreds of years old yet always new. It was as if everything had been placed here only yesterday.

I would sometimes come back on my own, but often my friend Louis came along. He was always ready for adventure. Once I shared with him the existence of the grapes that served as our ready excuse when we asked our parents to let us go up there. (They couldn't always see the benefit of wandering the mountains with no specific end in mind.)

Even Joseph must have come along at least once. I know because I embarrassed him thoroughly one day in front of half the community. I'd carried some of the "gold" sand home packed in sealable plastic bags. I stored them under my bed. On the day of the embarrassment, a miner arrived in the community. "Just passing through," he said. He'd stopped in, attracted by the gathering that day on top of the church hillside. It couldn't have been a Sunday or a wedding. Perhaps it was the last day of school or some such thing. The men grouped around him, listening with great interest to his tales of the metals he'd mined in Honduras. They peppered him with questions.

Gold was mentioned, and my ears perked up. This could be my day to find out for sure. Was the gold on the mountain real? I needed to know. And so I raced home for my stored plastic bag of sand filled with glittering pieces of ore.

Arriving back on the hilltop, the crowd was still there. Dozens of Amish men and boys were listening to the tall American holding forth about Honduras's hidden treasures.

I caught my breath and approached Joseph with my bag in hand. There was no way I could ask the question myself. Not with my stammering speech.

"Could you ask him if this is fool's gold?" I whispered in Joseph's ear.

"But you know it's not real," he whispered back.

"I want to know for sure," I insisted.

I had no concept of public relations back then or how this might appear to the gathered men: a couple of stupid Amish boys who thought they'd found real gold in the mountains. Joseph was astute enough to know, but he still went forward on my behalf. Being a true friend, I suppose.

"We found this in a mountain stream," Joseph told the miner. "What kind of metal is it?"

The glitter in the bag clearly said what kind of a metal we hoped it was.

The miner opened the plastic bag, running the sand through his fingers. Silence hung over the hillside. I watched with bated breath. It couldn't be real, I thought. But still, maybe it was.

"No," the miner shook his head, rattling off some Latin term I couldn't pronounce. I knew the meaning from his tone though. It wasn't *gold*.

He smiled. "This is an oft-found metal in Honduras but perfectly worthless. Sorry to disappoint you, boys. It's fool's gold."

Joseph kept his composure, but he was deeply embarrassed. That's what he told me later. I was too unaware to know I should be too. The men chuckled around us, but I was just glad to have my question answered.

Happy times on the mountain lay ahead, including an excursion to the top the young boys took upon themselves. I personally had no interest in conquering the peak, so I'd never ventured that far. But when I was told the group was going, I was willing to tag along.

Several of the men claimed they'd reached the top accompanied by stateside visitors and had returned the same day. I'd always been skeptical of that claim and wasn't shy about voicing my opinion. The mountain peak could perhaps be reached in one day, but you couldn't get back before dark. Whether the other boys believed me or whether they simply wanted to draw out the adventure for another day, I don't know. But a two-day trip was planned.

On the day appointed, we made our way on foot leisurely up the foothills following the path so familiar to me. The excursion quickly took on a festive air with so many boys traversing together. What provoked the following action, I don't know, but some of the boys shed their suspenders, blaming the extreme exertions they were under. The suspenders, they claimed, dug into their shoulders. I didn't think much of the matter, since suspenders were neither here nor there to me. But I did keep mine on. Not as much out of virtue as from the fact that my two school tormentors, Daniel Hostetler and Paul Schmucker, were the ring leaders in the suspender shedding.

We continued climbing the mountain. As the day dragged on, our large group made little progress on its leisurely journey. Some of them had never been up this high, and every so often they had to stop for the view. I enjoyed that too so I didn't complain. Plus we had two days for the venture.

By afternoon we splashed across the "gold" stream, stopping again for exclamations and running the sand through our fingers. Even with the sure knowledge that this wasn't gold, the fascination of it still lured us. We filled our canteens in the stream—at least the ones of us who thought of it. Drinking water at these heights was considered safe according to prevailing wisdom. And we never suffered any side effects that I know of. The water we feared was contaminated by people, animals, and laundry washing, which was far below us now.

A final, high ridge lay just below the woods line, and we arrived around dusk. There was no thought given to pushing on higher with the little daylight we had left. We were tired, and many boys were now burning up with thirst. If we needed further reason to stop, this was also a spectacular view for the night. Even I had never been up this high. The valley lay before us bathed in the late evening sunlight. The glory of Honduras lay in front of us to behold. Felix, a local boy who had converted to the Amish faith, joined me in the wonder of it. Round, effusive, and perpetually happy, Felix was enthralled.

"*Que linda!* [How beautiful!]" he said over and over again. "I didn't know Honduras had anything like this to offer."

I drank it all in, spreading my blanket out under a few tall trees that grew on the hilltop, preparing to settle in for the night. But it was not to be. Water became a pressing problem, and the last stream we passed lay way below us. No one wanted to return there or drag all the canteens back up the steep slope.

Somehow I ended up in the search party for a better solution. "There has to be water up here somewhere," I said. And when no one disagreed with me, I proceeded to put a plan into action. Below our hill was a deep ravine, and it was much closer than the stream behind us.

"There's water down there," I claimed.

Several of the boys talked the matter over and decided I could be right.

"I'm going," I said. "Who's coming with me?"

Felix volunteered, and we gathered up everyone's canteens, draping the straps over our necks. Down we went, hanging on by our hands and feet. At the bottom there indeed was a small stream. Not much, but enough to fill all the canteens with water. Clean and clear water, cold from the mountain spring it must have come from.

Back up we went on our hands and knees, and we distributed the canteens to their owners. The whole thing quickly became a shuffled mess. No one could remember whose canteen belonged to whom. Or perhaps they didn't care, slurping greedily out of the first canteen they could grab ahold of. I watched in horror. Later, as my own thirst increased, I discovered my intense squeamishness in never drinking out of the same glass as anyone else vanished. I did keep insisting that a certain red canteen was mine though.

"*La cantina roja is mia!*" I told Felix.

Felix thought this usage of the word "cantina" absolutely hilarious. Apparently in its Honduran usage, "canteen" had never come to mean only a water container—referring instead only to the local liquor establishment.

Felix never let me live down this mistake. Not that I held it against him. Even today, though I don't see him that often, we have shared laughs over *la cantina roja* that invoke shocked looks from bystanders that necessitates a quick explanation from Felix as to the meaning of our inside joke.

Eventually everything quieted down on the mountain, and the lights of the huts came on below us, twinkling in the darkness. After dusk they went out, one by one, until only the moonlight remained to bathe the valley with an ethereal glory bright enough that we could read under the full moon.

I lay there taking a long time to fall asleep.

In the morning we pressed on, hacking our way through dense undergrowth, at times resorting to being on our hands and knees for the climb. By late-morning we arrived at the top...or thought we did. We couldn't really see out. We only got a few glimpses of the valley through the trees.

We carved our initials on the mountainside and looked for what lay on the other side, which would be the most convincing evidence we had indeed reached the top. And sure enough, another valley lay below us. And beyond that were rows and rows of mountain ridges as far as the eye could see.

It was soon time to leave because we had to make our way home on foot before dark. Going down was much faster than coming up. We paused at our camping ground for one last look at the valley, taking in the majesty and the glory.

I've been back to Honduras numerous times, but I've never climbed that far up again. I'd like to someday. Perhaps I haven't because I'm afraid it won't be like I remember through the eyes of my youth, back when the world was an open book begging to be read and I couldn't turn the pages fast enough.

Once we arrived back home, the Stoll boys promptly informed their parents of the suspender transgression.

Mom, once she heard, approached me, demanding to know whether I'd joined in.

"No," I told her. Quite virtuously, I'm sure, now that the gravity of this sin was apparent. "I'd never think of doing that."

Mom sighed with relief. "I'm sure glad to hear that. And don't you ever part your hair like those boys do either."

I had no plans to. Besides, I didn't care how my hair was combed as long as it stayed where I wanted it to. My brothers and I had devised our own system of keeping our hair combed forward in place. We purchased a local concoction called *Sol de Oro*. It was a wax that we smeared into our hair. It gave off a spicy smell and kept things where we put them. We also looked like wax figures, but who cared? At least our hair was combed correctly.

Much later, we became the joke of the local Amish community when we landed in Belle Center, Ohio. I'm sure they thought, "These strange Amish boys with their waxed heads." Our dresser drawers were faithfully stashed with our supply of precious *Sol de Oro,* which we'd brought up with us from Honduras. What we planned to do when it ran out, I don't know. Luke Miller, a local Amish boy and a ringleader in the Ohio community, finally took compassion on me. He told me his sister Lois wanted me to stop using wax on my hair because she thought I might actually have fluffy hair. His sister was older than I was and not in danger of any romantic interest. Just observing, I guess. I listened and came to church the next Sunday with hair that floated all over the place. I had no idea what to do with it.

"Part it in the middle," Luke told me, which was what most of the other Amish boys were doing.

So I did.

Mom never said a word. Perhaps she had more important things on her mind by then. More likely she felt secure being surrounded by a solid Amish community. Apparently she saw no need to suspect parted hair as the first sign of her son sliding into the liberal ditch.

Chapter 29

By the fall of 1973, the date of Uncle Stephen's family leaving was firmly established. They would be gone by the spring of 1974. I don't know when the deal was brokered, but Dad committed himself to buying Uncle Stephen's place. The land adjoined ours and had three or four times the acreage of our small farm. Imagining Dad as a farmer was difficult, but he would prove up to the task. That is, eventually—and with Fausto's help.

For the present, plans were made to rent out the place. Cousin Ira with his new bride, Lizzie, would move in. Their wedding had occurred back in May of 1972. At the time they were making do by living in one of the cottages that had come with the original farm.

Knowing that he would soon be installed in Uncle Stephen's former place, Cousin Ira was seized with a harebrained idea. He would introduce goats into the Honduran culture. Were not goats hardy creatures? he reasoned. Didn't goats eat anything—well, almost anything? So why not turn the garbage-strewn Honduran yards and highways into tasty goat milk? It was a plan destined for smashing success…at least Cousin Ira thought so.

The Heifer Project, Inc., a stateside charity livestock program promoting the introduction of quality animals into foreign countries, would be the means for implementing his plan. Through them, quality breeding goats could be obtained at much-reduced prices. The shipment of twenty-three goats arrived soon after Cousin Ira and his wife moved into Uncle Stephen's old place, and Ira was in business.

When it came to the reproduction of his goats, Cousin Ira's plan worked to perfection. The animals multiplied like mice, and they soon overran the hillsides of Uncle Stephen's farm. Fences were no impediment. As a result, the goats were constantly into the neighbors' produce. Uncle Joe was hardest hit, but he bore the suffering with great patience. This was, after all, a worthy project.

At least the Amish thought so. The locals were the ones who didn't. They had never heard of creatures like goats. And hearing the hoarse cries emanating from Cousin Ira's goat-covered hills did nothing to persuade them. Personally, I disliked the smell the most. And Mom refused to come close to either goat's milk or goat's meat. And the locals totally agreed. I never heard of a goat being stolen, even when they ran open and unguarded everywhere. And stealing is the ultimate test in Honduran culture on a subject's desirability. An opinion expressed with zeal for the Holstein cattle the Heifer Project kindly assisted the Amish in obtaining.

A prize bull and some heifers were flown in and turned out in Leroy Hostetler's pasture. A few mornings later Leroy found a pile of hide, bones, and entrails rolled out in the grass where the bull once walked, courtesy of Honduran opinion on prized Holstein cattle. Something like "Better is a piece of meat in the pot today, then a pasture full of hardy calves tomorrow."

Mom's opinion of Cousin Ira's goats also extended to the owner. The two never got along for reasons I couldn't quite fathom. Perhaps because they both believed in fully expressing their minds, saying things to each other they would have refrained from uttering were "more worthy" human beings in earshot. Mom informed Cousin Ira in no uncertain terms that his pants were a disgrace to mankind. That is, his way of wearing of them was. I have to admit his pants were of the raggedy sort in their own right. But it was downright immodest, Mom told him. The way he pulled his suspenders so tight that the top of the pants ended up around his middle.

Cousin Ira informed Mom that she was a meddlesome woman, and that she should stay on her side of the fence if she didn't like his personal appearance. Somehow the quarrel never reached into their community life or into the business of renting the place. But in walking back to our cultivated river bottom, a walk that required going past the hill on which sat the rented house, Mom found ways to avoid meeting Cousin Ira. The sight of him seemed to loosen her tongue no matter how hard she tried to keep silent.

⌦

October seemed to be the month for tragedies in the community. It had been in October of 1970 that Uncle Stephen was injured. Then in 1971, Grandfather Stoll died in October, followed by Miriam Peachey's passing away from cancer in October of 1972.

Now tragedy came calling at Uncle Joe's house in October of 1973. Their tenth child, a daughter whom they named Eunice, was born on October 9. I didn't exactly keep track of babies being born in the community, but this one registered—mostly for what followed after the birth.

The eldest daughter, Rosanna, I believe, came up the hill to tell us the great news. Her mom had delivered a baby girl the night before. Rosanna beamed with the news even above and beyond the normal joy Rosanna constantly radiated. I didn't pay that much attention. Not until we were soon told that baby Eunice was sickly. The next day already jaundice had set in, and the baby had turned quite yellow. This was nothing to be concerned about, Uncle Joe thought. Lots of babies had jaundice.

To me a yellow baby sounded ominous. They weren't that good-looking to begin with.

Then we were told that Uncle Joe had rushed the baby to the doctor in the capital city. The mother was still not well enough to travel, so Uncle Joe had taken Rosanna along to help care for the baby—no light matter considering the four-hour bumpy bus ride. Uncle Joe reported later that when they boarded the small bus he asked if Rosanna could sit in front with the sick child. Upon hearing this, the bus driver not only immediately agreed, but made the announcement to the rest of the passengers. This produced quite an outpouring of sympathy from the busload of locals. So much so, they were even willing to forgo the usual halfway stop, where a light breakfast was normally consumed, to ensure quicker arrival at the capital. Not an easy sacrifice, as anyone who has made that trip knows.

Arriving in Tegucigalpa, the baby was rushed into the offices of the same child specialist who had taken care of my illness. At least this time he was more proficient than he had been in my case. Blood tests were taken, and the awful news learned. Uncle Joe had arrived too late. Little Eunice had an extremely high bile pigment in her blood from an RH factor in the parents. Her blood should have been changed immediately, but by now the damage had been done to her brain cells. Changing her blood was too late.

Understandably, Uncle Joe was guilt-ridden, as surely Rosanna must also have been. But it is the parent who carries the heaviest burden of the responsibility. And to make things worse, Uncle Joe was the medical expert in the community. This should have happened to someone who didn't know better, but not to Uncle Joe. I can't imagine the anguish he felt. But the father and daughter somehow rallied. The doctor thought the baby might not survive the night. Still, Uncle Joe admitted her to the hospital, and they stayed in the capital until the morning, unable to communicate with the family at home. The Guaimaca buses didn't run again until the next day.

Uncle Joe made peace with God that night, but he didn't get far with himself. The agony of his mistake bore into his soul. If the baby were alive by morning, she would be crippled or brain damaged, not unlike a cerebral-palsied child, the doctor had said.

The two returned to the hospital in the morning to find baby Eunice still alive. They left the baby and walked out to where the buses loaded for Guaimaca. There they providentially found a group of visiting Mennonite students with their own rented bus headed out to the community. Of course they could ride along. And of course they were all sympathetic. As the bus bounced and wound around the hilly dirt road, the students sang, no doubt trying to offer what comfort they could. Singing the old song they all knew from memory: "Farther along we'll know all about it. Farther along we'll understand why."

Uncle Joe must have wept as those young voices filled the bus. His arms were empty, and he would have to explain why to the rest of the family when he arrived home. Yet who could explain such things? How did one give an answer for a baby lying back in the hospital? Once healthy and now turned into a vegetable? The mistake avoidable. And yet there must be reasons that lay on the other side. Reasons too high for mortals to comprehend. Explainable someday by the God who named the stars. To think otherwise is but to harden the soul until it feels no more.

Arriving home, the younger children, eager for news, came running out to meet the returning pair, and the truth had to be told. What was said to them, to the mother, to the rest of the family, I don't know, but it couldn't have been easy.

Baby Eunice was soon brought home and placed in the sunlight for the prescribed amounts of time during the day to drive the last of the poison from her blood. She would live, but she would never be like other children.

~

School opened that October with me in the seventh grade with Fred Yoder teaching the upper-graders. He was down from stateside for a school year on sort of an Amish mission trip to instruct us youngsters in the finer points of education.

I planned to write a large chapter on him, reflecting back on how much that school year meant to me. But it has all flown away now that I'm here. I can't find a single solid thing to mention. I do know I almost worshiped the man. It was just one of those unexplainable things. Now I have no idea why that year with him as my teacher was so special. I met teacher Fred years later and approached him almost trembling as I introduced myself. He didn't remember me. After all, I was one face among many. A tall, scrawny boy who caught a glimpse of a man he wished he could become.

The big event that November was Uncle Stephen's cattle auction, a thing hardly known in Honduras. But we were *gringos* who knew the value of auctions. And surely, the Amish men thought, the Honduran culture could stand the enlightenment.

A search was made, and the only auctioneer in the country engaged. At least he claimed he was the only auctioneer. The date was set months in advance, and fliers were distributed. I believe even radio announcements from the big stations in Tegucigalpa were used—though, of course, none of the Amish listened to radio unless they were rebellious teenagers.

On the day of the auction, a crowd showed up, mostly white *gringos* living in other parts of Honduras. Some local farmers did come with money. Bleachers were set up on the side of the knoll south of Uncle Stephen's house. Each cow was led past the auctioneer's elevated platform, its pedigree read, and the minimum bid named. From there the bidding soared. Nothing remained unsold. The country had apparently been hungry for quality livestock from reputable sources.

I sat watching, fascinated. I spent a few lempiras on drinks and tasty food being offered by the Amish women. I'm sure they made a sizable haul themselves. By late afternoon a thunderstorm rolled in, and the crowd began to scatter. The auctioneer was beside himself, no doubt seeing his five percent fee dwindling away.

"*Es nube pasaero*," he shouted into his mike. ["It's just a passing cloud."]

Most people stayed, more convinced by the bright sunshine off in the distance than the shouted optimism.

When all was said and done, everyone was happy with the results. Especially the auctioneer, who made off with a considerable sum for his day's work. And no one would ever doubt again whether auctions would work in Honduras.

Chapter 30

The year 1974 opened with Uncle Stephen's leaving in February. His family quietly slipped away like ghosts into a mist. The mine canary had died, but we were too busy with our lives and too taken up with all the wonders of this land to notice.

Dad now had full responsibility for the acres left behind. Cousin Ira had the grasslands up front under control with his goats, but beyond those lay a rich river bottom on the western border. I was called upon to work in Dad's new venture: farming.

I learned how to harness the Belgian horses, of which we only had a few left in the community at this point. The work of plowing was something I never did learn to like. It was just long days of driving back and forth, seeming to get nowhere.

Dad kept a huge Belgian stallion in the pasture around Fausto's shack. I don't think I used him for plowing. He was kept for breeding purposes, and he was about as big a failure as the rest of the Belgian project was. For the most part, the stallion refused to mate with any Belgian mares. There was nothing wrong with his prowess. He loved the local mares, but his use as a stud was impractical at best since the larger colts he sired risked killing the females when they delivered.

Potatoes were the real cash crop, and Dad was now able to give farming his full attention. True to his nature, he either invented or modified our horse-drawn machinery at the shop to aid in the effort. We turned the black soil along the river into long rows of mounds, into which the sliced potato seeds imported from Holland were placed. I don't know how the other Amish planted their potatoes, but we were spared doing the arduous process by hand because of Dad's inventiveness.

The green potato plants soon sprouted. Pure gold in that culture where making a living wasn't easy. Thievery being what it was, Fausto volunteered to keep our potato fields safe. We cultivated by day, and as the harvesttime approached, he guarded by night. At least Fausto claimed he did. Since I was around him more than anyone else, he told me he was sleeping down near the potato fields with his gun. We didn't ask too many questions. Having an armed guard on our property would not have gone over well with the rest of the community. I doubted the story though. Fausto wasn't a man given to sleeping outdoors at night. He was much too practical. He had other methods, I was certain. I could tell by the twinkle in his eye when he spoke on the matter. My guess is he dropped the word around Guaimaca at a few choice spots that he was guarding *Don* Samuel's potato fields, and that he wouldn't look kindly on any night visitors. From there he would stroll down once in a while to the river bottoms along about dusk, making sure that Dad saw him go past the house a few nights a week.

He could then be back in his house, sound asleep, an hour later. We would never know the difference, nor did we wish to ask. Fausto was smart enough to figure that all out. Dad didn't pay Fausto extra for these guarding favors. It would have been pushing things too far to pay for a guard and all, but Fausto did get to keep a few bags of potatoes, which must have been a small fortune in his world. He still worked for eighteen lempiras a week, and his family had grown to at least two children by then.

Harvesttime was entered upon with a flourish. We worked long and late hours. It was one of the few times we stayed out after dark, something we didn't normally do. I know Dad came under ridicule for his peculiar practice of getting inside the house soon after dusk. Not by the Stolls though. They had some of the same sentiments. But the Amish who came from Northern Indiana thought this practice the strangest thing—not burning the midnight oil as most of them did by working in the barn by gas lantern.

Dad ignored the laughter, telling us children that it wasn't how late you stayed up that mattered, but how much work you got done once you were awake. I never saw any reason to disagree with Dad since he worked us children hard all the years we worked for him. At least I thought it was hard, but then I suppose most children do. We are all still quite alive and know how to work hard to this day.

Out in the fields we turned up the long rows of now-dying plants with our potato digger pulled by a single horse. If we didn't keep the feathered blade deep enough in the ground, sliced potatoes were the result—a problem I struggled with. But after some practice, we didn't have too many spoiled potatoes.

Every hand was required to bag the scattered harvest. The entire family turned out for the event. We children left the filled bags lying in the rows for the adults to pick up in a wagon that would haul the load up to Uncle Stephen's old barn. From there a truck came to take the potatoes into either Tegucigalpa or San Pedro Sula, wherever Dad had heard the market was best. Eventually I gathered enough courage to help with the loading, following the example of the adults by lifting the bags over my shoulder to walk up the ramps. This was no OSHA-approved weight either. No forty- or fifty-pound load—more like 120 pounds. Not the smartest thing in the world for a twelve-year-old to try, but I couldn't resist. Plus I was tall for my age, so I probably looked like I could handle it. I felt manly—I know that.

In the years we raised potatoes on Uncle Stephen's river bottom, we never found any signs of potato digging besides our own. Whatever Fausto did while guarding our land, he was good at it.

⁓

Danny and Sadie Stoltzfus arrived that April. They were an older couple to me, but in reality they were only in their early thirties. Childless, they came to take over the role of administrator at the children's home and, hopefully, to adopt a local child. Soon after their arrival, they took on a boy they named Nathan.

Danny would play a memorable role later in my life, one I don't think he was ever fully aware of. It's strange how these things happen.

You dislike some people—intensely in this case—and they end up being the ones who touch your life the deepest.

My relationship with Danny Stoltzfus grew out of my habit of roaming the neighborhood on weekends with my little pellet gun, which was about the only weapon left in the community the locals didn't feel like stealing. I stalked the blackbirds and parrots that populated the community. They were regular pests at the vast orchard behind Grandmother Stoll's place, so no one complained when I hunted there.

Where I crossed paths with Danny was at the pond where we often swam. During our swims, I'd notice the local wildlife that gathered at this watering hole. Later I'd creep back alone to hunt the colorful diving ducks and kingfishers. Both would have been worthy opponents with a .22, let alone a pellet gun.

The ducks I never succeeded in bagging. But I must have succeeded with the kingfishers because Danny got bent all out of shape over it. He confronted me and requested that I refrain from hunting on the pond. I told him Dad owned a major share, and that I would hunt there if I wanted to. Considering my stutter, I remember no difficulty in telling him this, which is a shame really. I could have used the restriction on my tongue at those times instead of the times I had justification for speaking up.

Anyway, we parted on hostile terms—not having exchanged harsh words exactly, but having established a low opinion of the other on both sides. Why he didn't speak with Dad, I don't know. He certainly had every right to.

Perhaps our personal quarrel wasn't helped by Dad's conflict with Danny. This conflict wasn't about hunting, but about German singing on Sunday mornings. The liberal winds were blowing increasingly at our church, now manifesting by an attempt to introduce English singing on Sunday mornings. Stateside, English singing at the evening hymn singings is fine, but on Sunday mornings it's a mortal sin. Here the change proposed came with the most logical of explanations. The local converts and visitors couldn't make the least sense out of the great German hymns of the faith, so why not use English or Spanish songs, which would benefit everyone?

Dad, of all people, was the most visible in opposing English singing on Sunday mornings. I shouldn't have found his little tiff with Danny Stoltzfus funny, I suppose, but I did. We would sit in church on Sunday mornings after the first song had been sung, waiting for the next number to be given out. Amish tradition dictated that the second song always be *Da Lob Lied*. The old classic *Praise Hymn*. Whether Danny knew what he was doing or not, I don't know. I suspect he did. Plus, he felt the need to sing a fitting song, and a fitting song for the occasion to Danny Stoltzfus was number thirty three: "Brethren, We Have Met to Worship." (It has been a long time since those days, but if we sing that song in church today, it's still Danny Stolzfus's song to me.)

Dad was sure Danny was up to no good. Certain that Danny was leading the charge to replace the sacred *Da Lob Lied* with an English impostor, Dad muttered about the matter at home. He lifted his voice in song out in the shop almost in vengeance, I think. And Dad was a great singer, his voice rising far above the noise of the machinery. That's where I first learned to appreciate the style of the old German music and the sheer majesty of its passion. The depth of its expression is unequalled in most modern singing.

Both men knew they couldn't sing their songs every Sunday. This would be too obvious. So who would dare start their song today? That was the question. Danny, being more brash than Dad, won most of the time. But Dad didn't fail to get in his licks. He'd lead forth in his high tenor, drawing out the notes in glorious triumph.

For one Sunday at least, *Da Lob Lied* would reign, clothed again in the glory of the Amish fathers.

Chapter 31

The Amish church on the hilltop didn't lack in enthusiasm that spring of 1974. Things were growing and moving, both in members and in mission opportunities. A call came in from San Marcos, a town beyond Guaimaca that lay near the mountains to the south. The locals wanted someone from our community to come and hold services.

Bishop Monroe thought the opportunity should be pursued, and talk began on the logistics. The ride back to San Marcos was on a road in worse shape than the main one into Tegucigalpa, and it took about an hour and a half to traverse. Some people from the community began making the trip one night a month to hold services in one of the local people's homes. Enough interest was shown at these meetings to warrant further investigation, so Bishop Monroe decided to move into the area himself for three months.

Mom and Dad took us all for a visit not long after Bishop Monroe moved. I wasn't impressed with the area, but then no one asked my opinion. The road didn't help my mood, nor did the crossing of an immense river without a bridge, which our driver took at a fast clip, water spraying out on all sides of the truck.

When we arrived at Bishop Monroe's house, I found the area quite closed-in, as in not being able to see around. To me, that's a big thing. I like a view of some sort. Here I could barely see the nearby mountains.

Spiritually though, things were going well with the new church, at least according to Bishop Monroe. The locals were attending the services and appreciative of the help. Mom had packed a lunch large enough for both families, and we ate on the table set on the dirt floor of Bishop Monroe's house. Not that I minded a dirt floor. I was used to eating in much worse conditions in Honduran huts.

Some weeks later, Bishop Monroe's boys would try to scale the peaks of the mountain behind the village. It wasn't the first attempt at such a venture, but, like previous attempts, it was without success. This didn't help my opinion of the mountain. It had a quite hostile attitude, I thought. Decidedly unfriendly.

Bishop Monroe stayed his three months and returned with glowing reports on the progress of the new church he'd founded. Minister Richard soon felt the call to take on the new responsibility and moved to San Marcos permanently. He would keep the post even during the final tumultuous years at the main community and right through the eventual breakup of the Amish settlement. I always thought he was thankful for the distance and anonymity San Marcos provided him.

In the meantime, at our house, plans were well underway to visit the States and Canada that year. I really didn't care one way or the other. It had been almost five years since we'd moved, and life up there had grown a bit blurry, dimmed in my memory by the life in the tropics that I loved. Mom and Dad thought the trip necessary. I wasn't told why. We were just going. So when the time came, we locked up the house and left the keys and the dog at Fausto's shack. We made our way to Tegucigalpa on the early bus with our suitcases in tow.

The airport ran several flights between both New Orleans and Miami back in those days, with stops in between, of course. These stops changed seemingly on the whim of the airlines. At one time or another in my travels to and from Honduras, I saw the outsides of the airports in San Salvador, British Honduras (now Belize), and San Pedro Sula. The planes originated stateside, landing around lunchtime, and made their way back home an hour or so later.

Few things run on time in the third world, even stateside planes. We waited and waited until the afternoon had nearly dwindled away. The airline claimed the plane was late coming out of Miami. This wasn't exactly a cheerful start to a three-month trip.

Once in the air, there was a stop that day in British Honduras. Darkness had fallen by the time we were airborne again. We soon found out why there had been the delay earlier. We were flying into a fierce storm. We couldn't see much out of the windows except thick banks of clouds illuminated when lightning flashed for a few moments. The seat-belt light stayed on the whole time, and we bounced around for almost the entire ride. I don't think they even served us food. No one was in an eating mood anyway. We children clung to our seats and hoped to arrive without meeting our watery death far below.

When we got to Miami, our connecting flight was already gone. Consulting the ticket agent, Dad leaned on the counter with his ever-present briefcase strapped over his shoulder. That was a habit learned in the third world, where thieves snatched anything loose. He came back and held a whispered conference with Mom. There was a night flight available into Kentucky, and from there we could take the Greyhound. I really didn't care. But when we boarded the next plane, I perked up considerably. This was a Delta flight. An immense plane by my standards, with the seats set wide apart and the aisles roomy. Nothing like the cramped planes they flew into Honduras. I tilted my seat back, feeling like royalty as I watched the twinkle of city lights far below us. This was living indeed. And the flight attendant even brought us food—nice food. By then we were really hungry, so anything probably would have tasted good.

We landed and went by taxi to the Greyhound station, which was followed by hours and hours of riding, the whine of the bus soon an almost-permanent buzz in my ears. I lost all the pleasant memories of the plane ride amidst the agony of the following day and night. Already Honduras was a faint memory, hardly recallable in this new world I found myself in.

We eventually crossed the border into Canada and soon arrived in Aylmer. Everything still looked the same—and yet it didn't. We drove down the gravel road past Bishop Yoder's old store, where Susanna and I had made our winter trek scared stiff of wolves just to buy a kerosene lamp shade for Mom to keep the darkness at bay for another night. The silver dollar Mom had bribed me with was back in Honduras, safe among my prized possessions. The date on the coin was sometime late in the nineteenth century. I envisioned it bringing me great riches someday, once I found a coin collector who would realize its true value. (I ended up losing the coin somewhere and sometime in the passing years. And now have no idea whether there was value there much beyond a dollar or not.)

We drove past the old, red Stoll mansion, standing empty at present. We drove on and, as I looked around, I saw nothing but stark emptiness. The charm of this land had flown away, driven to flight by the smells of mangoes and oranges in Grandmother Stoll's orchard, scattered by the glorious visage of our mountain lying beyond the church house hill. This land was no longer where my heart resided.

We drove past our old house. Here I had cut my toe off in the whirling blades of the push mower. And in the yard we'd watched the glow of Grandfather Stoll's house burn in the distance. I looked long and hard at the houses as we drove by. It was hard to imagine I'd really lived here. I left as an eight-year-old boy, and now I was back as a thirteen-year-old. It felt as if a lifetime had passed. I was no longer who I once was.

We drove past Uncle Johnny's place—the uncle of maple syrup fame. No one was in the yard, but the farm still looked the same, the dark-green siding hanging limply on the house, the barn running parallel with the road still dim and dusty with doves flying everywhere. This was a Gascho specialty, and one of the reasons I'd loved the place. Slowly I began to feel the first stirrings of home.

Driving past Pathway Publishers, we pulled into Grandfather Eicher's place. The doors of the house burst open and my aunts appeared. They hadn't seen us in five years, and their smiles stretched ear to ear. Nancy, Rosemary, and Martha enveloped us in hugs.

Grandmother Eicher came out last, always a little shy even around family. But I could tell she was glad to see us. Grandfather Eicher came from the barn, his whole face shining.

"So you've made it!" he called.

Obviously we had; it wasn't a question to be answered. He was welcoming us home. They all fussed over us and ushered us inside.

Soon supper was served, spread out on the long table in the living room. I listened as Grandfather Eicher led out in prayer, the sound of his chant bringing back so many memories. These were *my people,* and I did belong here.

This feeling clashed with my other world, and I was puzzled. How could one be two things at the same time? How could I belong in two places? These people had never looked at our mountain. They had never smelled tortillas frying on an open-drum barrel top. They'd never awakened to the sounds of parrots passing overhead. And yet they were a part of me. It simply was, and I let it be.

We soon moved over to the Red Mansion, and the next few weeks were spent in frequent trips to medical facilities. Honduras had no chiropractors that I knew of—that staple in every Amish community. All of us older children had to visit the chiropractor where our necks and various others parts of the body were given the wrench and the push.

On the top of the list though, was Mom and Dad's concern for my continued stammering. Apparently they'd begun to lose faith in the basic assurance everyone gave them—that children grow out of such things. The truth was, I wasn't growing out of it. And I was developing deep bouts with depression, which they thought might be associated with the stammering.

Sitting in the doctor's office, I filled out pages and pages of questions. Questions about my feelings, my faith, my experiences in life. I answered them the best I could. The doctor asked some follow-up questions, nodded sagely behind his huge desk, and then said there was nothing wrong with me. I would grow out of it.

That was advice Mom and Dad had already heard for free.

I don't remember feeling anxiety over the situation at that point in time. I was happy in my own way and keeping largely to myself. I'd learned how to stay out of situations where uncomfortable speaking was required. How I sounded the rest of the time, I already knew. But no one was making a big deal out of it—at least to my face.

We soon felt comfortable enough in the Red Mansion, a vast place of tall rooms and bare walls. One day when Mom and Dad were gone on business, John and Susanna went exploring in the basement—a place I stayed out of with its half-dug dirt walls and unlit darkness.

After exploring for some time, the two came rushing up the stairs, wild-eyed and dusty. They'd seen a ghost, they claimed. A real live one.

I was skeptical at first, but they ended up convincing all of us children. So we spilled out to the yard, afraid to stay inside until Mom and Dad came back. When we tired of waiting, we trooped down the road to Uncle Elmo's place, where John and Susanna repeated their tale. Uncle Elmo didn't say much, but he followed us back to the old house with eyes shining. I think he wanted to find a ghost for himself. But there was nothing in the basement. Even with Uncle Elmo's careful search of whole place.

"It might have been some pigeon trapped in the basement," he said, looking quite disappointed.

Chapter 32

Our time in Aylmer included a trip to one of the provincial parks lying along the edge of Lake Erie. These were the "Sand Hills," a local attraction where a mountain of sand borders the lake. We could drive there in a buggy, which helped make it Amish friendly.

Two of the Eicher aunts, Rosemary and Nancy, took us. We packed our lunches and headed out, arriving a long hour later. We rushed out of the buggy, dazzled by the sight—even after living in Honduras. We could run for long minutes, clawing our way upward on the sand. It was almost scary, the steepness, until we realized that rolling back down would cause no harm. In fact, my brothers loved to propel themselves down on purpose, their arms flying. I tried to stay on my feet.

We spent most of the day there, taking our time exploring the sand hills, making our way down to the water and splashing around, running along the tops of the immense dunes. It seemed like I would never tire of the place.

We ate our lunch under the trees at picnic tables near the entry. The minute we finished, we jumped up to run to the top of the dunes again. Eventually though, tired but happy, the aunts gathered us up and we headed home.

∽

The plan, we children soon discovered, was to spend four to six weeks of our vacation stateside. Part of the plan, though, was to travel to Pennsylvania to pick tomatoes to pay for our trip out of Honduras. A wise idea, I'm sure. And as it turned out, a memorable one for us children.

We said our goodbyes at Grandfather Eicher's place, not a lot of tears shed because we were a practical bunch of people. Relatives stood around smiling as we loaded up, even though we didn't know when we would see them again. They waved goodbye as we drove down the lane.

"*Machatest gut!*" Grandmother Eicher hollered after us. And we hoped we would "make it good."

Some three hours later, we stopped at Niagara Falls. This is an essential stop for all Amish children living in Canada. And also from other places if their travels take them anywhere close by. Amish life doesn't afford that many wonders, and few pass up a stop at Niagara. To stand looking at all that water plunging over the falls was a sight indeed. Even for us, though it didn't quite have the feel of Honduras with all the cars and people around. Still, we were impressed.

Later that evening we arrived at the place we were staying in Pennsylvania—an old, dusty, brown two-story house—a huge place it was, as it needed to be because it would be housing four families. That little tidbit of information we were soon told, along with the fact that our portion of the house consisted of two rooms upstairs. Even in Honduras math, that placed all of us children in one room. We commented on this, and not exactly favorably. Mom was having none of it. Three-year-old Sarah Mae, we were told, would sleep in the room with Mom and Dad. That left the six of us with the other room to ourselves.

We boys pushed the girls' beds as far to the other side of the room as we could manage, keeping our two beds near the door. I have no idea why, as everyone got along fine.

That evening we were introduced formally to the family already there, the Ed Schlabachs. A decent enough bunch of people, they were cousins of both Bishop Monroe and Emil Helmuth's families in Honduras. So the adults had a common bond. I don't think anyone arranged this. It's just the way things happen in Amish country.

Ed's oldest boy was also named Jerry, and he was around my age. We immediately hit it off, drawn together by our age more than anything.

The third family was Harry Warner and his wife. It soon became obvious to us that Harry was a novelty among the Amish. He took both the Lord's and the Amish's mandate to bear children quite literally. He arrived with over a dozen children in tow. I can't remember the exact number, but it would be in the high teens before Mrs. Warner passed away years later. His second wife would continue bearing him children.

Harry was breaking an unspoken taboo among the mainline Amish who don't have children above maybe twelve or thirteen before something is done—and that mainly for the woman's health. In this matter, they do have some sense and common decency. But Harry didn't believe in the prevailing opinion, as was obvious.

Harry also held forth on other religious matters during the long evenings after work when the men would gather to talk. Harry wasn't a minister at the time. He was more of a wanderer of sorts, moving about the smaller Amish communities—some he helped to found and others that had just started up.

Common opinion had it that Harry was fishing for a minister's ordination, which was frequently a necessity in the younger communities. But after the lot fell to another man on both the first and second ordinations, and the quota having been filled, Harry would move on again.

If we thought Harry was different, the final family outdid even Harry Warner. The David Byler family arrived a day or two after we did…by covered wagon.

They didn't believe in riding in *Englisha* modes of transportation—none whatsoever. They climbed out of the covered wagon, the men wearing robes that fell all the way to the ground, as if their modesty might somehow be exposed. They looked like biblical patriarchs.

The oldest boys were in their late teens, all of them attired like Dad. The women and girls looked fairly normal to us in their homespun dresses. We didn't ask any questions in the family's presence, but we had plenty for Mom and Dad later.

"Who are these people?" we asked. "What are they doing here?"

I don't think Dad knew either. We eventually got it all straight.

David Byler believed that the mainline Amish churches had drifted far from the truth. That plain living required a return to the ancient ways, including shunning *all* modern conveniences—as in motors, driving in vehicles, all modern food, and of all the crazy things...*breakfast.*

I have no idea where that one came from, and I never could follow the explanation when it was given to me. "Why is it wrong to eat breakfast?" we whispered, astonished at this new practice.

And it wasn't like we had to go looking for a display on how they lived. There was only one kitchen in the house, so all four families had to share it in common. I think the women had some arrangement between themselves on who cooked which mornings for everyone. Or perhaps they all worked together. I wasn't paying that much attention to this detail. What thunderstruck us was the sight of the long line of Bylers, the men in their robes strolling out to the main road with the women walking behind them. They were heading for the tomato patches while we sat there eating breakfast.

We felt an instant need to justify our own practice of eating breakfast. Because surely these people were the truly holy, suffering in the morning while we ate our fill. But it didn't take long for us to figure the whole thing out. I can't remember who came up with the logic, but it sounded right to me. All of the Byler men were overweight it was observed. And no breakfast naturally caused overeating on the next two meals. And that observation bore out. The Bylers loaded the food on their plates at night. Everyone cooperated with the Bylers' strange food requirements though. At least at the community meals. They also couldn't eat prepared foods from the *Englisha* stores. Everything had to be made by hand, but that didn't cause a problem.

I don't remember the backstory to the night our family purchased store-bought ice cream. My sisters think the Bylers couldn't eat desserts at all. I'm thinking there was no homemade ice cream maker on the place and no way to get one. What I do know for sure is our family loved ice cream. It's totally possible we would have purchased store-bought even with an ice cream maker on the grounds. We did have a hankering for the treat.

So Dad brought a gallon back to the house, and we had *Englisha* ice cream up in our rooms. Just our family. No one complained that I heard of. The Schlabach and Warner children didn't give us second glances, no doubt being used to such things themselves.

Susanna though, went outside later that evening and happened to walk past the trash bin where Mom had thrown the ice cream carton. There she found one of the Byler girls licking the last of the ice cream from the carton.

I think the sight did Susanna permanent psychological damage, watching the young Byler girl trying to get the last taste of ice cream off that carton. She never quite got over it.

On that first morning, after the Bylers had disappeared down the road and we had finished our breakfast, we gathered together and headed down the road. I had no idea what tomato picking meant or what lay ahead, but I would soon find out.

Acres of ripe tomato fields lay along the highway, well within walking distance of the old house. Scattered among the green, dying plants were the brown robes of the Byler males. Tractors pulling wagons sat waiting for their loads. Hampers were piled at regular intervals along the rows. We milled about until the owner showed up in his pickup truck. Dad seemed to know him; they shook hands. The owner rattled off his instructions in a no-nonsense tone. Clearly the man had other tasks awaiting. We would be paid by the hamper, he said. And each family was to keep its own count, turning in the number at the end of the day.

"I'll trust you," he told Dad. "But my workers will keep track of how many they load over all. And if the numbers start to conflict, I'll let all of you know."

Dad nodded and the owner moved on to the others.

Mom made sure all of us children understood how to carefully drop the tomatoes into the hampers without smashing them, and she told us we didn't have to worry about the stems. "That's from the bygone days," the owner had said with a smile after Dad asked him. "It doesn't matter anymore."

We picked away until close to dark, all of us staying in the field, including little Sarah Mae. Susanna and Miriam took turns tending her

if she needed anything, singing a jingle they had picked up that summer in Aylmer, and which Sarah can still repeat today. It comes from
a song called "Little Sally Walker." This song had been passed down
through so many mouths of Amish children by then—children who
had never heard the original—that the words had gradually changed:

> Little Sally Waters, sitting in the sun.
> Crying and weeping for another one.
> Cry, Sally, cry, wipe off your eyes.
> Point to the east, point to the west.
> Point to the one who loves you best.

Sarah could totter about at three years of age, but there wasn't any
place to lose her really. The open fields stretched for long distances in
all directions.

We children must have been allowed to take our time filling the
hampers because I never felt like complaining about the work. None
of us did. We just picked tomatoes, stretched our backs, and picked
some more.

At night we slept well, the evening spent lounging around the place.
David Byler and Harry Warner soon had heated religious discussions
going. Both Harry and David felt the need to convert the other to his
position. The other two men joined in only if they felt like it. Ed mostly.
Dad didn't hang around much. Deep religious arguments weren't down
his alley. He could confront Danny Stoltzfus at home about the *Da
Lob Lied*, but trying to convince a robed man he ought to ride in automobiles wasn't worth the effort. Harry, though, launched his best shots.

I listened the best I could, but I couldn't make a whole lot of sense
out of things. David mostly talked about the inconsistency of the thing.
If automobiles were wrong, he asked, then how was it right to ride in
them? Before we left, David had written up a long treatise on the subject and passed it around to the other three families. I think I was the
only one of our family who read any portion of it. I can't remember
much of the content, but there was lots of Old Testament scriptures
and a little logic thrown in here and there.

One evening toward the end of our stay, supplies had run low and the two oldest Byler boys were driving into town to replenish stock. I asked if I could ride along. I think I needed some small item—or thought I did. When they said I could, I ran inside to get permission from Mom. She okayed the venture, and I was already seated on the open buggy with the two Byler boys when Dad came out at the last minute.

"You'd better take a coat along," Dad advised, more of a suggestion, I thought, than a command.

I looked up at the sky, trying to see if there was an approaching storm. I couldn't see anything.

"It gets cold around here," Dad added.

I shrugged, finding that hard to imagine.

When I wasn't interested in taking the coat, Dad retreated.

Both of the Byler boys looked at me with incredulity written on their faces.

"Aren't you going to get your coat?" one of them asked.

"No," I said. "I'll be okay."

They looked at each other in horror, clearly expecting I would be struck down from heaven for this defiance of higher authority. When nothing happened, they shook the reins and we were off. Our destination was over an hour away, and it was well past dusk by the time we'd finished shopping. Sure enough, on the way home I froze most of the way. But I kept my mouth shut. Next time, I determined, I would listen to suggestions from Dad.

Chapter 33

Neil and Carol Wright were long-standing *Englisha* friends of Dad and Mom. We kids were told that the Wrights would drive us back to Honduras in their station wagon. We would travel overland all the way to Honduras, following the Pan-American Highway for much of the journey, once we were in Mexico. Dad figured he would save some money by paying Neil by the mile, and for Neil's part, he would have the time of his life making the trip. So when the tomato picking slacked off, Dad decided the time had come to leave. Neil was notified back in Aylmer, and the date was set.

When the couple pulled into the driveway for the beginning of our adventure, I was horrified. How in the world would eight of us, plus Neil and Carol, all fit in one station wagon?

"No problem!" Neil boomed.

He was a big man and always happy and sunny. Carol was the opposite—pessimistic and a little short-tempered. But this was our ride back to Honduras. Everyone must have arrived at the same conclusion I had though. We needed more room. The men talked and decided to purchase a trailer for the luggage. So Neil set off to find one while Dad got in one last day of tomato picking.

Finally Neil returned with the news that he'd found a trailer to buy. "I thought the man was going to finish me off," Neil joked when Dad and I went along to pick up the new purchase. "He was taking me way back in the sticks."

Dad chuckled and nodded. It was true, we were driving into the sticks. However, once we arrived, the trailer seemed suitable enough, though it was little more than a white box on two wheels. They hitched it up, paid the man, and then spent considerable time getting the lights hooked up to the car so they would work properly.

On the day of our departure, we all piled in. John squeezed in between Neil and Carol up front. Mom and Dad got into the backseat with Susanna and Miriam. That left three of us boys lying on our sides in the luggage compartment (minus the luggage, which was packed in the white box trailer).

Neil started the car and then pulled out his camera for a shot of the old house through the car windshield. David Byler was sitting on a bucket on the front porch. He leaped into the air, his robe flying, as he dove into the kitchen doorway. He wouldn't take a chance on being photographed, even accidently. In my mind's eye I can still see him scrambling. Neil and Dad roared with laughter all the way out the lane and long afterward. The story of David Byler's flying leap became a tale our family still remembers with smiles. When the picture was developed, the dim form of David's wife can be seen scurrying toward the kitchen doorway too, left behind to fend for herself by her panicked husband.

We headed south toward Texas, staying on the back roads at Neil's insistence. He said he could drive the same speed as the interstates, which was fifty-five miles per hour that year by virtue of a law passed by Congress in March to deal with the oil crisis and save on national fuel consumption.

We seemed to crawl toward Honduras. I think the real reason Neil liked the back way was for the scenery. He would stop and snap away with his camera at every pleasant view—and at us. I think we were the most photographed Amish family around that year. Dad probably figured it was useless to object; besides, Neil was his friend.

It's strange what you remember on such trips. For me it was the Dutch Pantry restaurants. Every evening we stopped there for supper at Neil and Carol's insistence. We ate only two meals a day, one late morning and at the Dutch Pantry around six. From there we would find a cheap motel and settle in for the night.

Mrs. Wright, Eicher kids, and Dad.

We hadn't gone too many days until it became obvious the trailer had serious problems with its tires. They simply wouldn't stand up to the sustained use, along with the heavy weight of what we were hauling back down. Every day or so a tire would blow. Neil and Dad would jack up the axle on some lonely road, remove the wheel, flag down a passing car, and hitch a ride into town while we all waited. Waiting each day for the next blowout drove both of them to severe states of mental distraction. Clearly something would have to be done. They tried buying new tires, but those didn't hold up any better than the old ones.

I didn't mind. From my spot lying on my side with my two smaller brothers in the luggage compartment, stopping was actually better than going.

John, the mischief maker, constantly made trouble up front for Carol, and there would be occasional temper flares. Carol said he wiggled. She claimed John punched her with his knee. They threatened to send him back with us, which kept things under control better than anything else did.

Carol played gospel tapes on those long miles. Endless loops of the same cassettes. Those songs played in my head for years afterward.

We finally crossed the border into Mexico, and my heart warmed at the sight. Gone in one mile was the sterile landscape, the lack of color, the order, the cleanness. Home was calling. I stared out the station wagon window at the confusion in the streets. Bicycles and donkeys mixed in with the cars. People were going everywhere. Huts sat hap-hazardly, dressed in their pastel pinks and yellows, oranges and greens paint jobs. Filth was thrown along the sidewalk, something I suppose only a homesick child could find beautiful. It stirred the deepest depths of my soul. A primordial emotion, I suspect, from before our race was civilized. Soldiers stood along the streets at checkpoints, waving us on without checking our papers. We were already back in favored *gringos* status.

We passed glimpses of the Gulf of Mexico, seen through the station wagon windows. Neil looked nervous as he clutched the steering wheel. We'd crossed the border late in the afternoon and were now out in the countryside. Dad didn't like traveling after dark, but we kept going. Neil felt the need to try for the next town. Showing his bravery, I sup-pose, which fled when headlights bounced around behind us, keeping pace with the station wagon.

"Do you think they're following us?" Neil asked Dad.

"I don't think so," Dad assured him.

"But they are!" Neil declared moments later.

He floored the accelerator, and we sped off into the night going more than ninety on the winding, unknown, rut-filled roads. Silence hung heavy in the car as the lights behind us kept pace.

Dad didn't say anything about slowing down. As we rocked into the next town, the lights behind us vanished. Neil wiped his brow and vowed to travel no more after dark. We were all thankful nothing worse had happened, so we refrained from caustic remarks. Even Carol kept her mouth shut as we found a motel and settled in.

The place we were at had a local band playing that evening. The music was in Spanish, of course. I crept out in the hallway to listen. The halls were full of cheerful, bouncy, soulish sounds. I couldn't believe my ears when music burst forth from Mom and Dad's room behind me. I snuck back for a look, peering inside the door. Dad was play-ing a mouth organ, keeping fairly good time with the sounds out in the hallway. I had no idea Dad played anything. Or that harmonicas were allowed by the Amish. I stared in disbelief. Had the world come to an end? Mom saw me and motioned me in. She explained that harmonicas were perfectly acceptable to most Amish people, and Dad had known how to play since his youth, all of which was news to me. I listened for a long time, enthralled. He was good. As good as the men outside. Apparently the trip north had brought back old memories for Dad. I have no idea, though, when or where in our travels he'd purchased the musical instrument.

We headed out again the next morning. Soon the continued trailer tire blowout stress finally came to a head. Dad and Neil had enough of it. They stopped at a machine shop and purchased a whole new set of tires. By the way they chuckled and laughed to each other when they came back, I knew something was up. Turns out they'd found tires stronger and better than anything sold stateside—something to do with government regulations.

We waited for most of the forenoon as the tires were installed third-world fashion—very slowly. Mom told us children Bible stories out beside the car. Stories I didn't even know existed, let alone that such stories could be in the Bible. She told the story of how Lot's two daughters kept their family lines afloat by intoxicating their own father and then sleeping with him. I listened in sheer horror.

Perhaps Mom thought it was time to begin the family's education in such matters, and that now was the moment. Or perhaps she was spurred on by her knowledge of the sexual mores that surrounded us daily in Honduras. Whatever the reasons, she wouldn't have had to worry. She did a good job with all her children. We turned out a fairly decent bunch.

With the new tires on, we climbed back into the station wagon and headed out. Our trailer tire troubles were finally over! No more blowouts from there to home.

Hanging to the coast, we drove through Veracruz, and then across Mexico to pick up the Pan-American Highway. The Continental Divide runs through there, with beautiful high mountains. The land felt as isolated as anywhere I've been.

I watched out the back windows as Neil snapped away with his camera. He was taking pictures even while he was driving. Carol kept yelling at him, but Neil couldn't resist the temptation. Somewhere in those mountains he pushed things too far. A group of native women chased the station wagon with rage on their faces after Neil slowed down to snap their picture.

Later, approaching a ravine, Neil stopped to capture the view. A native hut was sitting on the ridge with the valley below. It was breathtaking, and Neil snapped away, only to be interrupted by the wrathful hut owner who came bolting out, waving some kind of primitive weapon. Neil laughed as he sped off, but he stopped taking pictures for awhile.

In Guatemala, the mountains continued. When we entered Guatemala City, we got lost. Neil drove aimlessly around with the town spread out below us. Eventually Dad and Neil straightened things out, and we were on the right road again.

San Salvador wasn't much to see, but then the high mountains of Mexico and Guatemala are hard to compete with.

At the Honduras border we ran into our first problem with customs officials. Before that, Dad had been giving out apples from his stash in the trailer, and everyone had been happy to wave us on through.

"Duty," the officials said now. "It has to be paid."

"These are our own possessions," Dad explained to no avail.

We waited for hours on the Honduras side while negations proceeded. Officials would come by, rummage through the trailer's contents and leave again. I don't know how things were finally settled, but likely with the paying of some fee. Bribery really, but that goes without saying in that part of the world. You pay the small upfront fee and slip a little more under the paper to have it processed right away. And perhaps some more is slipped into a hand so the official who needs to sign off can be found today instead of tomorrow.

We drove on, happy as larks that our trip was finally close to over. Tegucigalpa looked different coming in from the Salvador side. Neil laughed at our horror stories of the four-hour bus trips to Guaimaca. Just another opportunity to snap pictures, he figured. He wasn't laughing by the time it was over. We pulled into the familiar valley after bouncing around in the station wagon for four hours. Even Neil was thankful to finally arrive.

I jumped out and made a beeline for Fausto's shack to see our dog, Jumper, and all things familiar. I announced my presence by hollering, *"Aquí estamos!"* ["Here we are!"] as I came around the edge of the shack at a dead run. Elsa grinned from ear to ear, but Jumper wasn't happy to see me at all. She groveled around on the dirt for awhile and growled at me.

"Se le ha olvidado" ["She has forgotten you"], Elsa said, all sympathetic. It didn't take long before things were back to what they used to be. Jumper followed us back to the house. We were home!

Neil and Carol hung around for a week or so and then headed north again.

Chapter 34

Soon after we arrived home, Hurricane Fifi struck the northern coastline of Honduras, drenching us all night with rain. The next morning torrents of water were running down the lane between David Peachey's house and the children's home. I thought nothing of it, thinking it just another hard-hitting nighttime storm. But news soon poured in, telling us otherwise. Unbeknownst to us, Hurricane Carmen had passed north of Honduras with its 150-mile-an-hour winds early that September—probably about the time we were traveling through Mexico, but it did little harm by the time it made landfall. Following right on Carmen's heels not two weeks later, Fifi struck, traveling lower in the Gulf this time. A weaker storm with its 110-mile-an-hour winds, it was the one that did the most damage. After raking most of the northern Honduras coast, the hurricane continued on across Guatemala and Mexico, passing close to the route we'd just come home on. When it reached land, it quickly became a tropical storm.

Honduras had little in the way of an early warning system back then. Locals in their huts had only the signs they knew to look for to prepare them before the storm smashed down. Estimates of the dead came close to 10,000—but those were Honduran figures, and thus open to question. One coastal town was reported to have been nearly wiped out.

The Amish community was quickly galvanized into action. Men were dispatched to Guaimaca to obtain passes needed to enter the afflicted areas. Contact was made with the Mennonite Relief Agency in the capital city. They reported that headquarters was sending down a man to survey the damage, and they would begin addressing the immediate need of housing people.

Letters to *The Budget* were written and mailed.

The little town of Choloma, population 10,000 before the hurricane, lies north of San Pedro Sula. It received the bulk of our Amish attention. Parties from the community left at regular intervals to shovel mud, at first, and then to rebuild the houses.

The papers in the capital implored the nations of the world for aid, and it did pour in. Shipments of not just food, but items of all description. All those donations, however, didn't end up as hurricane relief. In Honduras, aid seems to reach those who need it the least. This became a joke in the local community. All the strange items the locals showed up with to offer for sale to the *gringos* included things like small hand files, which we could use, especially at Dad's shop. We were miles from the coastal damage, so how the donated merchandise reached us was a stretch for even our imaginations that were accustomed to third-world corruption. It must have flowed through many hands, with each getting their dip.

In the meantime, only the adults were going to work at Choloma, as the area was considered too dangerous for children. Later a chaperoned load of schoolchildren was taken in on a chartered bus. For a long time we'd heard of the hurricane's terrible aftermath from the returning adults, so we greatly wanted to see this for ourselves.

There was little to see since most of the debris and damaged homes had been cleaned up by then. We could see some of the marks though. Honduras is a hilly country, consisting at times of land that goes up one hill and down the other. Near the foothills of San Pedro Sula, on all sides, were long brown marks running up and down them, like great claw marks of a wild beast trying to scale the heights.

Any hut caught in those landslides wouldn't have stood a chance. But it was the storm surge coming in from the ocean, we were told, and the flooding, that had done most of the damage.

Once we arrived, the chaperones gave us a tour of the building projects. We got to see where Minister Richard, as well as Bishop Monroe, had held church services. Enough monies had come in from *The Budget* write-ups to run a full-time, on-site Amish outreach program. Even Pathway's *Family Life* ran a short notice soliciting funds, all of which came directly from the Amish community in Canada and the States in checks they mailed down.

That night we slept on blankets laid out on the concrete floor in a municipal building.

~⧜~

Because of the publicity associated with the Amish community's involvement at Choloma, a government official representing aid outreach in Honduras arrived in the community with a bold proposal. The government would manufacture a horse-drawn plow, made right in Honduras. Then the Amish could teach the locals how to run the thing.

It would have seemed to me like Grandfather Stoll's dream come true. It was the fruition of his dream all those years ago. That of taking Amish farming ingenuity from a land where it really wasn't needed to a third-world country where it could produce maximum results.

The aid official had access to the highest levels of the national government, he claimed. And he was committed to the project. The prototype of the new plow was already made and ready for testing. Would the Amish try it out and give their expert opinion on the matter? Would they eventually supply multiple Amish men as trainers who would travel the countryside giving demonstrations and instructing the natives in this much superior use of horse plowing? It would certainly be better than the only option they now had—their oxen.

Amish recalcitrance set in at once. The decision for some reason fell to Uncle Joe, who was having none of it at first. This was the government, and no Amish person consorted with the government. I'm sure the liberal wing of the community would have loved the chance to hobnob with high-government officials, but those Amish either didn't like horse farming or didn't care to learn. Probably the former, since they'd already had their sights set on the mystical dream of tractor farming.

Honduran farmer plowing with oxen.

So things were thrown Uncle Joe's way. He relented a little. They would test the government's prototype and give their opinion. The official was overjoyed with even this offer, and he showed up on the appointed day with his plow. I'm sure Uncle Joe offered his definite opinion about the benefits of using local horses over the Belgians and Percherons brought in from stateside.

The prototype, under the skilled hands of Uncle Joe and his eldest son, Paul, proved fatally flawed. It was flimsy, and its nose dug into the ground. The government official wasn't discouraged. He would fix the plow in time for the big demonstration in the capital.

There important government officials would be in attendance and a final decision could be made. Would Uncle Joe send his team and an operator for the big day? All expenses paid, of course.

Again Uncle Joe relented. But that would be the end of it, he said.

Once the big day of the demonstration arrived, ox plowing was displayed alongside Uncle Joe's team of native horses and the new plow. Careful measurements were made of the furrows and the time taken. Officials muttered to each other, and everyone went home.

A few days later the original aid official returned to the community with a report of tremendous success. The government had approved the new plow and wished to proceed with the program. Could he hire on Amish boys or men to travel the countryside teaching the locals? All expenses paid, plus a wage four times what a local laborer made.

Uncle Joe said no. Things had gone far enough. He might do one more demonstration, but that was it.

The significance of Uncle Stephen's leaving had not gone unnoticed by Uncle Joe. He'd mourned often the departure of his brother, but he had soldiered on bravely. Up until now. This withdrawal was the end of the road, following so close to the great success of the Amish helping at Choloma.

So if Uncle Stephen was where the canary died, then Uncle Joe was where we lost our heart. The vision Grandfather Stoll had for the Honduras community was now ready to die. There remained only the details of how the long trek back home would occur.

Perhaps Bishop Monroe could yet have turned the tide if he'd known what to do. He didn't lack in enthusiasm, but he failed to grasp the gravity of the situation.

On the surface things were still going along quite well. The success with the Choloma project had invigorated everyone and seemed to solidify the role the Amish could play even in major national disasters.

⌒

School started again that fall. It was eighth grade, and thus my final year of formal education, according to Amish culture.

In February 1975, Uncle John Martin, who was married to my Aunt Sarah, placed the last touches on his new invention. Over near the creek by Grandmother Stoll's place, a puffed wheat popping machine began operation, looking like a cannon used in Civil War times. Uncle John set the thing on the upper floor of a shack, put in the wheat and heated up the cannon. When the proper temperature was reached, the whole contraption was thrown downward toward a chute leading to the lower level and the door flipped open by some trigger switch.

Kaboom! Like a real cannon it went off. And *presto!* Puffed wheat cascaded downward with white chaff flying everywhere.

I was a curious fellow, and after hearing the constant boom in the distance, I visited one afternoon. Uncle John was a friendly enough chap around his relatives, and he was glad to show me the machine in action. The puffed wheat was delicious too. I talked Mom into buying some at once, and we had it for breakfast. It didn't sustain us like oatmeal did, but it served as a refreshing break in our diet.

In the meantime, my life at school mirrored the hurricane wreckage on the coast. Destruction and turmoil with no one to mount a rescue operation. I don't know why I had such a hard time of things, but I did. I got into scraps all the time—mostly my fault, I'm sure. I was sensitive and touchy about everything. It was during this time the incident occurred that I shared earlier, where I cut up the papers that had drifted toward my desk and then returned them to the girl I had a crush on. What an odd way of showing my attraction! I was a mess.

One Saturday I passed her below the schoolhouse hill just beyond the children's home. I was on Lightfoot, and she was driving an open buggy with her little brother sitting beside her. With heart pounding, I looked straight ahead, not saying a word. In my defense, I couldn't have uttered anything if I'd tried.

"It's Jerry," I heard the little brother say loudly to the girl, stating the obvious.

"Shhh…" She clamped her hand over his mouth and turned bright red.

I rode grimly on.

In an unrelated incident, I stormed home one day at lunch hour and declared I wasn't going back to school after one of the girls said something to me on the playground. I can't remember what it was, but I was dead serious. The whole world hated me, and I hated it back.

Mom didn't say much, but the next day I was back in school, trying to keep out of everyone's way, which, of course, was the wrong thing to do.

The only bright spots in my life were my constant weekend wanderings to the mountain and the fun I had at the pond. The stocked fish were growing large by that time. Mostly some sort of scrawny local breed that we caught by the dozen, full of bones and hardly edible. Catfish were what we were after.

Uncle Mark had found the seed stock somewhere, dropping them in soon after the pond had been dug. Catfish that grew to thirty or forty pounds, we were told. They were monsters once they matured. Our mouths watered at the prospect of pulling one in on our lines.

"They ought to be getting on up there in size by now," Louis assured us. How he knew, I don't know. But it sounded right. He laid out plans for their capture.

I'm surprised Uncle Mark didn't object to our constant fishing, threatening the stock like we were. But I suppose he figured we wouldn't do much harm.

And in that he was correct. But it was fun trying.

Catfish are best caught at night, Louis informed us. And he had a secret bait that drew catfish from miles around. Some really good stuff, he asserted. We waited breathlessly for the revelation, expecting some complicated formula involving long-distance travel and great expense. It wasn't anything like that though. It was really rather quite simple and repulsive at the same time. Also quite effective. We hung chicken guts on the clothesline for a week until they turned leathery soft and oily. The smell was enough to gag us at a dozen yards. It stayed on our fingers for days, even after vigorous scrubbings. With that on our fishhooks, we were ready for business.

We camped out, fires burning along the shore. Our canvas tent was set up with candles inside for lighting. We were prepared for an all-night stay.

Louis told us we didn't have to stay up to catch the catfish. We were to take our fishing rod into the tent with us or lay on a blanket by the water. When a monster swallowed our hook, we would know it.

I never caught anything worth speaking of, but I awoke many times to the sight of Louis flailing around in the darkness all tangled up in his fishing line, his form silhouetted against the starry sky as he wrestled a monster on the other end.

We would leap up and stir the fire as we watched the fight. Louis would reel in line, and then the catfish would take it out again. Finally it would be over, and the fish was in the shallow water with its huge whiskers hanging off to the side, croaking in protest. Water flew when it thrashed its tail.

They never quite reached thirty pounds. Close to twenty sometimes.

And those were few and far between. Still, we were thrilled. The meat
had few bones and made excellent eating.

Good fishing was a subject for poetry, I figured:

> Boyhood dreams and boyhood ways,
> Stars within my heart that fade.
> When clear the heart, then clear the brain,
> When few the heartaches on me lain.
>
> The times beside a campfire bright.
> We fished until the morning light.
> Oh, sweetest thought on memories train.
> Of things all gone when manhood came.
>
> When free the hours I had to roam.
> In hill and dale and valley dome.
> When black the night and clear the stars.
> Are memories from boyhood hours.
>
> Oh, long gone days so dreamy bright.
> Are lost in manhood's streaming light.
> And sorrows come as sorrows can.
> For all too soon, I am a man.

Chapter 35

Bishop Monroe was holding forth with great zeal at the church house, preaching repentance from sins and holding forth Christ as the answer to all of man's problems. The spring instruction class for baptism started that April with my two school tormentors, Daniel and Paul, in attendance. They showed up one evening after dark, calling me out of the house to stand in the lane to speak with them. I was unable to say a word. I was worried, and I had no idea what they wanted. They had Daniel's older sister, Rebecca, along with her boyfriend. Rebecca was a kindhearted soul whom everyone liked. And she was the one who had knocked on the door to ask me outside. Likely they figured I wouldn't have come out without mediation from someone. And they were probably right.

They had come to apologize, they said, for their actions over the years. I nodded in acceptance, more observant of their lighthearted gaiety than of the apology. But one did forgive when asked. That much I knew. And a person did apologize for his or her sins upon taking up instruction class. That much I also knew from listening to Bishop Monroe's sermons. Their duty done, the group left, laughing among themselves, leaving me standing alone in the middle of our lane. I felt neither here nor there about the matter.

∽

I turned fourteen that May. I was a walking wanderer, alienated from most everyone in the community. I was slowly awakening to what I was: a social and community misfit who hated any public life or attention. I drew ever more inward, creating my own world and hanging out with Louis and Joseph Peachey, whom I considered my only friends.

I was in this condition when God found me. I don't know any other way of saying it. I didn't go looking for Him. And no one spoke to me of my need for a personal Savior, other than the holding forth of Christ I was constantly hearing in the sermons on the church house hill. I didn't respond to an altar call. And I said no sinner's prayer. I never asked Jesus to come into my heart. I just opened the door when He arrived.

Perhaps that seems too simplistic a conversion experience or even doctrinally dangerous. I intend neither. I'm just saying what happened. I was pursued by a love and conviction of sin that consumed me. Where I could find no fault before, there now lay glaring and weighty sins that crushed me. But it wasn't the awareness of my sins that had my attention. It was God's love that overwhelmed me. I felt lifted in arms so strong I knew they would never let go. I couldn't believe it. It boggled my imagination because I knew who I was and all I had done. So deep and certain was this awareness, so total was this transformation, that it has served as the bedrock of how I understand God. Not that I've never doubted or wavered, but it is to this experience that I always return.

Jesus said that those who are forgiven much love much. I could add that those who are unloved by this world have the most to be forgiven for because the anger and hatred goes the deepest. I was one of those people. I know how impossible love can seem. I wept for days when Jesus found me. My heart was moved to depths of gratitude and worship from the wonders of His life and from the horrors of what I was and what I had done.

Mom noticed and wanted to know what was going on with me. I stammered out the best explanation I could. Mostly about the things I'd done wrong. She agreed with me that they needed setting right. So I visited Grandmother Stoll's place, leaving the few lempiras I had on her table to replace the ones I'd stolen years before. Unable to explain myself face-to-face, I'd talked to Mom, and she told me this was good enough.

Rosa Sanchez and her chickens was harder, but I felt I had to do it. Calculating the value of the dead merchandise with Mom, we added some extra for good measure. I don't think Rosa could make heads or tails out of my stammering explanation when I arrived. She did get the fact that I had been involved in killing her chickens though, but she probably wasn't sure how. And she understood money, accepting it from me without hesitation. I left nearly bankrupt, but with a clear conscience.

Aunt Sarah was horrified when Rosa told her, but Mom smoothed things over for me. She told Aunt Sarah what was going on, and that likely kept me from being accosted by the uncles in their just outrage.

Danny Stoltzfus at the children's home was the worst task. I walked in and told him I was sorry for disrespecting him and for not listening to him. I think he understood most of my little speech. He was nice as could be about it—compassionate and understanding. I shed more tears in front of him than I got words out, embarrassing myself into the ground. I felt like the idiot I was. But I completed the task and left.

I was seized immediately with an intense desire to be baptized. Aware that this wasn't possible, I still told Mom. Whatever I said concerned her enough that she spoke to Bishop Monroe. A few days later he showed up one morning while I was washing the cream separator beside the shop. I doubt if Mom told him I couldn't talk, but I'm sure that was common knowledge by then because he didn't ask me any questions.

He said he'd heard that I'd recently become "born again."

I nodded, my head lowered. The tears starting to run down my face.

He was glad to hear that, he said, speaking quite kindly. And he said my mom had said I was worried I needed to be baptized immediately or I might be lost again.

I couldn't remember having said that, but it was close enough. I nodded.

"You don't have to worry about that," he said. "Baptism is only an *outward* symbol of an inward cleansing. It doesn't affect one's salvation at all. In our tradition, we like to take a little time. Have the person mature until he or she can make a reasoned, adult decision. We have had problems with young people who were baptized too quickly only to realize they weren't converted at all."

This sounded fine to me as long as he said so.

I appreciated his kindness and the fact he'd made a special stop to see me. But I didn't say anything lest I embarrass myself further. The cascade of tears was sufficient already.

"Once you're around sixteen," he told me, "you can ask to join instruction class. Okay?"

I nodded and he left. I don't think I said a single word the whole time.

That fall, since I was through with my schooling, Dad informed me the time had arrived to begin working. Not that I hadn't worked before, but now it would be full-time. This would mean no time during the day for mountain excursions or shooting pests in the mango orchard. I was not thrilled, to say the least. I showed up at the shop the next morning like I was supposed to. We started work around eight. Emil Helmuth still worked full-time for Dad back then, so there were three of us *gringos* in the shop. I quickly learned to plug my ears with tissue paper to avoid the pain of the shop noise, something neither Dad nor Emil ever did. They allowed the full volume of the motor and the clanging of metal to enter their ears at will. I figured it was a wonder they could hear at all.

Each day trucks rolled down the lane. Mostly lumber vehicles in various states of disrepair. The wealthier sawmill owners also brought in their pickups. They'd quickly learned of Dad's superior workmanship and quality over the shops in the capital. Besides, who wanted to endure that four-hour road trip?

Dad's tools in the shop included a band saw—a tool I'd already learned to use. Also an iron bender, twelve-inch grinder, drill press, metal pressing bench, keyway cutter, and an assortment of hand tools. A large metal table provided a working area to the rear and to the right of the shop.

Dad, believing that repetition was the key to learning, assigned me to the wheel rim department. There were stacks of them in the corner of the shop. It was a task neither Dad nor Emil liked or were behind on. Honduran roads were a rough lot, creating a lot of wear and tear on everything, especially on the wheel rims of trucks. The bolt holes would become so worn they'd increase in size until they were dangerous to use. Rather than throw the rims away, the current worn holes were filled with a metal plug, welded shut, ground off smooth, and new holes were drilled between the old ones.

This became my job. I cut, and welded, and ground, and drilled, working through an endless stack of rims. Week after week I came into the house in the evenings with my chest burned red from the heat of the welding rod. I showed Mom my wounds as evidence of my new accomplishments.

Eventually, either from lack of worn rims or because Dad figured I was now qualified for other things, I was given more complicated tasks. Most involved welding. I soon learned not to carry both the positive and negative welding cables at the same time when moving from one spot to the other. Emil and Dad laughed themselves silly over the little predicament I found myself in one day.

I'd headed across the concrete floor, carrying both of my welder cables to save time. The dial for the voltage on the welder could be adjusted, depending on what rod I was using to weld. I had it at around 120 to 130 volts that day.

I always wore leather gloves, but that didn't serve as enough protection apparently. Halfway across the floor, the negative and positive currents connected using my body as the conduit. The result was complete immobilization. I stood there with my arms arched out on each side, unable to let go of the cables. It was like a continuous tingling sensation. A strong, constant pulsating current running from one arm to the other through my shoulders.

But I could still yell. "Turn off the welder!" I hollered over the ever-present roar in the shop.

Emil didn't look my way and neither did Dad.

I yelled louder. "Turn off the welder!"

Dad finally glanced up from the lathe, a puzzled look on his face. I must have appeared before his eyes like a jack-in-the-box with its lid freshly pulled.

"Turn off the welder!" I yelled again.

Comprehension crept across Dad's face, but he was obviously still not understanding everything. Leaving the lathe he ran across the floor and threw the switch. Blessed relief came instantly, and I dropped the cables to the floor.

Emil must have noticed Dad's rush toward the welder because he came over now. The two gathered around me with worried looks as they rubbed my arms. After a while, I flexed my arms a few times and took a few steps. Everything still worked.

That was when the laughter started—and continued for a good long while. Dad would be working hours later, sober-faced and intent. When he paused for a moment, he'd look over at Emil, and the whole laughter thing would start up again.

Oh well. They hadn't been the ones fastened to the welder cables with a solid current of electricity pulsating through their bodies. I did notice that Emil took extra care for awhile whenever he carried his cables around.

Every noon hour, Dad shut down his shop for the lunch break. One day, while we were inside the house eating, we noticed a young boy who often brought small items to the shop for repair go racing past.

The first few times no one thought anything about it. His father was well-known to Dad, and perhaps he needed to return home suddenly. But when it kept happening, Dad became suspicious. A thorough search of the shop revealed dust disturbed on a little ledge in the engine room. Apparently the little fellow had been instructed to hide there. And when we went inside to eat, he was to lift a small amount of money from the cash register and sneak out. The boy was hoping we wouldn't miss it, I suppose. He'd lock the shop door behind him, and then go racing down the lane.

Our first thought was to set elaborate traps over the next few lunch hours and confront the lad. But Dad thought better of it.

Confrontation with Honduran thieves didn't always produce pleasant results. Instead we made sure the boy was well watched the next time he arrived, and we escorted him outside before shutting down for lunch. The obvious message was sent: The gig was up. No hard feelings were incurred on either side.

Chapter 36

Uncle Mark, who was usually the leader in harebrained ideas, came up with another one that summer. He would raft down the Patuca River, located in the Province of Olancho east of us. This river meanders around the wilds of Honduras, eventually emptying into the Caribbean Sea on the northern Honduras coast. The Patuca wasn't exactly of Mississippi River size, but it was big enough to raft on. It was also reported to contain some vicious rapids.

David Peachey and Emil Helmuth eagerly signed up for the adventure. The three consulted what local lore there was, pored over the maps, and were sure everything would work out fine. The river enters the vast eastern Honduras jungle, whereupon the men knew they would lose contact with civilization. That was part of the excitement. Guides were necessary, they decided, and so one was found—a local named Manuel, who professed great familiarity with the river's temperament and meanderings.

The party arrived at the river, well-stocked with supplies and ready to make their own raft Huckleberry Finn style—by lashing logs together.

As they pushed the contraption into the water, they watched it sink nearly to the top of the logs. There it was, bobbing up and down low in the water without people on it, daring them, it seemed, to crawl on board.

Should they continue? They looked at each other, finally verbalizing the question. But there was no turning back. Things would somehow work out. So one of them jumped on and bounced around.

"See!" he said. "It's not sinking in any deeper."

Encouraged, the others climbed on and strapped their supplies to the middle of the raft. They set out down the river. Things went peaceful enough for awhile. The river was smooth, and they were still in a slightly populated area. They camped for the night without mishap. They then picked up a waiting Mennonite couple, Wilmer and Miriam Dagan, who were scheduled to join them at a specific meeting place.

I have no idea how everyone fit on the raft. I've seen pictures of it, and it was about ten by fourteen at the largest. How they managed with all the men, let alone a woman, on board is anyone's guess. The trip continued smoothly for awhile, they claimed. Monkeys showed up in the trees as the jungle started closing in. An abundance of iguanas appeared, which they shot for meat.

The first day of rapids was enough for the Mennonite couple. Miriam was left behind on a rock after the raft got stuck, and she couldn't make it back on in time. Wilmer was thrown off from another impact, and the couple was soon joined in the river by both Uncle Mark and Manuel the guide. Eventually the remaining passengers cleared the rapids and made shore to wait for everyone to catch up.

When everyone had gathered, Wilmer and Miriam decided to turn back. The others, undaunted, vowed to press on. And like the Amish do, they prayed and cast about for some way of helping themselves. The occasion for self-help came after a short stop at the jungle community of New Palestine, a communal place that had been founded by two Catholic priests. As was done in the days of early Christianity, the community held all goods in common, a practice followed in the Anabaptist tradition by the Hutterites. Though the Amish people don't follow the tradition themselves, they find no end of fascination with anyone who does, so the rafting group had to visit the community.

What they found appeared prosperous enough. Over 100 people living quite peacefully in the middle of nowhere. Their belief, also from the Bible, was that if anyone didn't work, he didn't eat. With that rule in force, some of the community had left, but most had stayed.

Here the rafters obtained the first improvement for their journey—paddles of some sort. They proved far superior to the poles they'd been using. So armed, the journey continued. Perhaps nervous over the experience of the rapids encountered so far, the suggestion was made to hire another guide. All hands on board seconded the motion.

A young boy, Fernando, who claimed he knew the river, was hired for the measly salary of three lempiras and a way back home.

Skeptical over any claims of river knowledge from guides after Manuel's pitiful performance at the first rapids, Uncle Mark watched the two carefully as they approached the next roar ahead of them. Who would be in charge? Would Fernando be any better than Manuel?

Oblivious to Uncle Mark's scrutiny, Fernando took charge. Even though he was the youngest, he gave directions at the point where the river split. He warned, "Stay on this side. Don't go down there."

As they swept down the river, Uncle Mark looked over on the other side and saw huge rocks. Untold damage would have been done had they gone that way. He whispered his thanks to the Lord for guidance in hiring this young man. Uncle Mark also hung on.

One night, deep in the jungle, they made camp. None of them knew where their location was or how they would get out in case of an emergency. Uncle Mark said they watched the moon hanging over the treetops, shining down on them before slowly setting. They didn't think twice about the moon setting at the time, but it became a point of great interest when, sometime later, the moon was seen rising again as plain as day. Hadn't they just watched it set? Yes, they had. They stared at the sight but couldn't come up with a logical explanation. They finally figured maybe they were too tired or had seen too many rapids. Still puzzled the next morning, they wrote it off as one of those things that can't be explained, easy enough to believe in the wild country they were in.

The native Indians of Honduras were the first signs of civilization to appear again. They were more afraid of this raft full of bearded Amish men than the Amish were of them. The natives told them the worst of the rapids were behind them. Armed with this news, they began traveling nights to make better time since they were already long overdue. The folks back home would be worried.

I never could comprehend how Uncle Mark knew there would be airplane service back to the capital from the northern coast of Honduras, but there was. After they arrived at the coast, a flight was booked to Tegucigalpa. From there the men followed the familiar dusty route home, arriving at the community after dark.

Emil was the first to split off from the trio at the junction on Turk Road, heading toward his house in La Granja. Uncle Mark and David walked together up to the children's home, and then Uncle Mark split off and went around the lane on the pond side.

Uncle Mark claimed later he heard the guffaws all the way across the field that were elicited when David walked in on his children. I guess none of the men were aware how hairy and dirty they'd become on their adventure into the jungle—and smelly.

Emil and David proclaimed the trip well worth the effort, but they also vowed to stay home for awhile. Uncle Mark laughed. He would soon be on the road again, he said. Off to somewhere.

One evening we all gathered in Stephen Stoll's former basement, which Cousin Ira still rented. Uncle Joe's family, Uncle Alva, the Martins, Grandmother Stoll, and all of us were there as Uncle Mark held forth on the adventure of floating down the Patuca River.

⌒~⌒

That same year the Catholic priests were doing more than starting communities like New Palestine. There were also agitators among the priesthood who stirred the poor farmers in Olancho to a fever pitch, turning them into land grabbers known in the country as *campesinos*. Idle land owned by the rich ranchers was seized and squatter huts built, all with the blessings of the Catholic Church.

Uncle Joe reported being given a pamphlet on the subject that was circulating in underground fashion by the agitators. He said it was well written and contained considerable Scriptures. Obviously the Catholic priests felt themselves justified in their actions. The only recourse available to the ranchers was to call in soldiers from the capital. The soldiers then routed the *campesinos* from the land. In one case, this resulted in a gun battle that left dead on both sides. Eventually the soldiers had to leave, and the *campesinos* returned to occupy the land again.

Frustration and fear ran high. Fausto told me that *La Mansion*, where Elsa's father still lived, was under threat of attack. Most of the *La Mansion* ranch was in grassland with cattle on it. So whether the land was in use apparently wasn't always included in the calculations on where to occupy next. Lying near the town of Guaimaca, the ranch was apparently too tasty a target to pass up.

Rumors on the conflict swirled around the community. Truckloads of soldiers were seen passing by Bishop Monroe's store. The fighters were jammed into the back of the open beds with their guns sprouting skyward. The national papers soon carried stories of missing priests in Olancho. The main figures involved in the agitation couldn't be found, though their pickup was discovered abandoned and burned. Suspicion fell on a large ranch owner who had been the most vocal in expressing his hatred for the *campesinos* and their land seizures.

The rancher professed his innocence, but in Honduras you are always considered guilty, especially if you deny the charges. The rancher was taken into Tegucigalpa for "questioning," which usually means torture in that part of the world. The rancher soon confessed, whereupon bulldozers were brought in to check out the rancher's story. I was along with Dad on a trip into Olancho later and saw the dozers sitting there. They apparently had to dig deep, but eventually they did uncover the bodies of the murdered priests.

Chapter 37

In the months that followed the *campesino* trouble, Uncle Joe was still trying to bring peace between the increasingly hostile parties at church. Occasionally he came by the house to speak with Mom and Dad. Those were conversations which I wasn't privy to. Uncle Joe didn't believe in children being involved in church politics.

That didn't keep me from being interested or finding out at least the basics of what was going on. The big issues in the community at the time were tractor farming and the German language. I already knew about the German problem from Dad's quarrels with Danny Stoltzfus over the Sunday-morning singing, though Dad had largely abandoned that struggle since Spanish speaking had by now almost taken over at the services.

I didn't mind, since I could speak Spanish, but Bishop Monroe was trying for a compromise tailored for those who either hadn't or couldn't learn the language. The compromise was that a special German service was planned once a month. But even that was soon pushed to Sunday night. Uncle Joe, though, hadn't given up, and his hope of using German in the Sunday-morning services never quite died out.

I also heard mutterings around the house from Mom. She reported seeing women from La Granja going about the community without their *haulsduch* on. This was an outer piece of cloth that draped over the upper body of a woman's dress. This was not part of *Englisha*-made dresses, but it gave extra protection from prying eyes. Mom said she'd approached the women because she was outraged by this flagrant disregard of modesty, only to be rebuffed with lectures on liberty and Christian charity.

On my part, I feared having to leave Honduras more than anything. I knew that might be the result if things continued as they were. My church loyalties weren't deep, though I was definitely on Mom, Dad, and Uncle Joe's side. It didn't hurt that the other side seemed to reside primarily over in La Granja, where I still had memories of Daniel and his cousin Paul's school days antics.

Finally Uncle Joe wrote a letter to the three ministers: Bishop Monroe and Ministers Vernon and Richard. Dad signed on, as did most of the others who had concerns. It was a sizable number of the community's members. The result was that Bishop Monroe did more of his neutral dance, professing sympathy for both sides. Somehow they could all work together if they just tried harder. And there was return fire from the other side, justified in some cases. The emotions stirred Bishop Monroe deeply.

Dad caught most of the incoming missiles due to his shop, which had indeed been modernized well beyond most Amish *ordnung* standards stateside. Being a true man of action, Dad at once made offers to amend the situation. He would gladly sell his shop, he said, if that would help. He even had a standing offer in hand for a sale, he claimed. His overture was rejected. His shop wasn't the real reason for the problems.

By November of 1975, Uncle Joe said he'd had enough. His family was leaving. Still, hope lingered in the air. In the meantime, Uncle Joe kept on working his farm. Even if he were leaving, the move would take some time. Perhaps something would happen before then. Some miracle that would change everything.

I, for one, wished for it with all my heart.

～～

During this time, I was struggling with my new life as a Christian, which included deep bouts of depression for reasons no one could understand, least of all me. The confessions I'd made to Rosa Sanchez for her chickens and my arrogant attitude to Danny Stoltzfus no longer seemed sufficient repentance. I was still haunted with unrelenting and persistent guilt for the slightest error or slipup.

I was welding in the shop one morning when Emil asked me how I was doing. A normal morning greeting. "Fine," I said, not thinking twice about it. But as soon as I said it, I realized I really wasn't fine. Should I tell Emil I have been struggling? I wondered. He was hard of hearing anyway, and with the horrendous racket in the shop I could imagine our shouted conversation. Emil leaning toward me—trying to hear. Me—trying to do a stammering shout. This wasn't exactly an insight that warmed my heart. So I kept on working and agonizing for hours. Had I lied in saying I was fine? Was I putting my potential embarrassment up as an excuse not to say anything? I ended the day by not speaking up, held back mostly by my instinct that something wasn't right here. These urgings didn't feel at all like the impulses that moved me to confess before. Then there had been no doubt. I'd been filled with certainty that the confessions *needed* to be made. And in the end I'd felt humiliated but clean.

I knew that any shouted stammering to Emil wouldn't produce the same thing. These might be a charge of insanity, but not a feeling of cleanness.

The same thing happened one other time. I did something wrong that involved another person. The result was crushing guilt. To resolve it, should I or should I not write and confess? For the other person's part, I knew it would simply be a matter of apologizing. I asked around for advice from those I dared. Mom didn't really know, but from others and the sermons at church, the advice leaned heavily toward full confession of all minutia. When a person is trying to do right, it seems the pendulum swings fully to one side, helped on, I highly suspect, by the unseen tormentors on the other side. And that was what pulled me out of the depression more than anything. The certainty that this had become some sort of game. That no matter how many times I scored, the goalposts would be moved yet farther away.

I concluded that it didn't feel like this guilt came from God, who had pursued me with love. I've seen nothing since to persuade me otherwise. A conscience isn't a reliable barometer. It can be manipulated as well as seared.

From somewhere I obtained a copy of Hannah Whitall Smith's book *The Christian's Secret of a Happy Life*, which I devoured from cover to cover. It was the first theology book I'd ever read. I heard the call to remain faithful to the God who had called me and to the manner in which He had called me. I smiled at Smith's description of Christians who don't wish their heads removed in order to deal with their Christian headaches, but who don't know any other way out. They live with the headache. My Christianity certainly was giving me headaches, so I eagerly read on for whatever advice she would offer. Her message was simple enough. I was to give my burden to the Lord, and I was to fully depend on His sufficiency.

In one chapter she tells of a weary traveler who is offered a lift by a passing wagon, which he cheerfully accepts. Soon, though, the driver is perplexed as the traveler, now seated in the wagon, still has his luggage hanging over his shoulder.

"Why don't you set it down?" the driver asked.

To which the traveler responds, "I don't want your wagon carrying everything."

That message was clear enough! Rest in God while He is carrying you.

In Smith's book, the life of God was also clearly set forth as something we were given, not something we attain ourselves. This agreed with what I was hearing at the church house and with my own experience. I had not gone looking for God; He had come looking for me. Mrs. Smith held up faith over feelings by pointing out the many ways feelings can be misleading. Her words were water to my thirsty soul as I searched for truth through the torrents of emotions I was often overwhelmed with.

By believing comes certainty, she said. Not by feeling. And to believe, a person must know what God has said.

Mrs. Smith quoted Francois Fenelon, someone I'd never heard of, but I sure liked the quote: "True religion resides in the will alone."

Feelings, I read, follow the will. With that knowledge, I was determined to proceed forward in my Christian life.

I would quote Smith for years to come on the subject of guidance. That first a person must come to a complete surrender to the will of God, followed by the four-legged stool of the Scriptures, the advice of others, personal leading, and providential circumstances.

Mom noticed a marked difference in my attitude and wondered what was making the change. I told her it was the book I'd just read, mentioning the title and author's name. She asked me a few questions about what I'd learned and seemed satisfied with my answers.

I wasn't fully aware until years later the gift I had been given. That book, falling into my hands at that time, was a great blessing. It would affect in so many ways how I came to view the Christian life. And when years later I stumbled onto C.S. Lewis and George MacDonald, it was like coming home to the familiar.

Chapter 38

Isidro Gallo was a local man who lived near the end of our lane. I saw him a few times a week, mostly from a distance. He owned a nice house and considerable land for a native. We called him by his last name, Gallo, which in Spanish means "rooster." The name was perfect for him. The man strutted up and down the road like one of the roosters in his yard.

Gallo was hardworking. He grew produce across the river and picked up a lot about farming from watching what the Amish did. He learned our irrigation techniques and found seed lines we used. In his own way, Gallo was well-educated. He was always friendly to me, although I didn't have much in-depth contact with him. I could see his produce patch across the river when we tended the river bottom of Uncle Stephen's old farm, but Gallo rarely made a peep in our direction.

He wasn't a neighborly man...until he started showing up more often at Uncle Joe's. It seems Gallo's interest had expanded beyond learning Amish farming methods. His interest now included Uncle Joe's eldest daughter, Rosanna.

The fact became apparent to Uncle Joe when Gallo's business encounters with the family not only increased, but began to move far beyond that. It seemed like he was looking for every excuse possible to stop by and help out wherever he could. He even took to doing guard tours on Uncle Joe's farm every night, especially after midnight when the thieves were reputed to be the busiest. Gallo made sure that Uncle Joe's household was aware each night of his kindly ministrations.

However, one night his oversight took an odd turn. When Gallo arrived on his usual rounds, he was staggering drunk. His antics woke up Uncle Joe.

"Let me in!" he warbled, beating on the outside of the house with his machete. "I'm in love...so in love with your daughter."

"You're not coming in!" Uncle Joe told him from inside, astonished at this turn of events. "You're drunk. Now go home."

"I want in!" Gallo insisted, growing even angrier. "Don't you think I'm good enough? Is that the problem?"

"That's not true," Uncle Joe said. "We like you just fine. You just aren't getting my daughter."

Gallo charged the house and the door, threatening to beat both down. Uncle Joe wasn't too worried. They'd been through this enough times with thieves trying to get in. The house was secure.

Notorious for his temper even when sober, Gallo launched at the house with bloodcurdling screams, keeping up the fuss for quite some time.

"I'm not drunk," he insisted. "I'm in love. Let me take her home right now. You *gringos* think you're really something. A high-and-mighty people who will not let your daughters marry us. What is wrong with you? You pretend to help people, but you won't help me now."

Uncle Joe soon gave up persuading Gallo, and since most of the family was up by now and not likely to sleep anytime soon, they gathered in the living room and sang hymns for awhile even as Gallo hollered and whooped it up outside.

Eventually someone came up with the idea of getting a blanket out to him in the hopes he'd take the hint and settle down for the night.

Perhaps with the coming of daylight, they told each other, and with the wearing off of the whiskey, sanity would return. Gallo was consulted through the window and agreed. Throw out a blanket, and he would settle down on the front porch.

But how to get the blanket out to him?

A blanket wouldn't fit through the slatted windows, and if they opened the front door, that would be the end of the matter. Gallo would come charging in.

A solution was finally arrived at. They would throw the blanket out the small escape hatch in the back of the house that was built as an emergency exit sometime earlier.

So the trapdoor was opened, and the blanket was thrown out. Gallo's machete came back in after them, thrust with full force. They slammed the trapdoor shut and hoped things would soon quiet down outside.

And it did for short intervals, during which Gallo would fall asleep... only to awaken and set forth on his rants again. The words always punctuated by his horrible screaming. The entire family was worn out by the time daylight arrived. But with the dawn came no relief. Gallo was now sound asleep on the front porch. He'd awakened long enough to make it known he still had designs on Rosanna, after which he nestled into the blanket again. The family stirred restlessly inside the house. There were chores on the farm that needed doing, and Gallo obviously had no plans to leave so they didn't dare venture outside.

Now enter Mom on the scene. Mom had awakened Dad in the night, making him aware of the horrendous screaming coming from the direction of Uncle Joe's house.

Like men tend to do, Dad assured her that the sound came from Guaimaca, misdirected by the winds, no doubt. Dad said there was nothing to worry about.

Now with the dawn appearing, Mom was on a scouting trip, determined to hunt down the source of the awful sounds she'd been hearing all night. She felt foolish now that the sun was shining as she came sheepishly over the last knoll in front of Uncle Joe's place. There was probably a perfectly good explanation, one they could all laugh about and chalk up to the eccentricity of the country.

As she climbed the hill to the house, her uneasiness returned. There was no activity going on anywhere. Uncle Joe's place was always crawling with people, especially early morning when the chores needed tending to. So where was everyone?

Gathering her courage, she approached the front door, stepping over a pile of blankets in the process. As she knocked, Gallo awakened and stuck his head out to see who had arrived. Mom turned to see his grizzled, unshaven face, peering at her from the porch floor. She screamed—piercing shrieks of sheer terror. Mom ran like she hadn't run in years. Gallo told me his side of the story later, bending over with laughter.

"Whish!" he told me, swinging his hand through the air. "Could your mother ever run!"

Arriving back at the house, now panting for breath, Mom got out what she'd seen.

Dad believed her and set off in the other direction for help, finding Cousin Ira and two locals to accompany him on a rescue mission. As the men approached the house, Gallo sauntered off in the other direction. Uncle Joe's family poured out of the house to begin their chores.

As the milking began down at the barn, they looked up in astonishment to see Gallo coming back with his milk container to collect his morning's supply as usual.

Conversation ensued. Apologies were made. And peace returned… at least Uncle Joe hoped so.

Gallo did keep his peace with Uncle Joe's family for the time being, but his antics didn't stop.

Emil Helmuth's family was awakened one night by the blowing of someone's foghorn over in La Granja. The horns were a crude alert system fashioned after Dad's siren at the shop. If someone came under threat during the night, he would blow his horn, hoping either to scare away the thieves or summon help. Emil was gone that night on a business trip, and neither his wife, Edna, nor his boys entertained any thoughts of venturing forth on a rescue mission for whomever was in trouble. They did start their generator though, flooding the yard with light. This was a system also fashioned after the one in Dad's shop since Emil worked there. Only Emil hadn't bothered installing a shut-off switch in the house like Dad. After the danger passed, Emil would have to walk outside to turn off the diesel by hand. Not the most desirable exercise on a dark Honduran night.

When the foghorn had died down and no danger seemed evident

outside, two of the boys ventured outside and succeeded in turning off the diesel. They made their way back to the house. En route, their flashlights caught an odd bump protruding from the top of a wagon bed. Further investigation revealed a sleeping man, whereupon their retreat back to the house turned into a rout.

They met Edna halfway there, on her way to lend any aid that might be required.

"Get back!" the boys wailed, horrified at this impediment in their path. A mother couldn't be left behind.

Urging her into a run, they stumbled inside and bolted the door behind them.

Now what to do with the man outside?

The first order of business was to fire up the diesel again. Then the now-awakened household watched Gallo as he stumbled around the yard, stone drunk again and sending screams piercing into the night.

Emil's household kept watch as Gallo circled around the house. He didn't attempt to enter. He then seemed to head for home, nearly falling into the deep ravine that ran between Emil's place and Bishop Monroe's.

Unbeknownst to Emil's household, several of Bishop Monroe's boys were already watching from the other side of the drawbridge that connected the two places. They held back until Gallo finally decided to move on, motivated no doubt by signs of a rescue party approaching from the other side of Turk Road.

The Peachey family had heard the commotion and sent out two males with bright flashlights. They now approached, spotted Gallo, and urged him to leave, kindly thinking that by lighting his path ahead of him they might help the poor man find his way home.

Instead, Gallo launched himself straight at the boys all the while letting fly with his unearthly screams. The boys took off in the other direction on a dead run, not stopping until they were back home and safely inside with the doors barred. The Helmuth family would have to fend for itself until daylight.

Gallo decided to continue on home once the bobbing flashlights of the retreating Peacheys were out of sight. Then Bishop Monroe's boys stirred up enough courage to come across the drawbridge to make sure the Helmuth family was okay.

Whether Gallo retained negative memories about this night could never be fully ascertained. When approached on the matter, he freely admitted that he'd been there, laughing his actions off as those of a man who was a little out of it but perfectly harmless. He'd gotten lost, he claimed, and was only looking for shelter for the night. It was all good.

That it wasn't all good was apparent to everyone except Gallo.

Another incident occurred soon afterward when Bishop Monroe approached Gallo in his potato fields. After a friendly greeting from Bishop Monroe, Gallo simply exploded and began running toward Bishop Monroe with his machete waving.

With the machete swipes coming within inches of his chest, Bishop Monroe retreated beyond the gate.

"Let that be a lesson to you!" Gallo said in finality.

What the lesson was supposed to be wasn't very clear.

Eventually things flared up again at Uncle Joe's. There was a big ruckus one evening down at their place, and someone came running up the hill to let us know. We all went down to watch, walking as close to the house as we dared. There Gallo was prancing around outside with his machete, in broad daylight this time, holding the family hostage again.

This went on for an hour or so until the police from Guaimaca arrived in their pickup truck. I have no idea who drove into town to call them because it wasn't us. Perhaps Fausto, if I had to guess. He'd probably run down to flag a ride by the road.

Upon seeing the truckload of police approach, Gallo hightailed it toward the river, made it across, and disappeared into the underbrush. The police asked a few questions of Uncle Joe, and we meandered on down to offer what consolation we could.

All of a sudden a shout went up: "There he goes!"

Sure enough. Gallo was making a break for it below his house. I have no idea why. The police wouldn't have bothered looking for him in the underbrush by the river. Now the hounds had sight of their prey. The truck roared to life, and the police all piled in. They easily caught the running man before he could cross the main road to find refuge in the foothills. The truck stopped in a cloud of dust. The men jumped off and proceeded to beat Gallo to the ground with their rifle butts.

That was another reason besides their pacifist convictions the Amish didn't like involving the police. People seemed to get hurt without justification.

They threw Gallo into the back of the pickup truck like a sack of feed and took off. A week or so later, Gallo was back home much subdued. We never heard what happened during that time, but that was the end of our troubles with him. So I guess the Honduran version of justice was not without its benefits.

Chapter 39

In February of 1976, a 7.5 earthquake struck Guatemala near the capital, the worst such incident in Guatemala since 1917. Newspapers estimated the death toll at 23,000, and most of the adobe-type homes in the Guatemala City area were demolished. The quake lay along the Motagua fault, and aerial sightings would soon show a break along the surface running for a hundred miles.

When the news arrived in the Amish community, a meeting was called to plan a response. By then the heart had gone out of Amish mission ventures. Only three men were dispatched to Guatemala, and they were given the instruction that aid should be limited.

At the same time, as if he were taking lessons from the earthquake, Bishop Monroe chose to release his own tremor, which caused a spiritual rattling and shaking. I'm sure Bishop Monroe did what he thought was best, making what he considered a bold move that would satisfy the liberal side and thus show his good faith intentions. And too, he must have figured the conservatives would eventually get over it. Because, after all, his decision involved only bicycles.

Liberals and conservatives had been forming increasingly clear lines in the community, but no one wanted to leave over the differences. Too much was at stake. To a man, they enjoyed Honduras in spite of its obvious drawbacks of thievery and the problems in the church. The liberals asked for votes on the issues troubling them, no doubt feeling confident that their side would carry the day. The conservatives weren't objecting to the voting, at least not under the old way of doing things. The old way of voting required a unanimous vote before any changes could be made to the *ordnung*. The liberals wanted a simple up and down majority vote.

The problem was that a *unanimous* vote—or at least something very close to it—is the bedrock of Amish church politics. It's how they hold the line against drift. It's how they keep straying members in the fold. It's how they keep large, sentimental changes from happening. Either way the issue goes, there will always be someone who objects to the change, so the old way keeps change from happening. Or if change does happen, it happens very, very, slowly.

Bishop Monroe missed the cue entirely, falling for the emotional claptrap behind the push for a straight up or down majority rule. It's an old issue that percolates not just among the Amish. It's a much wider battle, reaching from the jungle tribes in Africa to modern nations. How does the majority rule without supplying some safeguards for the minority?

American democracy has never been, contrary to popular opinion, a pure 50/50 split. We elect representatives who then vote on our behalf during their prescribed terms. This removes decisions, at least in theory, from the passions of the moment. The congressional House functions on a 50/50 vote, but the Senate does not. They have the filibuster rule in place, where it takes a 60/40 vote to move most legislation. But even that's not the whole picture. Each state, whether large or small, sends in two senators. So in theory the 40 percent side of the vote could contain many senators from small states, which skews the results even further in terms of the popular vote. It could actually produce a split, where perhaps 20 percent of the population is holding up the wishes of the 80 percent.

And this system of protecting the minority goes even further. In presidential elections, states are assigned electoral votes based on their population. Once any candidate wins a majority of that state's votes, he is assigned that state's electoral votes but no more. The genius of the system is that it reduces the temptation for candidates to campaign only in states sympathetic to their cause.

If you had state A and state B, with equal size populations, and state C with a small population, under a straight 50/50 split, candidates would campaign primarily in either of the two large states. They would use the tactic of swelling their majorities to overwhelm state C.

With electoral votes assigned to each state: State A=5; State B=5; State C=1, State C is now in play. No matter how passionate the issue is in state A or B, their influence is no greater than the 5 electoral votes. So all candidates now have to visit state C to gain the one extra vote needed for a majority.

I'm sure Bishop Monroe wasn't fully aware of this complicated matter. It probably looked simple enough to him. How was it fair that over half the church should be held back by the minority? So the unanimous vote—the old way—was to be discontinued. A meeting was called, and it was simply announced. The ministers were all in agreement, Bishop Monroe said. And bicycles, one of the festering issues nearest the surface, were now allowed. Just like that.

I'd been aware of the push for bicycles for some time—as far back as my school days when Paul Schmucker had written a research project on bicycles. It had really been a clandestine effort to extol the virtues of bicycle riding. The article was all about the efficiency of man-powered equipment, its environmentally friendly nature, and its peaceful operation.

I got the message and was persuaded. I made no secret to Mom and Dad of my desire to own a bicycle. I even had one in town on standby. The bicycle was for sale if we were ever allowed to own one. But so far there had been opposition from the conservative Aylmer contingent.

Many of the Amish, especially those from Northern Indiana, came from communities that allowed bicycles. That may have played a large part in Bishop Monroe's reasons for overriding the dug-in conservatives. He failed to calculate the forces he would unleash.

First, there was the spiritual shock that was still sinking in after the stunned conservatives had gone home. Then within days, the community was filled with bicycle riding young boys—me among the lot. Mom and Dad, for whatever their reasons, went with the flow on this one. We went about whooping it up with our newfound freedom and creating an awful racket by blowing our horns and ringing our Honduran bicycle bells.

Cousin Ira and Uncle Mark accosted me at once and let it be known that this nonsense would be stopped. And within days, the rest of the horn blowing and ringing bells had been silenced. The Stolls weren't able to buck Bishop Monroe, but they knew how to take horns and bells off bicycles.

Uncle Joe, I'm sure, understood the deeper implications of the controversy. Without the unanimous vote, there would be no chance of keeping further changes out of the church. Any such proposals would simply need to gain the sympathy of the majority, and it would be done. The line had been crossed, and the whole community was little better than a tree caught in the currents of whatever winds blew up the valley. If the people felt like it, they could change anything if they could get half of the people plus one to agree to it. Today it could be this, and tomorrow it could be another thing. This was a prospect not acceptable to Uncle Joe.

The Amish firmly believe that it's not possible to practice and maintain truly biblical Christianity in today's culture. The Amish vision is simplicity itself. Freeze things at some point in the past, and so preserve the benefits of that time. They believe that the culture of 200 years ago had much to do with the mindset of that culture. Horses and buggies are really incidental. At stake is the best way to live out the practical applications of scriptural Christian living.

Women way back then generally wore some form of headdress. The general culture dressed modestly. Divorce was minimal or unknown. Young people didn't need chastity pledges to stay virgins until marriage. There were, of course, exceptions, but very few.

Children were raised by parents, not by their grandparents. Older people were respected and taken care of by their relatives. Community was a priority. People belonged to each other. This attitude and willingness of prior generations to live scriptural teachings, which even when known today are largely ignored, is the essence of the Amish vision.

Of course, nothing and no one are perfect.

The Amish are aware of the corruption that has crept into their older communities, and of the loss of their vision in those cases. It's the impetus behind many of the younger communities being founded. But it's also the experience of failed communities like ours—the mistakes that were made, the impossibilities revealed—that drives them to hesitate about missions and often to draw back from any attempted improvements. It's a difficult task, this balancing act they face. Their own thinkers struggle long and hard with the issue. How do you maintain a vibrant inner spiritual life while preserving the outer shell that gives shelter to that life?

So the bicycles raced around the community, and the ground shook and trembled from the aftershocks. Not unexpectedly, many of the community's members were soon deep into plans for a soon departure, including Mom and Dad.

I ignored the tumult the best I could, comforting myself with my new bicycle.

Into this charged atmosphere, Bishop Monroe appeared with a bold proposal. They needed a new minister, and he wanted to ordain one.

Where that idea came from, I have no clue. But looking back, the sheer magnitude of the proposal boggles my mind. Either Bishop Monroe had his head deep in the sand or he had great confidence in his own political brinkmanship. But the question that really fascinates me is why the conservatives agreed to this. Every single one of them, to a person, okayed the idea.

It couldn't have been because they hoped things would change. They'd already given up on the community. Most of them had plans to leave. And yet I wonder if it wasn't hope anyway. A whisper. A dream that perhaps a miracle could yet happen.

The influence of a minister was considerable. And what if they had one of their own in the power structure? That was an objective they had failed at so far. Would this turn the tide? Or at least slow things down to a manageable rate of change?

On the liberals' part, they simply found it unimaginable that God wouldn't be on their side and elect one of their own. I know because I heard their comments to that effect.

So a vote for a minister was agreed to. The date for the ordination was set for April. Five men were in the lot. Two of them liberals: David Peachey and Danny Stoltzfus. A neutral vote was Emil Helmuth. The two conservatives were Uncle Joe and Uncle John Martin.

When the time came for Bishop Monroe to open the books, the worst possible candidate—from the liberals' point of view—had the slip of paper: Uncle John Martin. The man could hardly speak Spanish, and he was a staunch conservative without any of Uncle Joe's diplomatic skills. The hammer had fallen hard, and conservative hopes soared. They now had their man on the bench. And a strong one at that. Or so they thought.

The liberals left the church house unable to comprehend this turn of events. This couldn't possibly be from God. So they acted like it wasn't. They pushed the new minister to learn Spanish quickly. They harassed him for his uncouth ways. They told him he needed to involve himself in outreach and mission work.

It's one of the mysteries of politics that those on the side of law and order usually fail to push their advantage, even when they win. Why do decent people have such a hard time closing the deal? Instead, they rely heavily on the virtue of their stand, shunning the gritty politics of consolidating power.

Much could have been made of this issue, both with spoken and spiritual bludgeoning. If God ordained a man who couldn't speak Spanish, then perhaps He wanted more sermons preached in German? If God ordained a man without mission skills, then perhaps He wanted more ministry given to the established saints? But none of this was done. And it soon became apparent that nothing was going to change. Minister Martin looked like a fish out of water on Sunday mornings, haltingly giving his Spanish sermons, agony on his face.

He looked subordinate and acted subordinate. To the liberals, that was, of course, the proper position for a conservative. He was a man who needed to learn their ways.

Chapter 40

While choosing the new minister was going on, Uncle Mark was planning his last hurrah before his wedding. He would take another trip or bust. This time he would travel by public transportation for most of the way down to the tip of South America. He said it looked like the Pan-American Highway was the best route to follow. It ran through the capital of Honduras and clear down to the tip of Chile and Argentina. The highway construction had been supported and financed by the United States in the 1940s and 1950s. Sure there were still some gaps not completed, he said, but nothing that couldn't be gotten around. The scenery would vary, he was told, from lush jungle to cold mountain passes of up to 15,000 feet in elevation. Some places were not passable during the rainy season.

Uncle Mark asked around for fellow travelers, but this time—after the Patuca River ruckus—there were no takers. He would be on his own. And so he set out in August. A few letters dribbled back at first and then nothing. Silence. Almost two months had gone by, and the whole community was in a stir. Deeply so in some quarters. Over in La Granja, Dora Miller had been busy with her wedding plans, and now Uncle Mark had disappeared. Their planned wedding date was in January.

One of Uncle Mark's planned stops was known to be the Mennonite community in Paraguay, but there was no way to contact the Paraguay folks by telephone, and mail was much too slow at this point. A telegram was considered but not tried. Who would they send it to?

Besides, Uncle Mark had probably already passed through there by now.

Uncle Mark solved the problem by walking in late one evening. He was surprised at both the concern and gladness expressed by the first people who saw him. They asked where he'd been. Uncle Mark responded by saying he'd been held up a little longer coming home than planned, but he'd written all about it in his letters.

When his greeters informed him the letters had not arrived and that Dora was sick with worry, Uncle Mark hightailed it for the far corner of La Granja to reassure his future bride.

What I was interested in was Uncle Mark's tale of his travels when he held forth at the family gathering in Cousin Ira's rented basement.

On the way south he'd stayed on the west side of the Andes, taking in some Inca ruins along the way. I can't remember their name, but they may have been at Ingapuca, just a little off of the Pan-American Highway near the town of Cuenca. These ruins are in southern Ecuador, near where Uncle Mark would have passed. They take up nearly 240 square kilometers of populated area and would have served as a magnet to someone like my uncle. For years those ruins had been uncared for, and the stones had been taken and used for the construction of present-day homes. Placed under historical care after 1919, many of the sites have been reconstructed and are now open to the public.

Uncle Mark loved Peru, he said, where the lower part of the country is irrigated by the far western tributaries of the Amazon. Here the Andes Mountains exceed 20,000 feet, leading up to the ruins of Machu Picchu and Lake Titicaca, the world's highest navigable lake.

He'd gone down to the tip of Chile to see the ocean before swinging over the mountains and north again on the Argentina side. The Southern Cross had been an awesome sight, he said. The constellation obviously visible every clear night, hanging high in the sky. (From the brief glimpses I've obtained of the Southern Cross in the summer, I would have given a lot to see the display in all its glory.)

Uncle Mark had stopped in at the Beachy community in Paraguay, he said, which had failed to impress him. And neither had the country of Paraguay. It wasn't like Honduras—something about being hot, dry, and dusty. And the Beachy community was a great disappointment after he'd entertained high expectations of seeing good things at another mission project run by Amish-related people. Perhaps he thought the Beachys would be making a better go of it, even as he watched the Amish failure in Guaimaca winding down. The Beachy community was in a discouraged state mentally and physically, he said. From the talk he heard, thieving seemed even a worse problem than in our community. One of the founders of the community had either left or was speaking of returning to the States.

From Paraguay he visited some city high in the Andes. Again, I don't remember the name, but there is a city up there that fits the description he shared. La Paz is the highest city in the Andes mountain range. At 11,910 feet in elevation, it would have been a site Uncle Mark needed to see.

He told of coming down the mountain and missing his bus. With dusk fast falling, he didn't wish to stay for the night—not with the trouble he was experiencing breathing in the high altitude. So he went out to thumb a ride. The fellow who stopped was middle-aged and driving by himself in a BMW.

Just outside of town, as they started down the mountain, the man clutched the steering wheel and violently shook the car back and forth.

Was he in the car with a madman? Uncle Mark experienced some serious doubts about the wisdom of riding with this fellow. Should he perhaps attempt an emergency exit? Keeping quiet, Uncle Mark soon learned the reason for the violent shaking. Apparently the fellow was testing the vehicle for roadworthiness because he took off down the mountain road going at least seventy miles an hour. Uncle Mark was unable to see the speedometer, being too busy hanging on, so he could only guess. Down mountain they went, the curves taken by driving randomly on either side of the road with tires squealing. Apparently no one came up the mountain that late in the evening. Somehow they made it down safely, but it had been quite some ride.

Going back to public transportation, Uncle Mark left Bolivia and traveled toward Brazil, expecting the Portuguese language to sound something like Spanish. But it didn't. He was unable to communicate

in that huge country. His eyes grew large as he tried to express the vast-
ness. To give us some idea he said the equator passed through Brazil.
And yet the distance of the land mass in Brazil, lying south of the equator, was greater than the distance between the equator and Honduras.

Other than his letters being lost, he said there had been no problems really.

Dora, smiling sweetly beside him, didn't look all that convinced.

It sounded like a grand adventure to me, and one I would have liked
to have been part of.

Uncle Joe now had one last thing he wished to accomplish before
retreating to Aylmer: a trip to Europe to research Anabaptist history
in Zurich, Switzerland, the town that was the birthplace of the faith.

Traveling by airplane is the preferred modern method, as passen-
ger ships no longer sail there that I'm aware of. And Uncle Joe needed
to go before his airplane access was removed, which it likely would
be. Enraged by the tales coming out of Honduras, the activist Amish
community in Aylmer had already taken steps to seal off the gangrene.
Their members, present and future, were now forbidden to use airplane
travel for any purpose. Never again would that community play any
part in an Amish mission outreach—especially a foreign one.

Uncle Joe's window of airplane travel was closing fast, so he asked
Dad to go along for the trip. Dad gladly accepted.

The two flew into Zurich and contacted some Mennonite fellow
Uncle Joe knew. The Mennonite drove them around town to see historical sites related to the beginning of the Anabaptist movement. They
got to see the river in the old city where Felix Manz was put to death by
drowning for his belief in adult baptism. They visited the church where
Ulrich Zwingli, a priest who operated separately from Martin Luther,
thundered forth his sermons. But Zwingli also believed the Anabaptists went too far regarding adult baptism, so he persecuted them. Then
Uncle Joe and Dad wandered down the side streets to visit Zwingli's
parsonage. But most important to them, they also saw the house where
the first Anabaptist converts had been baptized.

Uncle Joe spent considerable time researching old Anabaptist documents in Zurich and Berne. Dad had no interest in such research.

One evening at the supper table of their Mennonite host, a visitor arrived to meet the travelers from the States. Their host bounced up to welcome his friend, introducing Uncle Joe as the scholar who *hat zwei Bücher geschrieben.*

Dad was mortified, he claimed, because he was introduced simply by his name. There was no written book authored by him, let alone two as the host had just mentioned. But Dad didn't seem permanently wounded by the experience as he related the tale back at the church in Honduras with quite good humor.

Another highlight of their trip was a visit to a cave in the countryside. The place had once been used as a hiding place by Anabaptists in the sixteenth century. Here they could hold their meetings without being discovered by the authorities. The site is now preserved by the state and known as *Tauferhohle.* It is also the cave popularized by Christmas Carol Kauffman in her fictional work *Not Regina.* Uncle Joe and Dad took off their hats and sang the first stanza of that staple of Amish Sunday-morning church services *Da Lob Lied* when they were there.

On Sunday they visited the only remaining Mennonite church in the area, now so liberal it has joined the state church again, primarily to escape taxation. No doubt the church members were worn down from centuries of abuse. Dad spoke of the disconcerting experience of hearing a sermon in a liberal church, all of it spoken in real German—the holy tongue stateside—delivered by a minister in a suit and tie.

After they were finished in Switzerland, Uncle Joe, being the scholarly and sensitive type, wanted to see the tulips of Holland. Dad didn't think flowers worth the train trip, so they parted ways in Zurich. Dad flew straight home while Uncle Joe left by train. He would fly out of Holland for his return trip.

Chapter 41

At home in the Honduras community, things were winding down and yet going on at the same time. Some things even started anew. In the spring of 1977, I joined the instruction class with plans to be baptized in the summer. We met every other Sunday morning, walking out single file with the ministers after the church service began. This mirrored the format used by all Amish baptismal classes stateside. On the top of the hillside, benches were set up with the ministers on one side and applicants on the other. With the gentle morning wind blowing across our faces, we listened to Bishop Monroe read the eighteen articles of Amish faith.

After the assigned lesson had been read, there was time for additional comments by any of the ministers, either on the lesson or any instruction they wished to give. Bishop Monroe took these opportunities to quiz all of us on whether we'd actually been born again. He repeatedly asked if our conversion had been real or if we were we simply attending the class because it was the thing to do.

All of us kept insisting we had been born again.

Eventually Bishop Monroe offered some explanation as to why he was drilling us so intensely—something about past applicants who had slipped through and been baptized, only to discover later they hadn't experienced a true conversion. It even sounded as if he might be referring to classes he'd personally taught, but no names were mentioned.

I didn't doubt the sincerity of his motives, as I decidedly liked the man by then. But his questioning did produce considerable anxiety for me. Was I or wasn't I converted? And what did conversion consist of? Was it a specific action? Was it something tangible? Did someone have to vouch for me? It was quite a dilemma for me, even as I kept insisting Sunday mornings that I was converted. I still wondered, although I wasn't exactly doubting. I knew my experience had been real, but I was scared. What if I was wrong? What if my experience had been something other than being born again?

Enter Danny Stoltzfus, who invited me down to his place to share my testimony.

Now I was really scared. No one had ever asked me for my testimony before. It wasn't that I didn't know what to say, it was more along the lines of *how* to say it. And to have to say it to Danny, of all people. He was last person I wanted to be humiliated in front of.

But this ritual—that of inviting members of the community to quiz all applicants prior to their baptism—was one of Bishop Monroe's well-known traditions. So I made my way up to the children's home. Danny invited me in. We didn't sit down that I can remember, and he didn't smile much of a welcome. He just repeated his desire to hear my testimony per Bishop Monroe's invitation.

We stood there in the living room, and I went through the stammering rendition of what I had to say. What I actually said, I haven't the slightest recollection. Danny waited until I was done. Still not smiling, he nodded and said, "Jerry, yours is one of the clearest conversions I've ever witnessed."

Just like that. Without preamble or introduction, he gave me my answer when I was least expecting it. And he was someone I knew had no reason to fudge the truth. I was stunned—and I still am. That God would go to the trouble of answering what I hadn't even asked because it was important that I know. And beyond that, God answered because He cares for me.

And I had nothing to give Him in return. Literally nothing. I couldn't even talk. That fact had been well-demonstrated moments before. But with the assurance God gave me through Danny, I would have gone anywhere and done anything God asked of me.

I made my vows of service to His cause. If there would have been papers to sign, I would have gladly signed. I determined I would be His servant. He had loved me when I was the most unlovable, and I loved Him in return.

On the Sunday before my baptism, Joseph Peachey invited me to accompany him on a trek on foot to San Marcos. There would be six of us in the party, he said, his brother Daniel and sister Rhoda, and my brother John and sister Susanna. We'd make a quick morning hike of it, and arrive in time for Sunday morning services that were being held at Minister Richard's place.

I'd been to San Marcos by horseback before, taking the back trails to stay off the main road. That shortened the distance considerably. But I'd never walked it, and I should have told Joseph no. We had horses and could easily have ridden them. But Joseph wanted to walk. Lots of other people had done so, he said. He wanted to arrive with his Sunday clothing unruffled or some such reason. And Alvin Miller did the trip in three hours all the time. So we allowed ourselves an extra hour and set forth.

It was one of the stupidest, dumbest adventures I've ever been involved in. Looking back it's as if I'd lost my mind. It was on a Sunday morning, so maybe that's why I thought none of the normal rules applied. We didn't even take along canteens. All dressed up in our Sunday shirts and shoes, we were planning to walk though miles of wilderness. *Dumb.* We left around five o'clock in the morning. Soon after dawn we trudged through Guaimaca and then went down to the river and crossed on some stones so we wouldn't damage our Sunday shoes. We headed up the road and into the wilderness.

Thirst soon became an acute problem, which we solved by detouring higher up the mountain until we found a small spring, making sure no huts lay beyond before drinking the water. As the morning wore on, the San Marcos Mountains seemed to come no closer. At least the brief glimpses we could catch of them through the foothills.

We didn't have to tell each other. We were hopelessly lost.

So we asked for directions from the people at the huts we came to. The answers were a general waving of the arms toward the San Marcos Mountains and assurances that the river wasn't far away.

Time dragged on. My nagging fear was that somehow we'd get stuck in these mountains and not find our way out in time for my baptism the next Sunday. I knew that was ridiculous, but that was the dark cloud hanging over me nonetheless.

We finally reached the river sometime after ten, when the services in San Marcos would have been well under way. We pressed on, taking off our shoes and rolling up our pant legs to wade across the river. In some places the depths came to our knees. We continued across and made our way up the main road to San Marcos exhausted and thoroughly discouraged.

We arrived at Minister Richard's house before twelve, but there was no sign of any church people around. That they had all left we could clearly tell. That we were not only late, but *really* late, was also apparent.

"Where have you been?" Minister Richard asked, looking grim.

"We got lost," Joseph told him.

Obviously Minister Richard had heard that excuse before.

"What time did you start out?"

"Five o'clock," he answered.

We all did the calculation in our mind, glancing up at the clock on the wall. That had been more than six hours ago. We were not *gringo* tenderfoots. Joseph and I were well versed in the culture and language and in the mountains—something Minister Richard was well aware of.

"Over six hours," he said, leaving the implication hanging. We were lying, and something was seriously amiss here.

I knew there was no answer. What had just happened had no logical explanation. I would have been the first to admit the fact. If it had been up to me, I would have offered no further justification. There was none to give. And my tail would have been fried. I knew it by the look on Minister Richard's face. Baptismal candidates are watched closely for signs of moral weakness and for evidence their conversion had been faked. And I had just raised valid suspicions in both categories, none of which could have been satisfied in time for the baptismal the following Sunday.

"We got lost," Joseph repeated, not blinking an eye. "Really lost."

Minister Richard eyed him for a long moment.

I think we both ran Joseph's credentials in front of our eyes as the whole story hung on the peg of his credibility. And he came out smelling like a rose. Joseph was a pillar in the community and above rebuke. If he said we were lost, then however impossible that seemed, it was so.

"Okay," Minister Richard said. And he never brought the subject up again. On Monday morning we caught a ride back to Guaimaca and walked out to the community.

The next Sunday morning the church house was full as usual. We had one more session on the hillside where Bishop Monroe went over the last two articles of faith. Then he informed us male applicants that he would be requiring something from us that wasn't in the articles of faith. We perked up.

"I want our youth to mature rapidly in the faith," he told us. "And I want your input during church activities. So with that in mind, I will be asking each of you boys for your testimony on the sermons soon."

We knew what that meant. Amish tradition has two or three witnesses testify after each sermon on whether what was said was in accordance with the Scriptures. The male witnesses perhaps adding a few comments of their own to further edify the congregation.

It's not hard to figure out what that meant to me. I was going to be embarrassed in front of the whole church now, and not just in front of one person as was usual. But what could I do? I wanted to be baptized.

With the class finished, we filed back to our places in front of the church body. We sat down, and I felt exposed. Looked at. *Mortified.* Around me the service dragged on. I moved as little as possible until we were asked to kneel.

Bishop Monroe started with the oldest and moved down the line.

"Do you confess that Jesus Christ is the Son of the Living God?"

"Do you promise to lay aside the world, your flesh, and the devil?"

The water he poured on our heads trickled down our faces. Bishop Monroe believed in getting his candidates wet.

"I baptize you," he said, "in the name of the Father, the Son, and the Holy Spirit."

Going back to the head of the line, he gave each of us his hand of fellowship, lifting us to our feet at the same time, and kissing us—except the girls. He handed them off to his wife, who had slipped up to stand beside him for the final greeting.

I sighed with relief as the service closed and the crowd stirred behind us. No longer did it feel as if everyone was looking at me. I had survived my baptism.

Chapter 42

As events continued to head toward the final exit from Honduras that spring, another farm auction was planned. This would be a big affair, and Dad would contribute livestock. Uncle Joe and the other Stoll brothers found the auctioneer and managed all the details. The day arrived with the auction held out under Grandmother Stoll's mango orchard. Temporary seating had been knocked together stadium-style next to the ring where the animals would be driven through.

People came from every corner of Honduras it seemed, and even from some neighboring countries—mostly businessmen, I suppose. They bid wildly, buying what the Amish had to offer. Prices went to levels not seen before. It was as if, after all these years of work, the civilized world had come to say thanks for a job well done.

That evening the huge trucks—dozens of them—rumbled out the lane loaded mostly with cattle, along with a few horses. Through the sideboards we could see their heads and tails as they jostled against each other. I stood there and watched, thinking of so many years of work all gone in one day. But the worst for me was yet to come. The truck carrying Lightfoot drove by. The dusty-white horse I'd ridden around the community for years. I don't think he was looking at me, but I saw him as the truck disappeared over the knoll below our house.

I felt joy and pain in that moment. The love I had for that country. The loss I was experiencing. If heaven has horses, there will be a white one there. And he will know me because I've ridden him before into the places we both loved. He was tireless and could run like the wind. There was no place he wouldn't go when I asked. I didn't know who his new owner was. I hadn't watched my horse being sold. But I hoped whoever the person was he or she would love my dusty-white horse like I did.

~~~

Uncle Joe's family left soon after the auction, traveling back to Aylmer by public bus, already abiding by the "no air travel" rules that would soon be placed on them. Now their house sat forlorn and empty on the little knoll. I heard someone from the community had purchased the farm, but I never saw signs of anyone around the place.

Dad was busy trying to find buyers for our properties. He'd gotten a bite before the auction on Uncle Stephen's place from a rich businessman who lived in the capital city. And that man did buy our property as part of a package deal that included both of our places, plus the irrigation pump, plus the Brahman cattle. Fausto got thrown in the mix, sort of Dad's way of taking care of him. He would stay on as the manager for the new absentee owner. Fausto had already lived for some time in his new, block, two-bedroom home built by his old hut. No doubt he considered himself greatly blessed with the deal.

He regretted us going, he said, but he seemed confident he would fare well on his own. I had no doubt he would. The man was quite capable.

Dad had a Fruehauf semi-trailer brought in from the capital. It sat in our driveway for more than a month as we loaded his shop tools. Everything was going stateside in hopes that Dad could start another machine shop once we settled in. (I think the real reason was Dad couldn't find any buyers for the equipment.)

Mom and Dad talked, deciding that an exploratory trip north was needed in an attempt to ease our arrival stateside as a family. So Dad set out on a two-week trip. Once he left, Mom told us we were moving back to Aylmer. On that point, Mom was emphatic.

I took her word at face value, unaware that she was trying to overcome Dad's reluctance. I suppose she was trying to get us children on her side. I really didn't care where we went. It was the leaving that was my problem.

Five of my siblings: Miriam, Susanna, Sarah, John, and Jacob.

When Dad came back from his trip, we all raced out to see what news he had. With all of Mom's promoting, we wanted to know if everything was ready at Aylmer for our arrival. Dad grinned and refused to answer, looking as if he had eaten something he shouldn't have.

"I need to talk with Mom first," he said.

Mom looked quite grim-faced as they left for their private conference.

It turned out Dad was as determined not to return to Aylmer as Mom was convinced this was our only choice. After all, that was where we had come from. And it was where all the Stolls were returning to.

Perhaps Dad's memories of his trials in Aylmer had resurfaced. Whatever the reason, we were never told. What we were told was that while Dad was on his trip, he'd purchased a small place in Belle Center, Ohio. That was why he'd looked so sheepish upon his return. The house was in Bishop Wallace Byler's district, the same bishop who had helped Grandfather Stoll found the community in Honduras. Impeccable enough credentials for Dad, but Mom didn't look at all happy.

We were going to try the community, we were told. And if things didn't work out, we would continue on up to Aylmer. A compromise of sorts between the two of them, I suppose.

At church, I had one last nightmare to live through. Bishop Monroe's threatened testimony giving. He'd said he would soon ask all of us newly baptized male members to speak a word of testimony about a sermon. And "soon" to me meant any Sunday was possible. I sat in abject terror each Sunday as the names were called after the sermon for testimony. I couldn't imagine the horror of what would happen when I tried to speak in public. I had memories from another time to prove my point. During one of my school years, when we practiced for a program, a girl who also suffered from stuttering was given a piece to say. It was some Bible verses in Matthew. The Beatitudes—all of them starting with "B."

Strangely, I'd never had trouble speaking in school. I could recite pieces from memory at a school program without a stutter. But this girl practiced for weeks. Try as she might, she just couldn't get "Blessed" out. Mercifully, she was finally given another section of verses.

But I expected no mercy from Bishop Monroe. If he even thought about it, I figured he would think I needed "help" in growing out of my problem. I was, after all, baptized now. So Sunday after Sunday names were called to testify…but never me. At last, unable to stand the stress of the last two Sundays, I left some minutes before each sermon ended, going outside ostensibly for a bathroom break. This was something Bishop Monroe also didn't like, but I figured unauthorized leaving was better than the mess that would occur if he asked me to speak. Having escaped my terror, and with the last Sunday behind me, I sighed in relief.

Before we left, I walked down near Uncle Stephen's place where I'd built a tree house years earlier. I was too old for tree houses now, but I climbed up anyway. Sitting on the rotting boards, I looked over the countryside around me. I knew that I was leaving it all behind. That life would never be the same, even if I ever did return. Not just the mountain rising in its grandeur to the north, or the wispy clouds clipping its highest peak, or the fruit trees hanging heavy with tangerines, oranges, and mangoes, or even the smell of the tropics. But also that joy which is the balm of childhood. The awakening each morning convinced the day will be better than the one before. The natural ability to see beauty in the worst of circumstances. I knew there would be no coming back. After long moments I said my goodbye and climbed down.

We flew out of the capital that September of 1977 loaded down with our luggage. The plane was late, as usual, but it finally appeared, coming in low over the tiled rooftops. We got in line, and eight years and one month after our arrival, we boarded the aircraft for our new "old" world stateside.

The Honduras capital lay open and bare, awash in tropical warmth and splendor in the afternoon sun as we took off. We swept over the outer ring of mountains, climbing ever higher as I watched the countryside go past until we neared the coast. After landing for the stopover in San Pedro Sula, we were soon in the air again and over blue ocean water. I settled back into my seat. The land I loved now lay far behind us. Ahead of us was the unknown. A new community. A new life. A new beginning among our people. I knew I would never think of myself as a child again.

The Eichers and Mrs. Wright.

About Jerry Eicher

Jerry Eicher's bestselling Amish fiction (more than 400,000 in combined sales) includes The Adams County Trilogy, the Hannah's Heart books, and the Little Valley Series. After a traditional Amish childhood, Jerry taught for two terms in Amish and Mennonite schools in Ohio and Illinois. Since then he's been involved in church renewal, preaching, and teaching Bible studies. Jerry lives with his wife, Tina, and their four children in Virginia.

Visit Jerry's website!
http://www.eicherjerry.com/

Also check out Harvest House Publishers'
Amish Readers' page!
www.amishreader.com

If you enjoy reading about the Amish, you'll enjoy eating Amish

Bestselling author Jerry Eicher and his wife, Tina, offer this warm and inviting peek into an Amish kitchen, complete with recipes, Amish proverbs, and Amish humor, including:

Hannah Byler's Pecan Pie
Beat on low speed slightly or
with hand beater:
3 eggs
1/3 cup butter, melted
1 cup light corn syrup
1/2 t. salt
2/3 cup sugar
Stir in: 1 cup pecan halves
Pour into: 1 pie crust
Bake at 375° for 40 to 50 minutes.

It takes seven to cook for to make a really happy wife.
Amish proverb

The *Englisha* visitor suffered through a three-hour Amish wedding service, sitting on the hard, backless church bench.
"Why does it take so long to tie the knot?" he asked afterward.
"Well," the bishop said, stroking his long white beard,
"so that it takes 'em a lifetime to untie it."

Jerry Eicher's Amish Fiction offered by Harvest House Publishers

The Adams County Trilogy
Rebecca's Promise
Rebecca's Return
Rebecca's Choice

Hannah's Heart
A Dream for Hannah
A Hope for Hannah
A Baby for Hannah

Little Valley Series
A Wedding Quilt for Ella
Ella's Wish
Ella Finds Love Again

Fields of Home Series
Missing Your Smile
Following Your Heart
Where Love Grows

My Dearest Naomi
Susanna's Christmas Wish